PARTIES potlucks &BARBECUES

Taste of Home
B O O K S

REIMAN MEDIA GROUP, INC. • GREENDALE, WISCONSIN

Taste of Home®

A TASTE OF HOME/READER'S DIGEST BOOK

Editor: Janet Briggs
Associate Project Editor: Julie Schnittka
Art Director: Lori Arndt
Associate Layout Designer: Catherine Fletcher
Proofreader: Linne Bruskewitz
Editorial Assistant: Barb Czysz
Recipe Testing and Editing: Taste of Home Test Kitchen
Food Photography: Reiman Photo Studio
Cover Photo: Rob Hagen

Senior Editor, Retail Books: Jennifer Olski
Vice President/Executive Editor, Books: Heidi Reuter Lloyd
Creative Director: Ardyth Cope
Senior Vice President/Editor in Chief: Catherine Cassidy
President: Barbara Newton
Founder: Roy Reiman

Pictured on front cover (clockwise from top center): Citrus Mint Cooler (p. 36), Fire and Ice Tomatoes (p. 187), Bow Tie Garden Pasta (p. 196), Tropical Island Chicken (p. 94) and Fresh Strawberry Pie (p. 242).

Pictured on the back cover (top to bottom): Supreme Kabobs (p. 89) and White Chocolate Lime Mousse Cake (p. 231).

International Standard Book Number (10): 0-89821-516-1
International Standard Book Number (13): 978-0-89821-516-8
Library of Congress Control Number: 2006930006

For other Taste of Home books and products, visit
www.tasteofhome.com.
For more Reader's Digest products and information, visit
www.rd.com (in the United States)
www.rd.ca (in Canada)

Printed in China
1 3 5 7 9 10 8 6 4 2

Table of Contents

Getting Started

Celebrating special occasions and entertaining guests are the perfect opportunities to savor delicious food, share good conversation and create lasting memories. As the host, you know it's as much fun organizing a get-together as enjoying the hospitality! On the next few pages, you'll discover dozens of time-saving tips, stress-free shortcuts and mouth-watering menu ideas to help you make the most of any gathering.

Potlucks

Potlucks can make it easy to hold get-togethers even when your time's tight and your schedule is packed. When everyone contributes a dish, it cuts back on the time you'd need to devote to food preparation and gives you more time to spend with the guests.

Hosting a Potluck

As the host, you'll set the mood, like a simple cookout or block party, or theme of the party, such as Big Burgers Night, Mexican Fiesta or Fun in the Sun. You'll also set the date, plan the types of food needed to round out the menu and invite the guests.

Once the mood is set, choose a date that works well for you and your friends. If you're having a group over on a weeknight, select a recipe that can made the day before and held overnight, such as Crispy Fried Chicken (p. 74), which is delicious served cold, or Super Sandwich (p. 122). Or, choose a recipe that you can prep the night before and cook the day of the party like Dressed-Up Bacon Burgers (p. 98) or Marinated Flank Steak (p. 102).

The host usually provides the main dish or dishes for a potluck. Once you've decided what you are going to serve, next plan out the type and number of appetizers, sides and desserts you'll need. See "Food Quantities for a Crowd" (at right).

In your invitation, assign each guest an item to bring, offering some general suggestions, such as the types of sides or desserts to share. For those guests that are traveling farther, suggest they bring nonperishable items, such as rolls, cookies, condiments soda, napkins or plates.

Everyone likes to taste different dishes at potlucks, so plan ahead in case new favorites are found—

ask each guest to bring a few copies of their recipes to hand out. As a courtesy for those with food allergies, place a card by each dish with the recipe name and a list of the main ingredients.

A note of caution—keep in mind the location of the party and age range of your guests when planning your get-together. If you're serving indoors with lots of young children, you may want to avoid foods that stain, such as fruit punch, cherry soda, blueberries or spaghetti sauce. If your party is outdoors, you might also avoid breakable serving dishes or glasses and instead use plastic and disposable dishes, glasses and flatware.

Food Quantities for a Crowd

When planning a buffet, use this guide to estimate how much you'll need per person.

Keep in mind, if you offer more than one item from each category, the less you'll need per serving.

Beverages
- 3/4 cup of coffee or tea
- 24 ounces of soft drinks, juices, lemonade or bottled water
- 1 cup of milk

Breads
- 1 to 2 slices of bread
- 1 biscuit, roll or muffin

Salads
- 1 cup of green salads
- 1/2 cup of fruit, potato or pasta salads

Condiments
- 3 to 4 pickle slices or 1 pickle spear
- 3 olives
- 1 ounce of ketchup, mustard and pickle relish

Meats
- 4 to 6 ounces of meat, fish or poultry
- 2 hot dogs
- 1 to 2 ounces of sliced luncheon meat

Dairy
- 1 teaspoon (1 pat) of butter or margarine for bread and rolls
- 1 ounce of sliced cheese for sandwiches
- 2 tablespoons of cream for coffee

Desserts
- 1/2 cup of ice cream or frozen yogurt
- 1 portion of cake or pie

Miscellaneous
- 1 ounce of potato or corn chips
- 3 to 4 ounces of ice for beverages

Setting Up the Food

Set the food out in several areas to avoid congestion when the group goes to eat. Place the plates, utensils, main dish and sides in one area, then in separate spots set up the glasses and beverages, the desserts and, if desired, the condiments. Desserts can also be set out after the main meal items have been cleared.

Find a large surface to set up the main food line. If you're having a potluck in the backyard, set up a second picnic table for the food or set a large board over two sawhorses. Top with a cloth or plastic tablecloth. If the cloth tablecloth is large enough, tie a simple knot at each corner of the cloth (at right).

If the tablecloth is too short to tie, try one of these ideas:

- Clip the tablecloth to table with spring clamps.
- Clip the ends of the tablecloth around the table legs with spring-style clothespins.
- Weigh down a cloth tablecloth with metal washers sewn around the edges.
- Use clip-on tablecloth weights.
- Tape a disposable tablecloth under the table with duct tape.

After your tablecloth is ready, arrange plates at one end. Next, arrange the food, leaving room along the edge of the table for the guests to place the plates down as they fill them. At the other end, have the flatware and napkins. If it's a breezy day, use a rock to weigh down the napkins (at right).

To make it easy to grab the flatware and napkins, roll paper napkins around a fork and knife. Place the flatware bundles in a large jar or small bucket. To weigh the bucket down and prevent it from blowing over, fill a small resealable plastic bag with uncooked rice. Seal bag and place in the bottom of the bucket, then fill with flatware.

Place beverages in another shady spot away from the food so that there is less congestion around the food line. Fill a large ice chest or metal or plastic tub with ice and beverages. Or, set up cups

and icy pitchers of punch, tea or lemonade at one end of the buffet table.

Cleanup

Always have a spot designated for the trash. Clearly mark which bags are for recyclables and which are for other trash. Clear the clutter as it builds up. Ask some children to help clear guest's plates after they are done eating.

Rules for Safely Serving Food

Whenever you serve or handle food, keep in mind these rules of food safety:

- Keep everything clean, including hands, utensils, plates and work surfaces.

- Keep foods separate. Don't cross-contaminate foods, which means allowing the juices of raw meats, poultry and fish to come in contact with other foods. Anything that comes in contact with raw meat juices—hands, utensils, plates and work surfaces—should be thoroughly washed in hot, soapy water before reuse.

- Keep it at the right temperature. Keep hot foods hot, cold foods cold and cook food to the proper temperature. Cooked foods and uncooked foods that require refrigeration should only be left at room temperature for up to 2 hours, 1 hour if it is a hot day (90°F or warmer).

- To keep foods hot, use insulated containers, warming trays, slow cookers or chafing dishes. You can also serve a small amount of the hot food and replenish the dish as needed, while the rest of the food stays warm in a 200° oven.

- To keep foods cold, place dips, cut-up fruits and salads in a plastic bowl and set in a larger bowl filled with ice cubes or crushed ice (see above). Replenish ice for chilling and food bowls as it melts.

Bringing a Dish to Pass

Secure lids to dishes or cover with foil—it's disposable and won't break. Place just-cooked foods in insulated containers to keep hot or wrap warm dishes individually in clean towels or newspapers, then pack tightly in a cooler.

Keep cool food on ice in an ice chest. For nonperishable items, pack in a clean large laundry basket. Use towels, beach towels or crumbled newspaper as padding between any breakable items. A two-handled basket is easy to carry. Once unpacked, the basket can be stashed under a table for storage. And, don't forget to bring the serving utensils. After the party, just load up the basket and carry it back to your car.

7 Secrets to Successful Entertaining

1 Deciding the Three W's— What, Who and When:

- What kind of party do you want to have or what are you celebrating?
- Who are you going to invite?
- When will the party be? Pick a date and time that will work well for you and your friends.

2 Choosing the Menu: The food should go along with the type of party you are planning—backyard cookout, weekend brunch, party for your child's team, etc.

3 Sending Invitations: Match the invitation to the tone of your party. Let the guest know the reason for the party, when and where it will be, if they need to bring a dish to pass and how they should RSVP.

4 Setting a Timeline for Your Party: Divide the menu and decorating tasks into specific steps for the days leading up to your party. Plan to do as many things in advance as possible, such as pick up party decorations, soda and other beverages a week or so before the party.

5 Making the Perfect Party Food: Allow yourself enough time to prepare the food. Enlist your family or hire additional help if needed. Shop in advance, especially for the nonperishable items. Some foods can be made ahead, then frozen. Garnish platters with simple items, such as with cut fruits, vegetables or herbs.

6 Adding Special Touches for an Unforgettable Party: Decorations set a festive mood. Use mini white holiday lights, votive candles, tiki lights, etc. in your backyard. Potted plants can be placed around the area. Even a tablecloth and napkins can set the mood.

7 Using Helpful Hints:
- If there are going to be a lot of young children, hire a babysitter to watch and entertain them.
- Enlist older children to be the grounds crew. Have them collect used plates and refresh drinks.
- Recruit a friend or relative to serve as the bartender.
- For an outdoor party, have sunscreen, bug repellant and insect bite lotion on hand for guests.
- Have a few disposable cameras out. This way, people can snap a few party-memory shots.

Picnics

Picnics can be as simple as an impromptu lunch held in your backyard with your children or as involved as a well-planned day at the beach or park. If you enjoy the sun on your face, a fresh breeze and the great outdoors while dining, here are some pointers for perfect picnics.

Planning

Pick a location that allows picnickers. Invite family and friends to share the adventure. Plan the menu—keep in mind the number of people and how much you can carry. Meet at a designated spot and have everyone help carry the food and equipment to the picnic site.

Before the day of the picnic, make a checklist of all the items you think you might need. Check the items off as you pack to go and also when you pack to come home. That way, you won't leave your favorite serving spoon in the middle of a park. Here are some items that you might want on your checklist:

- Picnic basket, backpack or cooler
- Chairs, tables, blanket or tablecloth
- Paper plates, napkins and plastic utensils for serving and dining
- Clean foil, plastic wrap and resealable plastic bags to store leftovers
- Trash bags, paper towels moist towelettes, antibacterial soap that does not require water and a spray bottle with soapy water
- Sunscreen, insect repellant, sunglasses
- Radio, camera, flashlight, games, balls, bats

Packing

A few days before the picnic, make ice blocks, ice cubes or freeze reusable ice packs for the cooler. To make an ice block, use a disposable aluminum pan or pans that fit the bottom of your cooler. Place the pan on a baking sheet, then fill it about three-fourths full with water and freeze. For smaller ice packs, fill resealable freezer bags with water and remove most of air before freezing (leave some air in the bag to allow for the water to expand during freezing).

Foods and beverages that need to be cold should be refrigerated before placing them in the cooler. Chill the coolers beforehand, too, by placing some ice cubes inside and closing the lid about an hour before filling.

If your picnic involves a large group, you might want to have separate coolers for beverages and for fresh food. The beverage cooler will probably be opened more frequently than the food cooler. If the bevereages and food are packed together, the food may not stay cold.

If you made ice blocks, place them in the bottom of the cooler. For the beverage cooler, add the cans and bottles then top with ice cubes. For the food cooler, pack in the opposite order of how you'll use the items. The foods you need first should be on top, so they're easily accessible. Remember, a full cooler will stay cold longer. Once the food is in, fill the open spaces with the homemade ice packs, frozen gel packs, ice cubes or crushed ice.

Don't place the coolers in a car trunk. Place them in the back seat insted. On warm days, run the air conditioning.

Returning Home

When you arrive back home, promptly refrigerate all perishable items. If they are warm or wet, toss them out. Wipe out the picnic basket and wash all the picnic plates, glasses and utensils. Drain the cooler and wash it in hot soapy water. If meat juices have dripped over the cooler, you should clean it with a solution of 1 teaspoon bleach to 1 quart of water. Let the solution stand in the cooler for about 10 minutes. Drain carefully to avoid splashing and wash the cooler. Leave the cooler open until it is completely dried before storing.

Barbecues

Keep your kitchen clean and cool by entertaining and cooking outdoors. The aroma and flavor of food cooked on the grill is always a party pleaser. Best of all, you can prepare a wide variety of items on the grill, from juicy burgers to tender roasts or even a succulent turkey. Here are a few tips:

Planning

While gas grills only take minutes to heat up, charcoal grills don't. Charcoal briquettes are hot and ready when they are covered with a light gray ash—this takes about 25 to 30 minutes. You'll need about 30 briquettes to cook 1 pound of meat. Briquettes do cool off, so if you're planning on grilling over a period of time, place fresh briquettes by the edge of the coals and rotate them into the center as they get hot.

Direct heat is used for foods that take about 30 minutes or less, such as steaks, hamburgers, kabobs, boneless chicken breasts, fish fillets, hot dogs and vegetables.

Indirect heat is used for foods that take longer than 30 minutes to cook, are high in fat or are usually cooked in the oven rather than on the stovetop, such as roasts, ribs, whole chicken, bone-in chicken pieces and thick steaks.

If possible, cook food in batches. That way you'll have a steady supply of freshly grilled hot food. Keep uncooked food in the refrigerator or cooler until needed.

For kabobs, soak wooden skewers at least 15 minutes in cold water before using to prevent them from burning. Leave a little space between pieces of food as you thread them onto the skewer to promote thorough cooking.

Testing the Temperature of Your Grill

Check the temperature of your grill by cautiously holding the palm of your hand 3 to 4 inches above the grate. Count the number of seconds you can hold your hand in that position before the heat forces you to pull it away.

Hot (at least 450°)

2 seconds
coals glow red

Medium-hot (400°)

3 seconds
coals are gray with a red underglow

Medium (350°)

4 seconds
coals are gray with a hint of red

Medium-low (300°)

5 seconds
Coals are gray with a faint red glow

Grilling Safety and Tips

- Place the grill on a level solid surface, away from fences, shrubs, grass and overhangs.

- Grill in a well-ventilated area.

- The grill gets hot. It should be located away from the main activities so that no one accidentally bumps into it.

- The grill chef should wear long barbecue mitts to protect their hands and arms.

- Store charcoal in a dry place. Damp or wet charcoal may not ignite.

- Never add lighter fluid to lit coals. Never use gasoline or kerosene to light briquettes.

- Have two pairs of long-handled tongs—one to move the coals and one to turn food.

- Have a water bottle handy to spray any flare-ups.

- Bring foods to a cool room temperature before grilling to ensure more even cooking.

- Trim excess fat from steaks, chops and chicken.

- Use two sets of cutting boards, grill utensils and platters—one for uncooked foods and one for cooked items.

- Spray the food grate with nonstick cooking spray before starting the grill. Never spray directly over the fire (gas or coal) as you can cause a fire.

- To grease a hot grate, fold a paper towel into a small pad. Holding the pad with long-handled tongs, dip in vegetable oil and rub over the grate.

- When basting with marinade, reserve some for basting and add the meat to the remaining marinade. Discard the marinade from the meat.

- Brush on thick or sweet sauces during the last 10 to 15 minutes of cooking, basting and turning every few minutes to prevent burning.

- Always place cooked food on a clean plate—never place on a plate that held raw food.

- Cooking time will vary for many reasons: the starting temperature of the food, the temperature of the coals and the air temperature. Use the cooking time as a guide and test meat doneness with a meat thermometer. See "Temperature Doneness Chart" (below).

- The vents in a covered charcoal grill help regulate the coal temperature. When the vents are open, more air flows through the grill and the coals burn hotter. When the vents are closed, the coals are deprived of oxygen and will eventually extinguish themselves.

- Don't discard the ashes until they are completely cold. Cover the grill, close the vents and let stand until cold.

Temperature Doneness Chart

Temperature	Food Items
140°	fully cooked ham
145°	medium-rare: beef, lamb and veal
160°	medium: beef, lamb and veal; pork, fresh ham or partially cooked ham
165°	ground chicken and turkey and leftovers
170°	chicken and turkey breasts
180°	whole chicken and turkey, and thighs and wings

All-Occasion Party Menus

Picnic in the Park

Confetti Snack Mix, p. 28
Crispy Fried Chicken, p. 74
Antipasto Sub, p. 123
Creamy Coleslaw, p. 182
Marinated Tomatoes, p. 202
Caramel Brownies, p. 235
Strawberry Lemonade, p. 48
Serve with: chips and carrot
and celery sticks

Neighborhood Block Party

Super Ham Spread, p. 15
Brats with Onions, p. 94
Sandwich for a Crowd, p. 121
Antipasto Pasta Salad, p. 183
Barbecued Bean Salad, p. 184
Melon Fruit Bowl, p. 201
Frozen Ice Cream Delights, p. 236
Fruit Punch, p. 42
Serve with: assorted crackers,
olives, pickles and mustard

Sunday Brunch

Deluxe Ham Omelet, p. 50
Berry Cream Muffins, p. 62
Fresh Fruit Bowl, p. 53
Citrus Mint Cooler, p. 36
Serve with: coffee, tea, cream and sugar

Summertime Barbecue

Sweet 'n' Hot Mustard Dip, p. 18
Grilled Pork Appetizers, p. 24
Dressed-Up Bacon Burgers, p. 98
Dijon Four-Bean Salad, p. 193
Idaho Potato Salad, p. 194
Fresh Cucumber Salad, p. 188
Banana Orange Bars, p. 221
Lemony Iced Tea, p. 43 and
Sangria, p. 46
Serve with: breads, butter,
olives and pickles

Mother's Day Lunch

Herbed Garlic Cheese Spread, p. 34
Classic Cobb Salad, p. 74
Watermelon Ambrosia, p. 188
White Chocolate Lime Mousse Cake, p. 231
Sparkling Berry Punch, p. 47
Serve with: warm crusty rolls and butter

Family Reunion

Cold Chicken-Cheese Kabobs, p. 20
Mexican Corn Dip, p. 31
Creamy Deviled Eggs, p. 24
Sweet 'n' Moist Ham, p. 72
Bow Tie Garden Pasta, p. 196
Layered Fruit Salad, p. 192
Devil's Food Sheet Cake, p. 242
Old-Fashioned Lemonade, p. 40
Serve with: breads, butter, olives, pickles and
mustard

Menus continued on page 12

All-Occasion Party Menus

After-Game Party

Soft Taco Burgers, p. 172
Boston Subs, p. 177
Fresh 'n' Fruity Salad, p. 173
Trail Mix Snack, p. 164
Ice Cream Crunch, p. 179
Sparkling White Grape Juice, p. 44
Serve with: chips and bottled water

Grad's Day

Taco Appetizer Platter, p. 30
Barbecued Chicken.
  Sandwiches, p. 139
Citrus Spinach Salad, p. 202
Make-Ahead Vegetable
  Medley, p. 200
Lemon Sheet Cake, p. 237
Refreshing Raspberry Cooler, p. 48
Serve with: tortilla chips, mayonnaise,
  butter and watermelon wedges

Island Fun

Festive Cheese Beach Ball, p. 32
Marinated Shrimp, p. 33
Tropical Island Chicken, p. 94
Ambrosia Salad, p. 167
Raspberry Tossed Salad, p. 190
Hawaiian Dessert, p. 232
Citrus Quencher, p. 40
Serve with: assorted crackers, Hawaiian
  rolls and butter

South-of-the-Border Fiesta

Fresh Salsa, p. 20
Guacamole, p. 28
Grilled Steak Fajitas, p. 108
Fire and Ice Tomatoes, p. 187
Southwestern Rice and Bean
  Salad, p. 198
Fresh Strawberry Pie, p. 243
Fresh Lime Margaritas, p. 42
Serve with: tortilla chips

Father's Day Cookout

Grilled Wing Zingers, p. 16
Herbed Beef Tenderloin, p. 93
Garlic Green and Wax Beans, p. 206
Italian Potato Salad, p. 182
Fresh Blueberry Pie, p. 238
Iced Coffee, p. 38
Serve with: rolls and butter

Ice Cream Social

Chocolate Mint Ice Cream, p. 220
Creamy Vanilla Ice Cream, p. 225
Strawberry Ice Cream, p. 229
Fudge Sundaes, p. 227
Peanut Butter Ice Cream Topping, p. 244
Blueberry Ice Cream Topping, p. 223
Serve with: pirouette or sugar wafer cookies and
  assorted chilled beverages

Little
Bites

Appetizer Chicken Kabobs

—Gail Ponak
Viscount, Saskatchewan

Prep: 15 min. + marinating
Bake: 10 min.
Yield: 20-24 appetizers

These little chicken kabobs are a perfect appetizer. They're quick and easy to prepare, which means I can spend more time visiting with guests.

3/4 cup soy sauce
1/4 cup sugar
1 tablespoon vegetable oil
1/4 teaspoon garlic powder
1/2 teaspoon ground ginger
2 boneless skinless chicken breasts, cut into 1-inch chunks
6 to 8 green onions, cut into 1-inch pieces
1/2 pound medium fresh mushrooms, stems removed

In a large mixing bowl, combine first five ingredients. Pour half into another bowl. Add chicken to one bowl and the onions to another. Marinate for 30 minutes.

Drain and discard marinade from chicken. Drain and reserve marinade from onions. On each soaked wooden skewer, thread a piece of chicken, onion, mushroom and another chicken piece.

Place on a broiler rack. Broil 5 in. from the heat, turning and basting with reserved marinade after 3 minutes. Broil for 3 minutes longer or until chicken juices run clear. Serve immediately.

Smoked Salmon Dip

—Doreen McDaniels
Seattle, Washington

Prep/Total Time: 30 min.
Yield: about 3 cups

Salmon is practically a way of life here in the Pacific Northwest. My husband can make a meal of this dip. It's great for parties.

1 can (16 ounces) pitted ripe olives, drained
8 green onions, cut into 2-inch pieces
1 can (14-3/4 ounces) pink salmon, drained, flaked and bones removed
2/3 cup mayonnaise
8 drops Liquid Smoke, optional
Assorted crackers

Place olives and onions in a blender or food processor; cover and process for about 15 seconds or until finely chopped. Add the salmon, mayonnaise and Liquid Smoke if desired; cover and process until dip reaches desired consistency. Cover and refrigerate until ready to serve. Serve with crackers.

I reach for this recipe whenever I need a simple yet special snack for guests. As a matter of fact, I've been serving it for over 20 years, and it's always met with rave reviews.

Super Ham Spread

—Paula Pelis
Lenhartsville, Pennsylvania

Prep: **10 min. + chilling**
Yield: **2-1/2 cups**

1 container (8 ounces) cold pack cheddar cheese spread, softened

1 package (3 ounces) cream cheese, softened

1-1/2 cups finely chopped fully cooked ham

1/3 cup ground pecans

1/4 cup finely chopped green onions

1 tablespoon Dijon-mayonnaise blend

1 teaspoon Worcestershire sauce

1 teaspoon prepared horseradish

Snack rye bread *or* assorted crackers *or* pretzels

In a large bowl, combine cheese spread and cream cheese. Stir in the ham, pecans, onions, mayonnaise blend, Worcestershire sauce and horseradish. Cover and refrigerate for at least 1 hour. Let stand at room temperature 30 minutes before serving. Serve with bread, crackers or pretzels.

Set a platter of Cheesy Sausage Nachos on the table and stand back as guests dive in! This dish can be used as an appetizer as well as an entree.

Cheesy Sausage Nachos

—Jane Sodergren
Red Wing, Minnesota

Prep: **30 min.**
Bake: **10 min.**
Yield: **8-10 servings**

3/4 pound bulk pork sausage

1/4 cup chopped onion

3 cups diced fresh tomatoes, *divided*

3/4 cup picante sauce

4 cups tortilla chips

3 cups (12 ounces) shredded Monterey Jack cheese, *divided*

1 medium ripe avocado, diced

Crumble sausage into a large skillet; add onion. Cook over medium heat until meat is no longer pink; drain well. Add 2 cups tomatoes and picante sauce. Bring to a boil. Reduce heat; simmer, uncovered, for 20 minutes or until most of the liquid has evaporated.

Sprinkle tortilla chips over a 12-in. pizza pan. Top with 2 cups cheese and the sausage mixture; sprinkle with remaining cheese. Bake at 350° for 8-10 minutes or until cheese is melted. Sprinkle with avocado and remaining tomatoes.

Grilled Wing Zingers

—Angela Roster
Greenbackville, Virginia

Prep: 35 min.
Grill: 35 min.
Yield: about 6-1/2 dozen

My husband fine-tuned this recipe—and the results were spectacular! These spicy-hot grilled wings are true party pleasers. You can easily adjust the heat level by altering the amount of chili powder. The wings take a little time, but they're worth it.

40 whole chicken wings (about 8 pounds)
2 cups packed brown sugar
2 cups hot sauce
1/2 cup butter, cubed
2 tablespoons cider vinegar
1/3 cup sugar
1/2 cup Italian seasoning
1/4 cup dried rosemary, crushed
1/4 cup paprika
1/4 cup chili powder
1/4 cup pepper
2 tablespoons cayenne pepper
1 cup blue cheese salad dressing
1/2 cup ranch salad dressing
Celery sticks

Cut chicken wings into three sections; discard wing tip section. Set the wings aside. In a saucepan, bring the brown sugar, hot sauce, butter and vinegar to a boil. Reduce heat; simmer, uncovered, for 6-8 minutes or until butter is melted and sauce is heated through. Cool.

In a gallon-size resealable plastic bag, combine the sugar, seasonings and 1 cup sauce. Add chicken wings in batches; seal bag and toss to coat evenly.

Cover and grill wings over indirect medium heat for 35-45 minutes or until juices run clear, turning and basting occasionally with remaining sauce.

In a small bowl, combine blue cheese and ranch salad dressing; serve with chicken wings and celery sticks.

Editor's Note: This recipe was prepared with the first and second sections of the chicken wings.

Ready-Made Chicken Wings

Chicken wings are always a hit when entertaining, but planning ahead makes it easier to prepare them. Buy whole chicken wings in bulk, cut them into three pieces, discard the wing tips and store the pieces in freezer bags. They just need to be thawed before using.

This is a nice way to serve mushrooms as an appetizer...and it also makes a great side dish for any type of meat. Sometimes I add these tangy mushrooms to salads for extra flavor.

Marinated Mushrooms

—Brenda Swan
Alexandria, Pennsylvania

Prep: 15 min. + marinating
Yield: 4 cups

2 pounds fresh mushrooms
1 envelope (.7 ounce) Italian salad dressing mix
1 cup water
1/2 cup olive oil
1/3 cup cider vinegar
2 tablespoons lemon juice
1 tablespoon sugar
1 tablespoon minced fresh parsley
1 tablespoon soy sauce
2 teaspoons crushed red pepper flakes
3 garlic cloves, minced
1/2 teaspoon salt
1/8 teaspoon pepper
Leaf lettuce, optional

Remove mushroom stems (discard or save for another use). Place caps in a large saucepan and cover with water. Bring to a boil. Reduce heat; cook, uncovered, for 3 minutes, stirring occasionally. Drain and cool.

In a jar with a tight-fitting lid, combine the salad dressing mix, water, oil, vinegar, lemon juice, sugar and seasonings; shake well.

Place mushrooms in a bowl; add dressing and stir to coat. Cover and refrigerate for 8 hours or overnight. Serve in a lettuce-lined bowl if desired.

Serve a colorful array of vegetables with this delicious dip to add even more appeal. This popular appetizer would be a welcome snack just about anytime.

Picnic Veggie Dip

—Susan Schuller
Brainerd, Minnesota

1 cup mayonnaise
1 cup (8 ounces) sour cream
1 package (1.7 ounces) vegetable soup mix
1 package (10 ounces) frozen chopped spinach, thawed and squeezed dry
1 can (8 ounces) water chestnuts, drained and chopped
Assorted fresh vegetables

In a large bowl, combine the mayonnaise, sour cream and soup mix. Stir in spinach and water chestnuts. Cover and refrigerate for at least 2 hours. Serve with vegetables.

Prep: 5 min. + chilling
Yield: 3 cups

Sweet 'n' Hot Mustard Dip

—*Rita Reifenstein*
Evans City, Pennsylvania

Prep: 20 min. + chilling
Yield: 2-1/3 cups

With pretzels, this sweet and spicy mustard is a fun snack. It also sparks the flavor of grilled chicken strips or sausages.

1-1/2 cups honey

1 cup white vinegar

3 eggs

2 containers (1-3/4 ounces *each*) ground mustard

1/2 teaspoon salt

Pretzels, cooked chicken fingers *or* sausage slices

In a blender, combine the first five ingredients; cover and process until blended.

Pour into a saucepan; cook and stir over low heat until mixture thickens and reaches 160°. Pour into small jars. Cover and refrigerate for up to 1 week. Serve with pretzels, chicken fingers or sausage.

Creamy Chicken Spread

—*Charlene Barrows*
Reedley, California

Prep/Total Time: 25 min.
Yield: 3 cups

Every time I take this eye-catching log to a party, it's gone in no time. It spreads easily onto any kind of cracker.

1 package (8 ounces) cream cheese, softened

1/4 cup mayonnaise

2 tablespoons lemon juice

1/2 teaspoon salt

1/4 teaspoon ground ginger

1/8 teaspoon pepper

1/8 teaspoon hot pepper sauce

2 cups finely chopped cooked chicken breast

2 hard-cooked eggs, finely chopped

1/4 cup sliced green onions

Diced pimientos and additional sliced green onions

Assorted crackers *or* snack rye bread

In a small mixing bowl, combine the first seven ingredients. Stir in the chicken, eggs and green onions.

Shape into an 8-in. x 2-in. log. Garnish with pimientos and onions. Cover and refrigerate until serving. Remove from the refrigerator 15 minutes before serving. Serve with crackers or bread.

Here's a great way to bring something colorful, nutritious and fun to a buffet. Everyone likes fresh fruit, and these skewers are great served alongside the creamy coconut dip.

Fruit Kabobs

—Cheryl Ollis
Matthews, North Carolina

1 medium tart apple, cut into 1-inch chunks

1 medium pear, cut into 1-inch chunks

1 tablespoon lemon juice

1 can (8 ounces) unsweetened pineapple chunks, drained

24 grapes (about 1/4 pound)

24 fresh strawberries

Coconut Dip:

1-1/2 cups fat-free vanilla yogurt

4-1/2 teaspoons flaked coconut

4-1/2 teaspoons reduced-sugar orange marmalade

Toss apple and pear with lemon juice. Divide fruit into 12 portions and thread onto wooden skewers. Combine dip ingredients in a small bowl; serve with the kabobs.

Prep/Total Time: **15 min.**

Yield: **12 kabobs**

When my friend's husband needed lower-fat snacks, she served him this fresh-tasting shrimp spread. Cucumber slices are a fun and healthy alternative to crackers.

Cucumber Shrimp Appetizers

—Patricia Kile
Greentown, Pennsylvania

Prep/Total Time: **10 min.**

Yield: **32 appetizers**

1 can (8 ounces) unsweetened crushed pineapple, drained

1 can (4 ounces) tiny shrimp, rinsed and drained

1/4 cup reduced-fat mayonnaise

1 tablespoon finely chopped green onion

2 teaspoons Dijon mustard

1-1/2 teaspoons minced fresh dill

1 medium cucumber (8 inches), cut into 1/4-inch slices

Fresh dill sprigs, optional

In a bowl, combine the pineapple, shrimp, mayonnaise, onion, mustard and dill. Spoon onto cucumber slices. Garnish with dill sprigs if desired.

Fresh Salsa

—Terry Thompson
Albuquerque, New Mexico

After the mild green chilies I grow in my garden are roasted, I peel, dice and freeze them to use all year. This colorful salsa is a favorite.

6 Anaheim peppers, roasted and peeled

4 large tomatoes, chopped

3 green onions, sliced

2 tablespoons minced fresh cilantro

1/2 to 1 jalapeno pepper, seeded and minced

1 garlic clove, minced

1/3 cup red wine vinegar

1/3 cup olive oil

1/2 teaspoon pepper

1 teaspoon salt, optional

In a large bowl, combine the peppers, tomatoes, onions, cilantro, jalapeno and garlic. In another bowl, combine the vinegar, oil, pepper and salt if desired; stir into vegetable mixture. Cover and refrigerate for at least 2 hours.

Editor's Note: When cutting or seeding hot peppers, use rubber or plastic gloves to protect your hands. Avoid touching your face.

Prep: **15 min.** + chilling
Yield: **4-1/2 cups**

Cold Chicken-Cheese Kabobs

—Sherine Gilmour
Brooklyn, New York

These appealing kabobs will add pizzazz to any party...and you don't even have to get out the grill!

1/2 teaspoon salt

1/2 teaspoon chili powder

1/8 teaspoon pepper

1/2 pound boneless skinless chicken breast, cubed

1/2 cup balsamic vinegar

2 teaspoons olive oil

1 block (5 ounces) part-skim mozzarella cheese, cubed

18 cherry *or* grape tomatoes

Combine the salt, chili powder and pepper; rub into chicken cubes. Place bowl; add vinegar. Cover and refrigerate for 3-4 hours.

In a skillet, cook chicken in oil until juices run clear. Cool slightly. Alternately thread chicken, cheese and tomatoes onto wooden skewers. Serve cold.

Prep: **20 min.** + chilling
Yield: **8 servings**

It's hard to stop munching this yummy snack mix! Melted vanilla chips make a delightful coating for the crisp corn chips, cereal and popcorn. This snack mix is simple to toss together. I like to keep it on hand for when our grandchildren visit.

Corny Snack Mix

—Sandy Wehring
Fremont, Ohio

Prep/Total Time: 25 min.
Yield: 7-1/2 quarts

3 quarts popped popcorn

1 package (15 ounces)
Corn Pops

1 package (15 ounces)
corn chips

2 packages (10 to 12
ounces *each*) vanilla
or white chips

In several large bowls, combine the popcorn, Corn Pops and corn chips.

In a large saucepan over medium-low heat, melt chips; stir until smooth. Pour over popcorn mixture and toss to coat. Spread onto two 15-in. x 10-in. x 1-in. baking pans. Cool. Store in airtight containers.

I slice this tasty snack into pinwheels for an appetizer or serve them as handheld sandwiches with salsa on the side for dipping.

Olive Chicken Roll-Ups

—Lisa Hymson
Aurora, Colorado

1 package (8 ounces)
cream cheese, softened

2 cans (4 ounces *each*)
chopped green chilies,
drained

1 can (2-1/4 ounces)
chopped ripe olives,
drained

1 jar (2 ounces) diced
pimientos, drained

1/4 teaspoon garlic powder

1/4 teaspoon chili powder

1/4 teaspoon hot pepper
sauce

8 flour tortillas (8 inches)

1-1/4 pounds deli smoked
chicken

Salsa *or* picante sauce, optional

In a large mixing bowl, beat cream cheese until smooth. Fold in the chilies, olives, pimientos, garlic powder, chili powder and hot pepper sauce.

Spread on one side of each tortilla; top with chicken and roll up tightly. Wrap in plastic wrap; refrigerate for at least 1 hour. Cut into 1-in. slices or serve whole with salsa if desired.

Prep: 20 min. + chilling
Yield: 8 servings

Ham Roll-Ups

—*Kathleen Green*
Republic, Missouri

Prep: **10 min.** + chilling
Yield: **40 appetizers**

Green onions and ripe olives give lively flavor to these bite-size appetizers. They're quick to assemble and can be made the day before. I find that they are very popular with my friends and family.

1 package (8 ounces) cream cheese, softened

1 can (2-1/4 ounces) chopped ripe olives, drained

1/3 cup thinly sliced green onions

8 to 10 thin slices fully cooked ham

In a large mixing bowl, beat cream cheese until smooth; stir in the olives and onions. Spread over ham slices. Roll up, jelly-roll style, starting with a short side. Wrap each in plastic wrap; refrigerate for at least 1 hour. Just before serving, cut into 1-in. pieces.

Mexican Pizza

—*Sandra McKenzie*
Braham, Minnesota

Prep: **20 min.** + chilling
Bake: **10 min.** + cooling
Yield: **12-16 servings**

My husband and I created the recipe for this hearty snack. Our whole family enjoys it.

2 tubes (8 ounces *each*) refrigerated crescent rolls

1 package (8 ounces) cream cheese, softened

1 cup (8 ounces) sour cream

1 pound ground beef

1 envelope taco seasoning

1 can (2-1/4 ounces) sliced ripe olives, drained

1 medium tomato, chopped

3/4 cup shredded cheddar cheese

3/4 cup shredded part-skim mozzarella cheese

1 cup shredded lettuce

Unroll crescent roll dough and place in an ungreased 15-in. x 10-in. x 1-in. baking pan. Flatten dough to fit the pan, sealing seams and perforations.

Bake at 375° for 8-10 minutes or until light golden brown; cool. In a small bowl, blend cream cheese and sour cream with a wire whisk; spread over crust. Chill 30 minutes.

Meanwhile, in a large skillet, cook beef over medium heat until no longer pink; drain. Stir in taco seasoning. Add water according to package directions and simmer for 5 minutes, stirring occasionally. Spread over cream cheese layer. Top with the olives, tomato, cheeses and lettuce. Cut into serving-size pieces. Serve immediately or refrigerate.

Because blue crabs are so plentiful in Maryland, we are always looking for new ways to enjoy them. This recipe is easy, elegant and delicious. It makes a delightful treat when you have company. And best of all it whips up in just minutes.

Deviled Crab Dip

—Debbie Jones
California, Maryland

- 1 cup mayonnaise
- 2 tablespoons *each* finely chopped celery, green pepper and onion
- 2 to 3 teaspoons lemon juice
- 1 teaspoon ground mustard
- 1 teaspoon Worcestershire sauce
- 1/4 teaspoon salt
- 1/8 teaspoon lemon-pepper seasoning
- 1/8 to 1/4 teaspoon hot pepper sauce
- 1-1/2 cups cooked crabmeat, flaked and cartilage removed
- Assorted fresh vegetables *or* assorted crackers

In a large bowl, combine the mayonnaise, celery, green pepper, onion, lemon juice, mustard, Worcestershire sauce, salt, lemon-pepper and pepper sauce. Stir in crab. Cover and refrigerate for at least 1 hour. Serve with vegetables or crackers.

Prep: **15 min. + chilling**
Yield: **about 2 cups**

Fresh Crabmeat Fact

If you're using cooked fresh crabmeat like Debbie Jones, it should only be refrigerated for up to 2 days before using. If you can't use the crabmeat within that time frame, store in it the freezer.

Creamy Deviled Eggs

—Barbara Towler
Derby, Ohio

These deviled eggs are nicely flavored with a tang of mustard and a spark of sweetness from pickle relish.

36 hard-cooked eggs

1 package (8 ounces) cream cheese, softened

1-1/2 cups mayonnaise

1/3 cup sweet pickle relish

1/3 cup Dijon mustard

3/4 teaspoon salt

1/4 teaspoon pepper

Paprika and sprigs fresh parsley, stems removed

Slice eggs in half lengthwise; remove yolks and set yolks and whites aside.

In a large mixing bowl, beat cream cheese until smooth. Add the mayonnaise, relish, mustard, salt, pepper and reserved yolks; mix well. Stuff or pipe into egg whites. Garnish with paprika and parsley. Refrigerate several hours before serving.

Prep: **15 min.** + chilling
Yield: **36 servings**

Grilled Pork Appetizers

—Susan LeBrun
Sulphur, Louisiana

Marinated in a sauce that is slightly sweetened with honey, the party starters also make a wonderful entree when served over rice.

1 pound boneless whole pork loin roast

3 tablespoons reduced-sodium soy sauce

3 tablespoons honey

1 tablespoon lemon juice

1 tablespoon vegetable oil

3 garlic cloves, minced

1/2 teaspoon ground ginger

Cut pork into 1/8-in. slices, then cut each slice widthwise in half. In a large resealable plastic bag, combine the remaining ingredients; add the pork. Seal bag and turn to coat; refrigerate for 2-4 hours, turning occasionally.

If grilling the kabobs, coat grill rack with nonstick cooking spray before starting the grill. Drain and discard marinade. Thread pork onto metal or soaked wooden skewers. Grill, uncovered, over medium heat or broil 4-6 in. from the heat for 2-3 minutes on each side or until meat juices run clear, turning once.

Prep: **10 min.** + marinating
Grill: **10 min.**
Yield: **8 servings**

This sensational salsa is a colorful combination of lots of fresh-tasting flavors. My husband, son and I think it's great as a dip or with main-dish burritos or chimichangas.

Black Bean Salsa

—*Charlene Denges*
Elgin, Texas

2 cans (15 ounces *each*) black beans, rinsed and drained

1 can (15-1/4 ounces) whole kernel corn, drained

1 can (10 ounces) diced tomatoes and green chilies, undrained

1 jar (7-1/2 ounces) roasted red peppers, drained and diced

2 plum tomatoes, chopped

1 medium red onion, finely chopped

4 green onions, finely chopped

1/3 cup minced fresh cilantro

2 garlic cloves, minced

1/3 cup orange juice

1 teaspoon ground cumin

1 teaspoon grated orange peel

1/8 teaspoon coarsely ground pepper

Tortilla chips

In a large bowl, combine the first 13 ingredients. Cover and refrigerate for at least 2 hours. Serve with tortilla chips.

Prep: **10 min.** + chilling
Yield: **8 cups**

These quick hors d'oeurves may be mini, but their bacon and tomato flavor is full-size. I serve them at parties, brunches and picnics, and they're always a hit. Even my kids love them.

BLT Bites

—*Kellie Remmen*
Detroit Lakes, Minnesota

16 to 20 cherry tomatoes

1 pound sliced bacon, cooked and crumbled

1/2 cup mayonnaise

1/3 cup chopped green onions

3 tablespoons grated Parmesan cheese

2 tablespoons snipped fresh parsley

Cut a thin slice off of each tomato top. Scoop out and discard pulp. Invert the tomatoes on a paper towel to drain.

In a small bowl, combine all remaining ingredients. Spoon into tomatoes. Refrigerate for several hours.

Prep: **25 min.** + chilling
Yield: **16-20 appetizer servings**

Bacon Cheese Spread

—Sharon Wilson Bickett
Chester, South Carolina

Prep/Total Time: **15 min.**
Yield: **4 cups**

This recipe is great for any occasion. Every year, I share Christmas cheer by setting up a buffet at my family's hardware store.

1 package (12 ounces) bacon strips, chopped

4 cups (1 pound) shredded sharp cheddar cheese

2 cups mayonnaise

1/2 cup chopped pecans

1 small onion, chopped

2 tablespoons finely chopped sweet red pepper

1/8 teaspoon cayenne pepper

Assorted crackers

Cook bacon over medium heat until crisp. Using a slotted spoon, remove to paper towels; drain.

In a large bowl, combine the cheese, mayonnaise, pecans, onion, red pepper and cayenne. Stir in bacon. Transfer to a serving dish. Serve with crackers.

Pineapple Pecan Cheese Ball

—June Stone
Brewton, Alabama

Prep: **10 min.** + chilling
Yield: **12-14 servings**

This cheese ball will keep for several days in the refrigerator. It's delicious! I've found it's especially popular at a party or get-together.

2 packages (8 ounces *each*) cream cheese, softened

1 can (8 ounces) crushed pineapple, well drained

1/2 cup chopped green pepper

1/2 cup chopped green onions

1 teaspoon lemon-pepper seasoning

1 teaspoon seasoned salt

2 cups chopped pecans, *divided*

Assorted crackers

In a large mixing bowl, beat cream cheese until smooth. Stir in the pineapple, green pepper, onions, seasonings and 1/2 cup nuts. Turn out onto a sheet of plastic wrap and shape into a ball. Cover and refrigerate several hours or overnight.

Before serving, roll cheese ball in remaining nuts. Serve with crackers.

I've served these easy appetizers many a time at a party and they're always a hit! Strips of chicken are nicely seasoned to give them a savory flavor. The chicken strips and bits of onion sit in jalapeno halves that are wrapped in bacon and grilled. Serve them with blue cheese or ranch salad dressing for dipping.

Jalapeno Chicken Wraps

—Leslie Buenz
Tinley Park, Illinois

- 1 pound boneless skinless chicken breasts
- 1 tablespoon garlic powder
- 1 tablespoon onion powder
- 1 tablespoon pepper
- 2 teaspoons seasoned salt
- 1 teaspoon paprika
- 1 small onion, cut into strips
- 15 jalapeno peppers, halved and seeded
- 1 pound sliced bacon, halved widthwise

Blue cheese salad dressing

Cut chicken into 2-in. x 1-1/2-in. strips. In a large resealable plastic bag, combine the garlic powder, onion powder, pepper, seasoned salt and paprika; add chicken and shake to coat. Place a chicken and onion strip in each jalapeno half. Wrap each with a piece of bacon and secure with toothpicks.

Grill, uncovered, over indirect medium heat for 18-20 minutes or until chicken juices run clear and bacon is crisp, turning once.

Serve with blue cheese dressing.

Editor's Note: When cutting or seeding hot peppers, use rubber or plastic gloves to protect your hands. Avoid touching your face.

Prep: **15 min.**
Grill: **20 min.**
Yield: **2-1/2 dozen**

Setting Up Coals for Indirect Grilling

To set up a charcoal grill for indirect heat, arrange half the coals on one side of the grill and half on the other side, leaving the center open. Set a foil drip pan in the center and place food on grill rack over the drip pan.

Guacamole

—Anne Tipps
Duncanville, Texas

Prep/Total Time: **10 min.**
Yield: **about 1-1/2 cups**

The lemon juice will keep your dip looking fresh and will prevent discoloration until serving. Or, before chilling, place plastic wrap directly over the surface of the guacamole.

1 medium ripe avocado, halved, seeded and peeled

4-1/2 teaspoons lemon juice

1 small tomato, seeded and finely chopped

1/4 cup finely chopped onion

1 tablespoon finely chopped green chilies

1 clove garlic, minced

1/4 teaspoon salt, optional

Tortilla chips

In a large bowl, mash avocado with lemon juice. Stir in the tomato, onion, chilies, garlic and salt if desired. Cover and refrigerate until serving. Serve with tortilla chips.

Confetti Snack Mix

—Billie Blanton
Kingsport, Tennessee

This colorful snack mix will satisfy a sweet tooth or salty tooth! It's great to mix up when friends drop over unexpectedly since it just takes a few minutes to make.

1 package (16 ounces) plain M&M's

1 package (16 ounces) peanut M&M's

1 package (15 ounces) golden raisins

1 can (11-1/2 ounces) mixed nuts

1 package (11 ounces) butterscotch chips

Combine all ingredients in a large bowl. Transfer to airtight containers; store in a cool dry place.

Prep/Total Time: **5 min.**
Yield: **11 cups**

If you're thinking about taking a fruit tray to a breakfast social, consider whipping up this creamy treat, too. Not only does the pretty dip come together easily in a blender, but it only calls for five ingredients.

1 cup sliced fresh
   strawberries

1/4 cup sour cream

1 tablespoon sugar

1/4 teaspoon vanilla extract

1/2 cup heavy whipping cream

Assorted fresh fruit

In a blender, combine the strawberries, sour cream, sugar and vanilla; cover and process until smooth. Transfer to a bowl.

In a small mixing bowl, beat cream until stiff peaks form. Fold into strawberry mixture. Cover and refrigerate for at least 1 hour. Serve with fruit.

Strawberry Fruit Dip

—Lydia Graf, Norton, Ohio

Prep: 15 min. + chilling
Yield: 1-1/2 cups

I make these stuffed eggs once a month for a fellowship meal at church and I've yet to bring one back home! Different from typical versions, these hard-cooked eggs get a subtle crunch from chopped veggies, and the deviled ham adds zing.

8 hard-cooked eggs

1/4 cup deviled ham spread

1/4 cup finely chopped green onions

1/4 cup sweet pickle relish

1/3 cup finely chopped celery

1/3 cup mayonnaise

1 teaspoon prepared mustard

1/8 teaspoon salt

1/8 teaspoon pepper

Paprika

Slice the eggs in half lengthwise; remove yolks and set the whites aside. In a small bowl, mash yolks with a fork. Add the next eight ingredients; mix well. Stuff or pipe into egg whites. Cover and refrigerate until serving. Sprinkle with paprika.

Deviled Ham Stuffed Eggs

—Margaret Walker Pace, Florida

Prep/Total Time: 15 min.
Yield: 8 servings

Taco Appetizer Platter

A crowd usually gathers when I set out my barbecue-flavored taco dip. It's gone before I know it! You can cook the ground beef a day ahead then reheat in the microwave before assembling the dish.

—Iola Egle, Bella Vista, Arkansas

1-1/2 pounds ground beef

1/2 cup water

1 envelope taco seasoning

2 packages (8 ounces *each*) cream cheese, softened

1/4 cup milk

1 can (4 ounces) chopped green chilies, drained

2 medium tomatoes, seeded and chopped

1 cup chopped green onions

1-1/2 cups chopped lettuce

1/2 to 3/4 cup honey barbecue sauce

1 to 1-1/2 cups shredded cheddar cheese

Corn chips

Prep/Total Time: **15 min.**
Yield: **8-10 servings**

In a large skillet, cook beef over medium heat until no longer pink; drain. Add water and taco seasonings; simmer for 5 minutes.

In a large bowl, combine the cream cheese and milk; spread on a 14-in. serving platter or pizza pan. Top with meat mixture. Sprinkle with chilies, tomatoes, onions and lettuce. Drizzle with barbecue sauce. Sprinkle with cheddar cheese. Serve with corn chips.

Taco Appetizer Platter Toppings

To jazz up this tasty dip, you can also sprinkle 1 cup thawed frozen corn and 1 cup canned black beans over the meat mixture.

Refrigerated crescent rolls shape the crust for this party pleaser that features flavored cream cheese and fresh vegetables.

Vegetable Pizza

—Pat Walter
Pine Island, Minnesota

- 1 tube (8 ounces) refrigerated crescent rolls
- 1 package (8 ounces) cream cheese, softened
- 1/2 cup mayonnaise
- 1-1/2 teaspoons ranch salad dressing mix
- 1-1/2 cups fresh broccoli florets
- 1-1/2 cups fresh cauliflowerets
- 1/2 cup chopped radishes
- 1/4 cup chopped ripe olives
- 1/2 cup shredded cheddar cheese

Unroll crescent dough and separate into triangles; arrange to fit on an ungreased 12-in. pizza pan. Press perforations together to seal. Bake at 375° for 8-10 minutes or until golden. Cool.

In a small mixing bowl, beat the cream cheese, mayonnaise and salad dressing mix until smooth. Spread over crust. Sprinkle with the vegetables, olives and cheese.

Prep/Total Time: **25 min.**
Yield: **12 slices**

This tasty, make-ahead dip goes fast at office parties or any gathering. Be sure the corn chips are large enough to scoop up a hearty helping.

Mexican Corn Dip

—Laura Cameron
Delaware, Ohio

Prep: **15 min.** + chilling
Yield: **8-10 servings**

- 2 cups (8 ounces) shredded cheddar cheese
- 1 can (11 ounces) yellow and white whole kernel corn, drained
- 1 can (11 ounces) Mexicorn, drained
- 4 ounces pepper Jack cheese, shredded
- 1/4 cup chopped green onions
- 1 can (4 ounces) chopped green chilies
- 1 jalapeno pepper, seeded and chopped
- 3/4 cup mayonnaise
- 3/4 cup sour cream
- 1/8 teaspoon sugar
- Additional chopped green onions, optional
- Tortilla *or* corn chips

In a large bowl, combine the first seven ingredients. In a small bowl, combine the mayonnaise, sour cream and sugar; stir into corn mixture. Cover and refrigerate overnight. Sprinkle with additional green onions. Serve with chips.

Editor's Note: When cutting or seeding hot peppers, use rubber or plastic gloves to protect your hands. Avoid touching your face.

Festive Cheese Beach Ball

—Florence McClelland
Fredonia, New York

Prep/Total Time: 25 min.
Yield: **7 cups**

This beach-ball-looking cheese ball is filled with a variety of cheeses. I cover each section with a different topping—from chopped yellow peppers to shrimp. You can add your own toppings, such as nuts or chopped red pepper.

6 packages (8 ounces *each*) cream cheese, softened, *divided*

2 cups (8 ounces) crumbled blue cheese

2 cups (8 ounces) shredded cheddar cheese

1/2 cup chopped green onions

1 garlic clove, minced

Toppings:

1/4 cup cooked tiny shrimp

2 tablespoons chopped pimiento-stuffed olives

2 tablespoons crumbled cooked bacon

2 tablespoons chopped sweet yellow pepper

2 tablespoons chopped green onions

2 tablespoons chopped ripe olives

2 tablespoons chopped pimientos

2 tablespoons minced fresh parsley

Assorted crackers

In a large mixing bowl, combine two packages of cream cheese and the blue cheese. In another mixing bowl, combine two packages of cream cheese and the cheddar cheese; set aside. In a third bowl, beat the remaining cream cheese; add the onions and garlic.

In a 2-qt. bowl lined with plastic wrap, layer each portion of cream cheese. Invert onto a serving platter; remove plastic wrap and shape into a ball. With a sharp knife, score eight sections on the ball. Sprinkle each section with one of the toppings and press lightly. Cover and refrigerate until serving. Serve with crackers.

Shrimp Math

One pound of medium shrimp will have about 45 shrimp. This means each person will have 5 shrimp. If your group loves shrimp, you may wish to double the recipe.

These bite-size snacks are delicious any time of the day. Simply combine the cream cheese, dried beef, vegetables and salad dressing mix, spread over tortillas, roll up, refrigerate, slice and serve.

- 1 package (8 ounces) cream cheese, softened
- 4 teaspoons ranch salad dressing mix
- 1 package (2-1/4 ounces) dried beef, chopped
- 1/2 cup chopped fresh broccoli
- 1/2 cup chopped fresh cauliflower
- 1/4 cup chopped green onions
- 1/4 cup sliced pimiento-stuffed olives
- 5 flour tortillas (8 inches)

Salsa, optional

In a large mixing bowl, beat the cream cheese and salad dressing mix until blended. Stir in the beef, broccoli, cauliflower, onions and olives. Spread over tortillas; roll up tightly and wrap in plastic wrap. Refrigerate for at least 2 hours.

Unwrap and cut into 1/2-in. slices. Serve with salsa if desired.

Veggie Tortilla Pinwheels

—Doris Ann Yoder
Arthur, Illinois

Prep: **15 min. + chilling**
Yield: **about 5 dozen**

My husband's cousin introduced us to this recipe. Every time I bring it to a party, everyone wants the recipe. It's so easy to prepare.

- 1 pound cooked medium shrimp, peeled and deveined
- 1 small red onion, thinly sliced
- 2-1/2 teaspoons capers
- 1/3 cup vegetable oil
- 1/4 cup white wine vinegar
- 1/2 teaspoon salt
- 1/2 teaspoon celery seed

In a large serving bowl, combine the shrimp, onion and capers.

In a jar with a tight-fitting lid, combine the oil, vinegar, salt and celery seed; shake well. Pour over shrimp mixture and toss to coat. Cover and refrigerate for 6 hours or overnight, stirring occasionally. Serve with a slotted spoon.

Marinated Shrimp

—Stephanie Marchese
Whitefish Bay, Wisconsin

Prep: **15 min. + marinating**
Yield: **8-10 servings**

Herbed Garlic Cheese Spread

—Christine Duffy
Concord, New Hampshire

Prep: **5 min. + chilling**
Yield: **about 3 cups**

I've taken this creamy spread to many parties and holiday gatherings—and there's never any left to bring home! Well-seasoned with a blend of herb flavors, this cheesy treat tastes great on slices of French bread, too.

2 packages (8 ounces *each*)
  cream cheese, softened

1 cup butter, softened

1/2 teaspoon *each* dried basil,
  marjoram, oregano,
  thyme, dill weed, garlic
  powder and pepper

Assorted crackers

In a large mixing bowl, beat the cream cheese, butter and seasonings until well blended. Cover and refrigerate for at least 2 hours. Serve with crackers.

Peachy Avocado Salsa

—Shelly Platten
Amherst, Wisconsin

Prep: **15 min. + chilling**
Yield: **3 cups**

This bright and colorful, fruity salsa is a welcome change from the store-bought varieties. It's wonderful served with tortilla chips. I usually make a double batch since my husband and our two children can't seem to get enough of it.

1 can (15-1/4 ounces)
  sliced peaches, drained
  and chopped

1 medium ripe avocado,
  peeled and chopped

1 tablespoon lime juice

2 cups chopped seeded
  tomatoes

1/4 cup diced onion

2 tablespoons minced fresh
  cilantro

1 tablespoon cider vinegar

1 to 2 teaspoons seeded
  chopped jalapeno pepper

1 garlic clove, minced

1/4 teaspoon salt

Tortilla chips

In a large bowl, combine the peaches, avocado and lime juice. Add the tomatoes, onion, cilantro, vinegar, pepper, garlic and salt. Lightly toss just until combined. Cover and refrigerate for at least 30 minutes. Serve with tortilla chips.

Editor's Note: When cutting or seeding hot peppers, use rubber or plastic gloves to protect your hands. Avoid touching your face.

Refreshing
Coolers

Cranberry Quencher

—Dorothy Smith
El Dorado, Arkansas

Prep/Total Time: **5 min.**
Yield: **6 quarts**

You need just three items to stir up this rosy fruit punch. Float a few fresh cranberries on top or garnish each glass with a pineapple wedge for a fast finishing touch.

1 bottle (64 ounces) cranberry-apple juice

1 can (46 ounces) pineapple juice, chilled

1 can (6 ounces) frozen lemonade *or* orange juice concentrate, thawed

In a large container or punch bowl, combine the juices. Stir in the lemonade concentrate. Serve immediately.

Citrus Mint Cooler

—Kathy Burkholder
Bakersfield, California

Prep: **30 min. + chilling**
Yield: **about 15 servings**

My grandmother used to make this refreshing drink for those hot Oklahoma summer days. The family would sit on the front porch relaxing while sipping this drink. Here in California, where lemons, oranges and mint are so abundant, my family has found equal enjoyment sitting in the shade and drinking a tall glass of this thirst-quenching cooler.

1 cup fresh lemon juice (about 6 lemons)

1 cup fresh orange juice (about 6 oranges)

2 cups sugar

2-1/2 cups water

10 mint sprigs

1 bottle (32 ounces) ginger ale, chilled

Water

Ice cubes

In a large saucepan, combine the first five ingredients. Bring to a boil over medium heat; cook until the sugar is dissolved, stirring occasionally. Cover and remove from the heat; cool to room temperature.

Line a mesh strainer with a double layer of cheesecloth or a coffee filter. Strain, discarding mint. Cover and refrigerate.

To serve, fill chilled glasses or a pitcher with equal amounts of the fruit juice, ginger ale and water. Add the ice cubes and serve immediately.

The ingredients in this slushy beverage tastes just like orange Creamsicles. If you don't have time to freeze the orange juice, use orange sorbet instead.

Orange Cream Slush

—Nina Hall
Spokane, Washington

8 cups orange juice

8 scoops vanilla ice cream

8 orange slices, optional

Pour the orange juice into 2-qt. freezer container; cover and freeze for 2 hours or until slushy, stirring twice.

To serve, pour slush into eight glasses. Add a scoop of ice cream to each glass. Garnish with orange slices if desired.

Prep: 10 min. + freezing
Yield: 8 servings

Mint juleps are a favored beverage of folks at the Kentucky Derby. Our home economists offer two versions here—one traditional, one nonalcoholic.

Mint Julep

—Taste of Home Test Kitchen
Greendale, Wisconsin

Prep: 30 min. + chilling
Yield: 10 servings

Mint Syrup:

2 cups sugar

2 cups water

2 cups coarsely chopped loosely packed fresh mint

Beverage:

2/3 to 1-1/4 cups bourbon

Cracked ice

10 mint sprigs

For syrup, combine the sugar, water and mint in a saucepan. Bring to a boil over medium heat; cook until sugar is dissolved, stirring occasionally. Remove from the heat; cool to room temperature.

Line a mesh strainer with a double layer of cheesecloth or a coffee filter. Strain syrup; discard mint. Cover and refrigerate syrup for at least 2 hours or until chilled.

For each serving, combine 1/4 cup mint syrup and 1-2 table-spoons bourbon. Pour into a glass over cracked ice. Garnish with a mint sprig.

Mock Mint Julep: Prepare mint syrup as directed; after straining, add 1/2 cup lemon juice. Cover and refrigerate for at least 2 hours or until chilled. For each serving, combine 1/2 cup club soda and 1/4 cup mint syrup. Pour into a glass over cracked ice. Garnish with a mint sprig.

Strawberry Shakes

—Ruby Williams
Bogalusa, Louisiana

Prep/Total Time: 5 min.
Yield: 4 servings

Full of summer fruit, these thick berry blends are the perfect way to savor hot days. I serve tall glasses with strawberry garnishes.

2/3 cup milk

3 cups strawberry ice cream

1 cup fresh strawberries

2 tablespoons strawberry syrup

In a blender, combine all ingredients; cover and process until smooth. Pour into chilled glasses. Serve immediately.

Editor's Note: Double this recipe when cooking for a crowd.

Iced Coffee

—Jenny Reece
Lowry, Minnesota

Prep/Total Time: 5 min.
Yield: 2 cups

When I first tried iced coffee, I didn't think I'd like it. But now I created this fast-to-fix version, and it's a refreshing alternative to hot coffee.

4 teaspoons instant coffee granules

1 cup boiling water

Sugar substitute equivalent to 4 teaspoons sugar, optional

1 cup fat-free milk

4 teaspoons chocolate syrup

1/8 teaspoon vanilla extract

Ice cubes

In a large bowl, dissolve the coffee in water. Add the sweetener if desired. Stir in the milk, chocolate syrup and vanilla; mix well. Serve over ice.

Editor's Note: This recipe was tested with Splenda No Calorie Sweetener. For a crowd, prepare coffee for as many servings as desired and chill. When ready to serve, combine the chilled coffee and remaining ingredients in a large pitcher. Serve over ice.

This pleasing punch is wonderful for special occasions. To make it even more festive, float an ice ring in the punch.

Champagne Party Punch

—Taste of Home Test Kitchen
Greendale, Wisconsin

1 cup sugar

1 cup water

2 cups unsweetened apple juice

2 cups unsweetened pineapple juice

1/2 cup lemon juice

1/3 cup frozen orange juice concentrate, thawed

1/4 cup lime juice

2 cups ice cubes

1 quart ginger ale, chilled

1 bottle (750 ml) champagne, chilled

In a large pitcher, combine the sugar and water; stir until sugar is dissolved. Add the apple juice, pineapple juice, lemon juice, orange juice concentrate and lime juice. Refrigerate until serving.

Just before serving, pour into a punch bowl and add ice cubes. Slowly add the ginger ale and champagne.

Prep: **15 min. + chilling**
Yield: **16-18 servings (3-1/2 quarts)**

For more fun variations, try using your favorite gelatin and sherbet flavors (such as orange, strawberry or lemon).

Springtime Lime Slushy

—Joyce Minge-Johns
Jacksonville, Florida

2 packages (3 ounces *each*) lime gelatin

2 cups boiling water

2 cups cold water

2 quarts lime sherbet

3 cups ginger ale, chilled

In a freezer container, dissolve the gelatin in boiling water. Stir in the cold water and sherbet until combined. Freeze for 4 hours or until set.

Remove from the freezer 45 minutes before serving. For each serving, place 1 cup of slush mixture in a glass; add about 1/3 cup ginger ale.

Prep: **10 min. + freezing**
Yield: **8 servings**

Old-Fashioned Lemonade

—Tammi Simpson
Greensburg, Kentucky

Prep: 15 min. + chilling
Yield: 2 quarts

Memorial Day and Fourth of July gatherings just wouldn't be the same without homemade lemonade. The fresh-squeezed flavor of this sweet-tart beverage makes it a winner.

2 to 2-1/2 cups sugar

5 cups water, *divided*

1 tablespoon grated lemon peel

1-3/4 cups lemon juice (about 6 lemons), *divided*

In a large saucepan, combine the sugar, 1 cup water and lemon peel. Bring to a boil over medium heat; cook until sugar is dissolved, stirring occasionally.

Remove from the heat. Stir in lemon juice and remaining water. Pour into a pitcher and refrigerate until chilled. Serve over ice.

Citrus Quencher

—Romaine Wetzel
Lancaster, Pennsylvania

Prep/Total Time: 10 min.
Yield: 3 quarts

Here's a refreshing beverage that's perfect on a hot summer day. It's a great complement to any chicken dish.

1 cup lemon juice

1 cup lime juice

1 cup sugar

1 container (64 ounces) orange juice

2 cups club soda, chilled

Lime slices, optional

In a large pitcher or container, combine the lemon juice, lime juice and sugar; stir until sugar is dissolved. Stir in orange juice. Refrigerate until serving. Add soda and ice cubes. Garnish with lime if desired.

For years, our family has toasted special occasions with this cool, quenching punch featuring wonderful rhubarb. It's easy to freeze, so we serve it throughout the year whenever we have a craving for it. Usually, we double the recipe and store it in the freezer in a clean, empty ice cream bucket. It always seems to disappear.

Rhubarb Slush Punch

—Diane Haug
Neenah, Wisconsin

6 cups chopped fresh *or* frozen rhubarb, thawed

7 cups water, *divided*

2 cups sugar

3/4 cup orange juice concentrate

3/4 cup lemonade concentrate

10 cups club soda, chilled

In a large saucepan, bring rhubarb and 4 cups water to a boil. Reduce heat; simmer, uncovered, for 5-8 minutes or until rhubarb is tender. Mash rhubarb; strain. Reserve juice and discard pulp. Add the sugar, concentrates and remaining water to rhubarb juice. Transfer to a freezer container and freeze.

Remove from the freezer 30-45 minutes before serving, scraping the surface as it thaws. Place equal amounts of slush mixture and club soda in each serving glass. Serve immediately.

Editor's Note: If using frozen rhubarb, measure rhubarb while still frozen, then thaw completely. Drain in a colander, but do not press liquid out.

Prep: **10 min.**

Cook: **10 min.** + freezing

Yield: **10 servings**

Fruit Punch

—Ruth Tacoma
Falmouth, Michigan

We had a diabetic child in our church youth group a few years ago and I tried to fix snacks that would be within his restrictions but enjoyable for the other kids as well. This punch really fills the bill.

1 package (.35-ounce) sugar-free tropical punch-flavored soft drink mix

4-3/4 cups water

1 (12-ounce) can unsweetened frozen orange juice concentrate, thawed

16 cups diet lemon-lime soda

In a large pitcher, combine soft drink mix and water. Add orange juice concentrate; mix well. Just before serving, pour mixture into a punch bowl; stir in the soda.

Prep/Total Time: **5 min.**
Yield: **20 servings**

Fresh Lime Margaritas

—Taste of Home Test Kitchen
Greendale, Wisconsin

Prep/Total Time: **15 min.**
Yield: **4 servings**

This basic margarita recipe is easy to modify to your tastes...try it frozen or with strawberries.

4 lime wedges

1 tablespoon kosher salt

1/2 cup gold tequila

1/4 cup Triple Sec

1/4 cup lime juice

1/4 cup lemon juice

2 tablespoons superfine sugar

1-1/3 cups crushed ice

Using lime wedges, moisten rim of four glasses. Holding each glass upside down, dip rim into salt; set aside.

In a pitcher, combine the tequila, Triple Sec, lime juice, lemon juice and sugar; stir until sugar is dissolved. Serve in prepared glasses over crushed ice.

For Frozen Lime Margaritas: Reduce lemon and lime juices to 2 tablespoons each. Increase the superfine sugar to 1/4 cup and the crushed ice to 4 cups. Add 3/4 cup limeade concentrate. Prepare glasses as directed. In a blender, combine the tequila, Triple Sec, lime juice, lemon juice, limeade concentrate, superfine sugar and crushed ice; cover and process until smooth. **Yield:** 5 cups.

For Frozen Strawberry Margaritas: Follow directions for the Frozen Lime Margaritas, except reduce the crushed ice to 2 cups and add 2 cups frozen unsweetened strawberries. **Yield:** 4 cups.

This beverage is one of our favorites to serve during the hot, humid summer months. We keep a jug in the refrigerator ready to serve family and guests.

Lemony Iced Tea

—Sharon Emery
New Burnside, Illinois

Prep/Total Time: **10 min.**
Yield: **8 servings**

- 8 cups water
- 3/4 cup sugar
- 1/2 cup lemon juice
- 1/2 cup white grape juice
- 1/4 cup unsweetened lemon-flavored instant tea mix

Lemon slices

In a large pitcher, combine the water, sugar, lemon juice, grape juice and tea mix. Stir until sugar dissolved. Serve in chilled glasses over ice with lemon slices.

This lemonade is a wonderful thirst quencher for a picnic or after a hot day of yard work or sports activities. It's my family's favorite. The addition of orange juice adds a fantastic flavor.

Orange Lemonade

—Tracie Loyd
Powell, Tennessee

- 2 quarts water
- 1 cup sugar
- 1 can (12 ounces) frozen orange juice concentrate, thawed
- 1 can (12 ounces) frozen lemonade concentrate, thawed

In a large saucepan, combine water and sugar. Bring to a boil over medium heat; cook until sugar is dissolved, stirring occasionally. Remove from the heat; cool to room temperature. Transfer to a large pitcher or container; stir in concentrates. Chill.

Prep: **10 min. + cooling**
Yield: **12 servings**

Sparkling White Grape Juice

—Taste of Home Test Kitchen
Greendale, Wisconsin

Prep/Total Time: **5 min.**
Yield: **7 servings**

The bubbles from the lemon-lime soda cling to the grape "ice cubes," giving this refreshing beverage lots of sparkle.

2-1/3 cups white grape juice, chilled

4-2/3 cups chilled lemon-lime soda

Green grapes

In a pitcher, combine grape juice and soda. Pour into chilled glasses. Thread grapes on skewers; add to each glass.

Fancy Berry Beverage

—Christine Wilson
Sellersville, Pennsylvania

Prep/Total Time: **10 min.**
Yield: **5 quarts**

We offer this fruity beverage to guests to add a festive touch to any gatherings. It pours up frothy, then separates into a dark pink base with a light foamy top. A slightly tart drink, it's wonderful with home-baked cookies.

8 cups cranberry juice, chilled

1 quart vanilla ice cream, softened

1 package (10 ounces) frozen sweetened sliced strawberries, thawed and pureed

1-1/4 cups sugar

1 teaspoon vanilla extract

2 cups heavy whipping cream, whipped

4 cups ginger ale, chilled

Fresh strawberries, optional

In a large bowl or container, combine the first five ingredients; stir until smooth and the sugar is dissolved. Fold in whipped cream. Slowly add ginger ale; stir gently to mix. Pour into glasses. Garnish with strawberries if desired. Serve immediately.

...flavor and lovely color to this pretty iced ...mon ingredients and offers make-ahead

1-1/2 c...

1 pac...ge (12 ounces)
frozen unsweetened
raspberries

10 individual tea bags

1/4 cup lemon juice

In a Dutch oven, combine water and sugar. Bring to a boil over medium heat; cook until sugar is dissolved, stirring occasionally. Remove from the heat. Add the raspberries, tea bags and lemon juice. Cover and steep for 3 minutes. Strain; discard berries and tea bags.

Cool to room temperature. Transfer tea to a large container or pitcher. Refrigerate until chilled. Serve over ice.

Raspberry Ice Tea

—Lois McGrady
Hillsville, Virginia

Prep: **10 min.** + chilling
Yield: **16 servings (4 quarts)**

This fruit smoothie is a blend of my family's favorite juices and fruits. It's a delicious beverage to serve at a brunch.

5 cups grapefruit juice

3 cups orange juice

1 cup water

4 medium firm bananas, cut up and frozen

12 frozen unsweetened whole strawberries

In a blender, place half of each ingredients; cover and process until smooth. Pour into a pitcher. Repeat. Serve immediately.

Citrus Fruit Smoothies

—Rose Press, Topeka, Kansas

Prep/Total Time: **10 min.**
Yield: **8 servings**

Strawberry Watermelon Slush

—Patty Howse
Great Falls, Montana

Prep/Total Time: **10 min.**
Yield: **5 cups**

Summertime's the perfect time for this thirst-quenching slush featuring fresh watermelon and strawberries.

2 cups cubed seedless watermelon

1 pint fresh strawberries, halved

1/3 cup sugar

1/3 cup lemon juice

2 cups ice cubes

In a blender, combine the watermelon, strawberries, sugar and lemon juice; cover and process until smooth. While processing, gradually add the ice cubes; process until slushy. Pour into chilled glasses; serve immediately.

Sangria

—Taste of Home Test Kitchen
Greendale, Wisconsin

Prep: **15 min.+ chilling**
Yield: **5 servings**

This is a great make-ahead beverage because it allows time for the flavors to blend together.

1 bottle (750 ml) Zinfandel *or* other fruity red wine

3/4 cup orange juice

1/3 cup unsweetened pineapple juice

1/4 cup superfine sugar

1 medium orange, sliced

1 medium lemon, sliced

1 medium lime, cut into wedges

In a pitcher, combine the wine, orange juice, pineapple juice and sugar; stir until sugar is dissolved. Add fruit, press lightly with a wooden spoon. Refrigerate for 2-4 hours. Serve over ice.

Sparkling Berry Punch

—*Kay Curtis, Guthrie, Oklahoma*

This beverage really rounded out our Valentine's Day dinner one year. But I've found it makes a colorful addition to any party menu no matter the season.

- 6 cups cranberry juice, chilled
- 2 cans (12 ounces *each*) ginger ale, chilled
- 1/4 teaspoon almond extract

Combine all of the ingredients in a punch bowl or pitcher. Serve immediately on ice.

Prep/Total Time: **10 min.**
Yield: **about 2 quarts**

Bottoms-Up Cherry Limeade

—*Awynne Thurstenson*
Siloam Springs, Arkansas

My guests enjoy this refreshing cherry-topped drink. It's just right on a hot southern summer evening. And it's pretty, too.

- 3/4 cup lime juice
- Sugar substitute equivalent to 1 cup sugar
- 2 liters lime carbonated water, chilled
- 1/2 cup maraschino cherry juice
- 8 maraschino cherries with stems
- 8 lime slices

In a bowl, combine lime juice and sugar substitute. Cover and refrigerate. Just before serving, stir carbonated water into lime juice mixture.

For each serving, place 1 tablespoon cherry juice in a glass. Add crushed ice and about 1 cup of lime juice mixture. Garnish with a maraschino cherry and a lime slice.

Editor's Note: This recipe was tested with Splenda No Calorie Sweetener.

Prep/Total Time: **10 min.**
Yield: **8 servings**

Strawberry Lemonade

—Denise Nebel, Wayland, Iowa

Prep/Total Time: 5 min.
Yield: 8 servings (2 quarts)

This refreshing beverage is the perfect reason for a break during a day of hard work! It's also nice for when family or guests are over for lunch.

3 cups cold water
1 quart fresh strawberries
3/4 cup sugar
3/4 cup lemon juice
2 cups cold club soda
Lemon slices, optional

Place half of the water, strawberries and sugar in a blender; cover and process until smooth. Transfer to a large pitcher. Repeat with remaining water, strawberries and sugar. Stir in lemon juice, then add soda. Serve immediately, garnished with lemon if desired.

Refreshing Raspberry Cooler

—Doreen Patterson
Qualicum Beach, British Columbia

Prep: 10 min.
Cook: 20 min. + chilling
Yield: 14 servings
(about 3-1/2 quarts)

This recipe explodes with raspberry flavor! It's a wonderful summertime treat.

8 cups fresh *or* frozen raspberries, thawed
1-1/2 cups sugar
2/3 cup cider vinegar
2-1/2 cups cold water, *divided*
2 liters ginger ale, chilled

In a large saucepan, crush the berries. Stir in the sugar, vinegar and 1/2 cup water. Bring to a boil; reduce heat. Simmer, uncovered, for 20 minutes.

Remove from the heat. Strain to remove seeds. Cool; refrigerate. Just before serving, stir in ginger ale and remaining water. Serve over ice.

Lazy
Weekend
Brunches

Deluxe Ham Omelet

—Iola Egle, Bella Vista, Arkansas

Ham, vegetables and two cheeses are what make this omelet deluxe. It's a hearty meal for one or two. If you like, substitute finely chopped, cooked sausage or Canadian bacon for the ham. For a little zip, use pepper Jack cheese instead of the cheddar cheese.

3 eggs

2 tablespoons half-and-half cream

2 tablespoons minced chives

1/2 teaspoon garlic salt

1/4 teaspoon pepper

1 tablespoon olive oil

1/2 cup finely chopped fully cooked ham

2 tablespoons chopped green pepper

2 tablespoons chopped tomato

2 fresh mushrooms, sliced

2 tablespoons shredded cheddar cheese

2 tablespoons shredded part-skim mozzarella cheese

Prep/Total Time: **20 min.**

Yield: **1-2 servings**

In a small bowl, beat eggs, cream, chives, garlic salt and pepper.

Heat oil in a large skillet over medium heat; add egg mixture. As eggs set, lift edges, letting uncooked portion flow underneath. When the eggs are set, spoon the ham, green pepper, tomato, mushrooms and cheeses over one side; fold omelet over filling. Cover and let stand for 1-1/2 minutes or until cheese is melted.

Editor's Note: For a group, figure 1 to 2 eggs per person. Increase the seasonings proportionally, based on the number of eggs you use. Using about a 1/3 to 2/3 cup per omelet, prepare omelets as directed. If desired, let each guest personalize their omelet by choosing their own toppings. To keep the omelets warm, place in a preheated 200° oven on heatproof plates.

This is a great dish to make ahead of time and freeze; then you'll have a fancy but easy-to-prepare breakfast whenever you host overnight guests or have people over for a breakfast buffet.

Overnight French Toast

—Sue Marsteller
Gouldsboro, Pennsylvania

9 eggs

3 cups half-and-half cream

1/3 cup sugar

1-1/2 teaspoons rum extract, optional

1-1/2 teaspoons vanilla extract

1/2 teaspoon ground nutmeg

24 to 30 slices French bread, cut into 3/4-inch slices

Praline Syrup:

1-1/2 cups packed brown sugar

1/2 cup light corn syrup

1/2 cup water

1/2 cup chopped pecans, toasted

2 tablespoons butter

In a large bowl, lightly beat eggs. Mix in the cream, sugar, rum extract if desired, vanilla and nutmeg. Place the bread in a single layer in two well-greased 15-in. x 10-in. x 1-in. baking pans. Pour the egg mixture over bread in each pan. Turn the bread over to coat both sides. Cover and refrigerate overnight.

Remove from the refrigerator 30 minutes before baking. Bake, uncovered, at 400° for 20-22 minutes or until golden.

Meanwhile, for syrup, bring the brown sugar, corn syrup and water to a boil in a saucepan. Reduce heat; simmer, uncovered, for 3 minutes. Add pecans and butter; simmer 2 minutes longer. Serve with the French toast.

Prep: 20 min. + chilling
Bake: 20 min.
Yield: 10-12 servings

I'm on a restricted diet, but my husband is not. So, I'll often make two different single-size recipes. This is a delicious breakfast or luncheon treat and can even be served as a dessert!

Yogurt Parfait

—Dottye Wolf, Rolla, Missouri

1 carton (6 ounces) flavored yogurt

1/4 cup granola

1/2 cup assorted fresh fruit

In a parfait glass or large glass mug, layer one-third of the yogurt, half of the granola and then half of the fruit. Repeat layers. Top with the remaining yogurt.

Editor's Note: This recipe takes just a few minutes to assemble so make the parfaits just before serving. For a group, have an assortment of yogurt flavors and fruit.

Prep/Total Time: 5 min.
Yield: 1 serving

Cranberry Velvet Freeze

—Pat Seville
Hagerstown, Maryland

Prep: 10 min. + freezing
Yield: 12-16 servings

Everyone in my family loves this dessert. I normally serve it at family gatherings when we're all together.

2 cans (16 ounces *each*) whole-berry cranberry sauce

2 cans (one 20 ounces, one 8 ounces) crushed pineapple, drained

1 package (10-1/2 ounces) miniature marshmallows

1 cup green maraschino cherries, quartered

1 cup red maraschino cherries, quartered

1 teaspoon lemon juice

3 cups heavy whipping cream, whipped

In a large bowl, combine the cranberry sauce, pineapple, marshmallows, cherries and lemon juice. Fold in whipped cream.

Spoon into an ungreased 13-in. x 9-in. x 2-in. dish. Cover and freeze overnight. Remove from the freezer 10 minutes before serving.

Spring Breakfast Strata

—Maryellen Hays
Fort Wayne, Indiana

Prep: 15 min. + chilling
Bake: 1 hour + standing
Yield: 12 servings

Eggs are the star of this hearty breakfast fare. Filled with tasty ingredients like ham, mushrooms, cheddar cheese and asparagus, this dish is super. You can prepare it the night before for a no-fuss breakfast, brunch or dish to pass.

8 eggs

3 cups milk

1 tablespoon Dijon mustard

2 teaspoons dried basil

1 teaspoon salt

2 tablespoons butter, melted

2 tablespoons all-purpose flour

2 cups (8 ounces) shredded cheddar cheese

1 pound fully cooked ham, cubed

1 package (10-1/2 ounces) frozen cut asparagus, thawed

2 cups sliced fresh mushrooms

10 cups cubed bread

In a large bowl, beat eggs; add the milk, mustard, basil and salt. Gently stir in remaining ingredients until well mixed. Pour into a greased 13-in. x 9-in. x 2-in. baking dish. Cover and refrigerate 8 hours or overnight.

Remove from the refrigerator 30 minutes before baking. Bake, uncovered, at 350° for 1 hour or until a knife inserted near the center comes out clean. Let stand for 10 minutes before cutting.

The glorious colors of assorted fruits make this a great summer salad. Slightly sweet and chilled, it makes a nice accompaniment to a grilled dinner or an early-morning meal.

Fresh Fruit Bowl
—Marlon Kirst, Troy, Michigan

- 8 to 10 cups fresh melon cubes
- 1 to 2 tablespoons light corn syrup
- 1 pint fresh strawberries
- 2 cups fresh pineapple chunks
- 2 oranges, sectioned

Fresh mint leaves, optional

In a large bowl, combine melon cubes and corn syrup. Cover and refrigerate overnight. Just before serving, stir in remaining fruit. Garnish with fresh mint leaves if desired.

Prep: **15 min. + chilling**
Yield: **3-4 quarts**

Melon Yields

A medium cantaloupe will yield about 4-1/2 cups of cubes, while a medium honeydew will yield about 4 cups.

Egg Blossoms

—Barbara Nowakowski
North Tonawanda, New York

Prep: 35 min.
Bake: 25 min.
Yield: 4 servings

These cute phyllo dough shells are filled with a savory combination of Parmesan cheese, egg and green onion. The flaky cups are served atop a warm homemade salsa.

4 sheets phyllo dough
    (14 inches x 9 inches)

2 tablespoons butter,
    melted

4 teaspoons grated
    Parmesan cheese

4 eggs

4 teaspoons finely chopped
    green onion

1/4 teaspoon salt

1/8 teaspoon pepper

Salsa:

1 can (14-1/2 ounces) diced
    tomatoes, undrained

1 small onion, chopped

1-1/2 teaspoons sugar

1-1/2 teaspoons white wine
    vinegar

1 garlic clove, minced

1/2 teaspoon salt

1/4 teaspoon dried oregano

Place one sheet of phyllo dough on a work surface; brush with butter. Top with another sheet of phyllo; brush with butter. Cut into six 4-1/2-in. squares. (Keep remaining phyllo dough covered with plastic wrap and a damp towel to prevent it from drying out.) Repeat with the remaining phyllo and butter.

Stack three squares of layered phyllo in each of four greased muffin cups, rotating squares so corners do not overlap. Sprinkle 1 teaspoon of cheese into each cup. Top with one egg. Sprinkle with the green onion, salt and pepper. Place on a baking sheet. Bake at 350° for 25-30 minutes or until eggs are completely set and pastry is golden brown.

Meanwhile, combine the salsa ingredients in a saucepan. Bring to a boil over medium heat. Reduce heat; simmer, uncovered, for 10 minutes or until onion is tender. Serve with egg cups.

Editor's Note: Double this recipe when cooking for crowd.

Dutch Honey Syrup

—Kathy Scott
Hemingford, Nebraska

Prep/Total Time: 15 min.
Yield: 2 cups

It was a special treat when Mom served this scrumptious syrup with our pancakes, waffles or French toast.

1 cup sugar

1 cup corn syrup

1 cup heavy whipping cream

1 teaspoon vanilla extract

In a saucepan, combine the sugar, corn syrup and cream. Bring to a boil over medium heat; boil for 5 minutes or until slightly thickened, stirring occasionally. Remove from the heat; stir in vanilla.

When you're short on time and scrambling to get a meal on the table, this recipe is "eggs-actly" what you need. There's a short ingredient list, and cooking is kept to a minimum. Plus, with green pepper and tomato, it's colorful.

Calico Scrambled Eggs

—Taste of Home Test Kitchen Greendale, Wisconsin

1/2 cup chopped green pepper

1/4 cup chopped onion

1 tablespoon butter

8 eggs

1/4 cup milk

1/8 to 1/4 teaspoon dill weed

1/8 to 1/4 teaspoon salt

1/8 to 1/4 teaspoon pepper

1/2 cup chopped fresh tomato

In a 12-in. nonstick skillet, saute green pepper and onion in butter until tender. Remove and set aside.

In a large bowl, beat eggs with milk, dill, salt and pepper. Pour into the skillet; cook and stir gently over medium heat until eggs are nearly set. Add pepper mixture and tomato; cook and stir until heated through and the eggs are completely set.

Editor's Note: Double this recipe when cooking for crowd.

Prep/Total Time: **20 min.**

Yield: **4 servings**

These golden, fluffy pancakes are great for Sunday brunches with friends. The buttermilk batter is refrigerated overnight to help ease the morning rush.

Overnight Pancakes

—Lisa Sammons Cut Bank, Montana

1 package (1/4 ounce) active dry yeast

1/4 cup warm water (110° to 115°)

4 cups all-purpose flour

2 tablespoons baking powder

2 teaspoons baking soda

2 teaspoons sugar

1 teaspoon salt

6 eggs

4 cups buttermilk

1/4 cup vegetable oil

In a small bowl, dissolve yeast in water; let stand for 5 minutes. In a large bowl, combine the dry ingredients. Beat the eggs, buttermilk and oil; stir into dry ingredients just until moistened. Stir in yeast mixture. Cover and refrigerate for 8 hours or overnight.

To make pancakes, pour batter by 1/4 cupfuls onto a greased hot griddle; turn when bubbles form on top of pancakes. Cook until second side is golden brown.

Editor's Note: These pancakes are topped with Ruby Breakfast Sauce on page 61.

Prep: **10 min. + chilling**

Cook: **10 min.**

Yield: **about 2-1/2 dozen**

Fruit Slush Cups

—Betty Webb, Nauvoo, Illinois

This frosty favorite is a great brunch snack. Pour the entire batch into one container to freeze, then scoop out single servings. Or, spoon the colorful medley into individual plastic cups before freezing.

4 cups water

1 to 1-1/2 cups sugar

3/4 cup orange juice concentrate

3/4 cup lemonade concentrate

3 medium firm bananas, sliced

1 can (20 ounces) unsweetened pineapple tidbits, undrained

1 can (11 ounces) mandarin oranges, drained

1/2 cup halved maraschino cherries

In a saucepan, combine the water, sugar and concentrates. Cook and stir over medium heat until sugar is dissolved. Stir in the fruit.

Pour into a shallow 3-qt. freezer container. Cover and freeze for 8 hours or overnight. Remove from the freezer 1 hour before serving.

Prep: 10 min. + freezing
Yield: 12 servings

Smoky Bacon Wraps

—Cara Flora Kokomo, Indiana

All you need are three ingredients to assemble these cute, little sausage-bacon bites. The simple breakfast item has a sweet and salty flavor, making the sausages great appetizers, too.

1 pound sliced bacon

1 package (16 ounces) miniature smoked sausage links

1 cup packed brown sugar

Cut each bacon strip in half widthwise. Wrap one piece of bacon around each sausage. Place in a foil-lined 15-in. x 10-in. x 1-in. baking pan. Sprinkle with brown sugar. Bake, uncovered, at 400° for 30-40 minutes or until bacon is crisp and sausage is heated through.

Prep: 20 min.
Bake: 30 min.
Yield: about 3-1/2 dozen

Garden vegetables and herbs give a savory zing to this fresh-tasting omelet. The tomato sauce makes this extra special.

Italian Omelet

—Dixie Terry, Marion, Illinois

1 cup sliced fresh
  mushrooms

1 cup sliced zucchini

3 tablespoons butter,
  divided

4 eggs

3 tablespoons water

1/4 teaspoon salt

1/4 teaspoon pepper

1/2 cup shredded part-skim
  mozzarella cheese

Sauce:

1 tablespoon butter

1 medium tomato, chopped

2 tablespoons minced fresh
  parsley

1 garlic clove, minced

1/2 teaspoon dried basil

1/8 teaspoon salt

In an 8-in. nonstick skillet, saute mushrooms and zucchini in 2 tablespoons butter until tender; remove and keep warm.

In the same skillet, melt remaining butter. In a small bowl, beat eggs, water, salt and pepper. Pour into the skillet, cook over medium heat. As eggs set, lift edges, letting uncooked portion flow underneath. When eggs are nearly set, spoon vegetable mixture over half of the omelet; sprinkle with cheese.

Fold the omelet in half over filling. Cover and cook for 1-2 minutes or until cheese is melted.

Meanwhile, melt butter in a small saucepan over medium heat. Add remaining sauce ingredients; cook and stir for 5 minutes or until heated through. Serve over the omelet.

Editor's Note: For a group, figure 2 eggs per person. Increase the seasonings proportionally, based on the number of eggs you use. Using about a 1/2 cup per omelet, or 1 cup per batch, prepare omelets as directed. To keep the omelets warm, place in a preheated 200° oven on heatproof plates.

Prep/Total Time: **30 min.**
Yield: **2 servings**

Oatmeal Nut Waffles

—Joan Scott, Dunbar, Wisconsin

When I found this recipe in a church cookbook early in my marriage, I was eager to try it. It was an immediate success and has been a family favorite ever since. I even serve these hearty waffles for a different kind of supper.

1-1/2 cups whole wheat flour
2 teaspoons baking powder
1/2 teaspoon salt
2 eggs, lightly beaten
2 cups milk
1/4 cup butter, melted
2 tablespoons honey
1 cup quick-cooking oats
1 cup chopped nuts
Sliced fresh peaches, optional

In a large mixing bowl, combine the flour, baking powder and salt. Whisk together the eggs, milk, butter and honey; stir into dry ingredients and mix well. Fold in oats and nuts.

Bake in a preheated waffle iron according to manufacturer's directions until golden brown. Garnish with peaches if desired.

Prep: **15 min.**
Bake: **30 min.**
Yield: **8-10 waffles**
(about 6-3/4 inches)

Quick Waffle Topping

To make these waffles extra special, sprinkle with fresh berries such as strawberries, raspberries or blueberries. Then melt some jelly with a squirt of lemon juice in the microwave and drizzle over the waffles.

I combine the dry ingredients for these muffins the night before baking. In the morning, I add the remaining items, fill the muffin cups and pop them in the oven. Brown sugar, cinnamon and pecans give them coffee cake-like flavor.

Coffee Cake Muffins

—Margaret McNeil
Memphis, Tennessee

1/4 cup packed brown sugar

1/4 cup chopped pecans

1 teaspoon ground cinnamon

1-1/2 cups all-purpose flour

1/2 cup sugar

2 teaspoons baking powder

1/4 teaspoon baking soda

1/4 teaspoon salt

1 egg

3/4 cup milk

1/3 cup vegetable oil

Glaze:

1/2 cup confectioners' sugar

1 tablespoon milk

1 teaspoon vanilla extract

In a small bowl, combine the brown sugar, pecans and cinnamon; set aside.

In a large bowl, combine the flour, sugar, baking powder, baking soda and salt. In another bowl, beat the egg, milk and oil; stir into dry ingredients just until moistened.

Spoon 1 tablespoon of batter into paper-lined muffin cups. Top each with 1 teaspoon nut mixture and about 2 tablespoons batter. Sprinkle with the remaining nut mixture.

Bake at 400° for 22-24 minutes or until a toothpick inserted near the center comes out clean. Cool for 5 minutes before removing from pan to a wire rack. Combine the glaze ingredients; spoon over muffins.

Prep: 20 min.
Bake: 25 min.
Yield: 1 dozen

Tall Pines is the name of our farm, and my husband and I love it here. I think fresh breakfast sausage tastes much better than the frozen variety, so I developed this recipe. It's great with scrambled eggs.

Tall Pines Farm Sausage

—Gloria Jarrett
Loveland, Ohio

Prep: 10 min. + chilling
Cook: 10 min.
Yield: 12 patties

2 tablespoons brown sugar

4 teaspoons salt

1 tablespoon dried sage

2 teaspoons ground savory

1 teaspoon pepper

1 teaspoon crushed red pepper flakes

1/2 teaspoon ground nutmeg

2-1/2 pounds ground pork

In a large bowl, combine first seven ingredients. Crumble pork over mixture and mix with hands to blend well. Cover and chill 6 hours or overnight.

Shape into twelve 3-1/2-in. patties. Cook patties in a skillet over medium-low heat for 10-12 minutes, turning once. Drain.

Speedy Cinnamon Rolls

—Nicole Weir
Hager City, Wisconsin

On special occasions when we were growing up, my mother would make as many as four batches of these delicious cinnamon rolls to satisfy the appetites of her children. Today this recipe is still a hit.

1 loaf (1 pound) frozen bread dough, thawed

2 tablespoons butter, melted

2/3 cup packed brown sugar

1/2 cup chopped walnuts

1 teaspoon ground cinnamon

1/2 cup heavy whipping cream

On a floured surface, roll dough into an 18-in. x 6-in. rectangle; brush with butter. In a large bowl, combine the brown sugar, walnuts and cinnamon; sprinkle over dough. Roll up jelly-roll style, starting with a long side; pinch seams to seal. Cut into 16 slices.

Place, cut side down, in two greased 9-in. round baking pans. Cover and let rise in a warm place until doubled, about 50 minutes.

Pour 1/4 cup cream over each pan. Bake at 350° for 25-30 minutes or until golden brown. Immediately invert onto serving plates. Serve warm.

Prep: **10 min. + rising**
Bake: **25 min.**
Yield: **1-1/2 dozen**

Orange French Toast

—Kristy Martin
Circle Pine, Minnesota

I use leftover slices of cinnamon bread in creating this awesome overnight brunch dish. With a hint of orange flavor, it's a special way to wake up the taste buds of weekend guests.

6 eggs, lightly beaten

3/4 cup orange juice

1/2 cup half-and-half cream

2 tablespoons sugar

1 teaspoon vanilla extract

1/2 teaspoon grated orange peel

8 thick slices cinnamon bread

1/4 cup butter, melted

In a shallow bowl, combine the first six ingredients. Dip both sides of bread into egg mixture; let soak for 5 minutes. Place in a greased 15-in. x 10-in. x 1-in. baking pan. Cover and refrigerate overnight.

Uncover; drizzle with butter. Bake at 325° for 35-40 minutes or until browned.

Prep: **15 min. + chilling**
Bake: **35 min.**
Yield: **8 servings**

This is a fairly new recipe for me, but my family loved it the first time I made it. A friend shared it with me.

Spinach Feta Strata

—Pat Lane
Pullman, Washington

10 slices French bread
(1 inch thick) *or*
6 croissants, split

6 eggs

1-1/2 cups milk

1 package (10 ounces)
frozen chopped spinach,
thawed and squeezed dry

1/2 teaspoon salt

1/4 teaspoon ground nutmeg

1/4 teaspoon pepper

1-1/2 cups (6 ounces) shredded
Monterey Jack cheese

1 cup (4 ounces) crumbled
feta cheese

In a greased 13-in. x 9-in. x 2-in. baking dish, arrange French bread or croissant halves with sides overlapping. In a large bowl, combine the eggs, milk, spinach, salt, nutmeg and pepper; pour over bread. Sprinkle with cheeses. Cover and refrigerate for 8 hours or overnight.

Remove from the refrigerator 30 minutes before baking. Bake, uncovered, at 350° for 40-45 minutes or until lightly browned. Let stand for 10 minutes before cutting.

Prep: **10 min. + chilling**
Bake: **40 min. + standing**
Yield: **12 servings**

Brighten up breakfast by draping this delicious cherry sauce over French toast, pancakes or waffles. With a hint of cranberry flavor, the mixture is also nice served over ham, pork or chicken.

Ruby Breakfast Sauce

—Edie DeSpain, Logan, Utah

Prep/Total Time: **10 min.**
Yield: **about 4 cups**

1 can (21 ounces) cherry
pie filling

1 can (8 ounces) jellied
cranberry sauce

1/4 cup maple syrup

1/4 cup orange juice

3 tablespoons butter

Pancakes, French toast *or*
waffles

In a microwave-safe bowl, combine the pie filling, cranberry sauce, syrup, orange juice and butter. Microwave on high for 3 minutes; stir. Microwave 2-3 minutes longer or until butter is melted and mixture is heated through; stir. Serve over pancakes, French toast or waffles.

Editor's Note: Recipe was tested in an 850-watt microwave.

Berry Cream Muffins

—Linda Gilmore
Hampstead, Maryland

Prep/Total Time: 30 min.
Yield: about 1 dozen

The sour cream makes these muffins so nice and light that you can serve them as a bread with a meal. But, here at our house, I've fixed them for everything from breakfast to a midnight snack.

2 cups all-purpose flour
1 cup sugar
1/2 teaspoon baking powder
1/2 teaspoon baking soda
1/2 teaspoon salt
1-1/2 cups fresh *or* frozen raspberries *or* blueberries
2 eggs, lightly beaten
1 cup (8 ounces) sour cream
1/2 cup vegetable oil
1/2 teaspoon vanilla extract

In a large bowl, combine the flour, sugar, baking powder, baking soda and salt; add berries and toss gently. Combine the eggs, sour cream, oil and vanilla; mix well. Stir into dry ingredients just until moistened.

Fill greased muffin cups two-thirds full. Bake at 400° for 18-22 minutes or until a toothpick inserted near the center comes out clean. Cool for 5 minutes before removing from pan to a wire rack.

Garden Frittata

—Catherine Michel
St. Peters, Missouri

Prep: 25 min.
Bake: 45 min. + standing
Yield: 8 servings

I created this dish one day to use up some fresh yellow squash, zucchini and tomato. To give it a different twist, try it with whatever veggies you have on hand.

1 small yellow summer squash, thinly sliced
1 small zucchini, thinly sliced
1 small onion, chopped
1 cup (4 ounces) shredded part-skim mozzarella cheese
1 medium tomato, sliced
1/4 cup crumbled feta cheese
4 eggs
1 cup fat-free milk
2 tablespoons minced fresh basil
1 garlic clove, minced
1/2 teaspoon salt
1/4 teaspoon pepper
1/4 cup shredded Parmesan cheese

In a microwave-safe bowl, combine the squash, zucchini and onion. Cover and microwave on high for 7-9 minutes or until the vegetables are tender; drain well.

Transfer to a 9-in. pie plate coated with nonstick cooking spray. Top with the mozzarella, tomato and feta cheese. In a large bowl, whisk the eggs, milk, basil, garlic, salt and pepper; pour over the cheese and tomato layer. Sprinkle with Parmesan cheese.

Bake, uncovered, at 375° for 45-50 minutes or until a knife inserted near the center comes out clean. Let stand for 10 minutes before serving.

I like to serve this impressive treat at parties. Pleasant banana-orange flavor makes it great for brunch. The crepes can be made ahead of time and stacked with waxed paper in between. Then place in a resealable plastic freezer bag and freeze. Thaw in the refrigerator before using.

Banana Crepes
—*Freda Becker*
Garrettsville, Ohio

2 eggs

3/4 cup milk

1 tablespoon butter, melted

1 tablespoon sugar

1/8 teaspoon salt

1/2 cup all-purpose flour

Additional butter

Orange Sauce:

1/2 cup butter

2/3 cup sugar

2/3 cup orange juice

4 teaspoons grated orange peel

6 medium firm bananas

In a large bowl, whisk the eggs, milk, melted butter, sugar and salt. Beat in flour until smooth; let stand for 20 minutes.

Melt 1 teaspoon butter in an 8-in. nonstick skillet. Pour 2 tablespoons batter into the center of skillet; lift and turn pan to cover bottom. Cook until lightly browned; turn and brown the other side.

Remove to a wire rack. Repeat with remaining batter, adding butter to skillet as needed. When cool, stack crepes with waxed paper or paper towels in between.

For sauce, combine the butter, sugar, orange juice and peel in a skillet. Bring to a boil; remove from the heat. Peel bananas; cut in half lengthwise. Add to orange sauce; cook over medium heat until heated through, about 1 minute.

Place one banana half in the center of each crepe; roll up jelly-roll style. Place folded side down on a plate; drizzle with orange sauce.

Prep: **20 min. + standing**
Cook: **10 min.**
Yield: **12 crepes**

Cabin Hash

—Mrs. Lyman Hein
Rochester, Minnesota

Prep/Total Time: **30 min.**
Yield: **8-10 servings**

My family named this dish because I served it when we vacationed at our cabin on the Mississippi River. Now it's become such a favorite that I often make it when we're home.

12 medium potatoes (about 4 pounds), peeled, cooked and cubed

3 cups cubed fully cooked ham (about 1 pound)

1/2 cup chopped onion

1/2 cup butter, cubed

1 package (10 ounces) frozen chopped broccoli, thawed

Salt and pepper to taste

Sour cream, optional

In a large skillet, cook potatoes, ham and onion in butter, stirring frequently, until potatoes are lightly browned. Add broccoli; heat through. Season with salt and pepper. Serve with sour cream if desired.

Italian Sausage Strata

—Amanda Reid, Oakville, Iowa

Prep: **20 min.** + chilling
Bake: **1 hour** + standing
Yield: **12 servings**

I like to serve this do-ahead dish to my family with fresh fruit and homemade rolls. Plus, it adds a nice touch to a celebration brunch.

1/2 cup butter, softened, *divided*

12 to 16 slices day-old bread, crusts removed

1/2 pound fresh mushrooms, sliced

2 cups sliced onions

Salt and pepper to taste

1 pound bulk Italian sausage, cooked and drained

3 cups (12 ounces) shredded cheddar cheese

5 eggs

2-1/2 cups milk

1 tablespoon Dijon mustard

1 teaspoon ground nutmeg

1 teaspoon ground mustard

2 tablespoons minced fresh parsley

Using 1/4 cup butter, spread one side of each bread slice with butter. Place half of the bread butter side down in a greased 13-in. x 9-in. x 2-in. baking dish.

In a large skillet, saute the mushrooms and onions in the remaining butter. Sprinkle with salt and pepper. Spoon half of the mushroom mixture over bread in prepared pan. Top with half of the sausage and cheese. Layer with the remaining bread, mushroom mixture, sausage and cheese. In a bowl, combine the eggs, milk, Dijon mustard, nutmeg and ground mustard. Pour over cheese. Cover and refrigerate overnight.

Remove from the refrigerator 30 minutes before baking. Bake, covered, at 350° for 50 minutes. Uncover; bake 10-15 minutes longer or until a knife inserted near the center comes out clean. Sprinkle with parsley. Let stand for 10 minutes before cutting.

I created this waffle recipe to recapture the memorable tropical tastes we enjoyed while visiting Hawaii.

Hawaiian Waffles

—Darlene Markel
Salem, Oregon

1 can (20 ounces) crushed pineapple, undrained
1/2 cup sugar
1/2 cup flaked coconut
1/2 cup light corn syrup
1/4 cup pineapple juice

Waffles:
2 cups all-purpose flour
4 teaspoons baking powder
1 tablespoon sugar
1/2 teaspoon salt
2 eggs, *separated*
1 cup milk
1/4 cup butter, melted
1 can (8 ounces) crushed pineapple, well drained
1/4 cup flaked coconut
1/4 cup chopped macadamia nuts
Additional chopped macadamia nuts, toasted, optional

In a large saucepan, combine the first five ingredients. Bring to a boil. Reduce heat. Simmer, uncovered, for 12-15 minutes or until sauce begins to thicken; set aside.

In a large bowl, combine the flour, baking powder, sugar and salt. Combine egg yolks, milk and butter; stir into dry ingredients just until combined. Stir in the pineapple, coconut and nuts. Beat egg whites until stiff peaks form; fold into batter (batter will be thick).

Preheat waffle iron. Fill and bake according to manufacturer's directions. Top with pineapple sauce and additional nuts if desired.

Prep/Total Time: 30 min.
Yield: 16 (4-inch) waffles

Three simple ingredients give bacon an entirely new taste. It's a real treat at any breakfast table.

Zippy Praline Bacon

—Myrt Pfannkuche
Pell City, Alabama

1 pound sliced bacon
3 tablespoons brown sugar
1-1/2 teaspoons chili powder
1/4 cup finely chopped pecans

Arrange bacon in a single layer in two foil-lined 15-in. x 10-in. x 1-in. baking pans. Bake at 425° for 10 minutes; drain.

Combine the brown sugar and chili powder; sprinkle over bacon. Sprinkle with pecans. Bake 5-10 minutes longer or until bacon is crisp. Drain on paper towels.

Prep/Total Time: 20 min.
Yield: 10 servings

Raspberry Cream Cheese Coffee Cake

—Brenda Knautz
West Chicago, Illinois

With cream cheese and raspberry jam, slices of this elegant coffee cake brighten any morning. I used to make this tempting treat only for special occasions. But now I prepare it whenever overnight company is coming. The wonderful aroma as it bakes seems to get my houseguests out of bed the following morning! My family prefers raspberry jam. But feel free to substitute another flavor, like strawberry or apricot.

2-1/2 cups all-purpose flour
3/4 cup sugar
3/4 cup cold butter, cubed
1/2 teaspoon baking powder
1/2 teaspoon baking soda
1/4 teaspoon salt
3/4 cup sour cream
1 egg
1 teaspoon almond extract

Filling:
1 package (8 ounces) cream cheese, softened
1/4 cup sugar
1 egg
1/2 cup raspberry jam

Topping:
1/2 cup sliced almonds

Prep: **25 min.**
Bake: **55 min. + cooling**
Yield: **16 servings**

In a large bowl, combine flour and sugar; cut in the butter until mixture resembles coarse crumbs. Reserve 1 cup crumb mixture.

To remaining crumb mixture, add baking powder, baking soda, salt, sour cream, egg and almond extract; blend well. Spread batter over bottom and 2 in. up side of a greased and floured 9-in. springform pan. (Batter should be 1/4 in. thick on sides.)

In small mixing bowl, beat the cream cheese, sugar and egg until smooth. Pour over batter in pan. Carefully spoon jam evenly over cheese filling. In a small bowl, combine reserved flour mixture and almonds; sprinkle over top.

Bake at 350° for 55-60 minutes or until cream cheese filling is set and crust is a deep golden brown. Cool for 15 minutes on a wire rack. Remove sides of pan. Serve warm or cool. Cover and refrigerate leftovers.

Main
Attraction

Turkey Breast with Apricot Glaze

*—Nancy Zimmerman
Cape May Court House,
New Jersey*

Prep: 10 min.
Bake: 2 hours + standing
Yield: 12 servings

One of my special-occasion entrees is this great-tasting turkey breast. I stuff the turkey breast with onion, cloves and an orange before roasting it, which fills the house with a wonderful aroma!

1 small onion

2 whole cloves

1 small orange, halved

1 bone-in turkey breast (4-1/2 pounds)

1 cup apricot preserves

1/2 cup unsweetened apple juice

1 teaspoon Dijon mustard

Peel onion and insert cloves. Stuff onion and orange into the neck cavity of turkey. Place on a rack in a shallow roasting pan. Bake, uncovered, at 325° for 2 to 2-1/2 hours or until a meat thermometer reads 170°. Let stand for 10-15 minutes before slicing.

Meanwhile, in a saucepan, combine the preserves, apple juice and mustard. Bring to a boil. Reduce heat; simmer, uncovered, for 4-5 minutes or until slightly thickened. Remove skin, onion and orange from turkey. Slice turkey; drizzle with glaze.

Orange-Glazed Pork Loin

—Lynnette Miete, Alna, Maine

Prep: 10 min.
Bake: 3 hours + standing
Yield: 12-16 servings

This is one of the best pork recipes I've ever tried. My family looks forward to this roast for dinner, and guests always want the recipe. The flavorful rub and a glaze sparked with orange juice are also outstanding on chicken.

1 teaspoon salt

1 garlic clove, minced

1/4 teaspoon dried thyme

1/4 teaspoon ground ginger

1/4 teaspoon pepper

1 boneless whole pork loin roast (5 pounds)

Glaze:

1/4 cup packed brown sugar

1 tablespoon cornstarch

1 cup orange juice

1/3 cup water

1 tablespoon Dijon mustard

Combine the salt, garlic, thyme, ginger and pepper; rub over entire roast. Place roast with fat side up on a rack in a shallow roasting pan. Bake, uncovered, at 350° for 2 hours.

Meanwhile, in a saucepan, combine the brown sugar and cornstarch. Stir in the orange juice, water and mustard until smooth. Bring to a boil; cook and stir for 2 minutes. Brush some of the glaze over roast.

Bake 1 hour longer or until a meat thermometer reads 160°, brushing occasionally with glaze. Let stand for 10 minutes before slicing; serve with the remaining glaze.

This herbed chicken has been a family favorite since I clipped the recipe out of a newspaper some years ago. It's often on our dinner table, since chicken is a staple in my freezer. If I'm out of lemon, I substitute a sprinkling of lemon-pepper.

Seasoned Lemon Chicken

—Pat Miller, Joplin, Missouri

2 tablespoons olive oil

2 bay leaves

2 teaspoons seasoned salt

1-1/2 teaspoons *each* garlic salt, pepper, dried basil, tarragon and thyme

1-1/2 teaspoons dried rosemary, crushed

8 bone-in chicken breast halves (7 ounces *each*), skin removed

1 large lemon, thinly sliced

1/4 cup lemon juice

In a large resealable plastic bag, combine the oil, bay leaves and seasonings; add chicken. Seal bag and turn to coat; refrigerate for 1 hour.

Discard the bay leaves. Place chicken in a 13-in. x 9-in. x 2-in. baking dish coated with nonstick cooking spray. Arrange lemon slices over chicken. Drizzle with lemon juice. Cover and bake at 350° for 30 minutes. Uncover; bake 10-15 minutes longer or until juices run clear.

Prep: **5 min.** + marinating

Bake: **40 min.**

Yield: **8 servings**

Skinning Chicken

Removing the skin from chicken can be a slippery task. To help improve your grip, use a paper towel to hold onto the chicken skin as you pull it off.

Raspberry Vinegar Pork Chops

—Maurita Merrill
Lac la Hache, British Columbia

This recipe originally called for chicken. In addition to pork, I've tried it with grouse for a change of pace. The area I live in is very rural, and so many of my visitors stay overnight. Some of those friends send me fresh raspberries before they arrive as a hint they'd like me to serve this dish.

1 tablespoon butter

1 tablespoon olive oil

3 pounds boneless butterflied pork chops (1 inch thick)

1/2 cup raspberry vinegar, *divided*

3 garlic cloves, thinly sliced

2 tomatoes, seeded and chopped

1 teaspoon rubbed sage *or* dried thyme *or* dried tarragon

1 tablespoon fresh *or* dried parsley

1/2 cup chicken broth

Salt and pepper to taste

Fresh raspberries

Fresh sage

Prep/Total Time: 30 min.
Yield: 8 servings

Melt butter in a large skillet; add oil. Brown the pork on each side. Pour off the oil; reduce heat to medium-low. Add 2 tablespoons vinegar and garlic. Cover; simmer for 10 minutes.

Remove pork and keep warm. Add remaining vinegar; stir up browned bits from bottom of skillet. Raise heat and boil until the vinegar is reduced to a thick glaze. Add the tomatoes, sage, parsley and chicken broth. Boil until liquid is reduced to half of the original volume.

Strain sauce; season with the salt and pepper. Spoon over chops. Garnish with fresh raspberries and sage.

This dish is quick and easy to prepare. Start cooking the ham about 5 minutes before the linguine is supposed to be done. That way all the ingredients will be ready at the same time.

Hay and Straw

—Priscilla Weaver
Hagerstown, Maryland

Prep/Total Time: **20 min.**
Yield: **8 servings**

- 1 package (16 ounces) linguine
- 2 cups julienned fully cooked ham
- 1 tablespoon butter
- 3 cups frozen peas
- 1-1/2 cups shredded Parmesan cheese
- 1/3 cup heavy whipping cream

Cook linguine according to package directions. Meanwhile, in a large skillet, saute ham in butter for 3 minutes. Add peas; heat through. Drain linguine; toss with ham mixture, Parmesan cheese and cream. Serve immediately.

My husband and I both retired. We've always loved to fish and we also enjoy skiing...so we like hearty meals. This is certainly that, and it's delicious!

Stuffed Beef Tenderloin

—Norma Blank
Shawano, Wisconsin

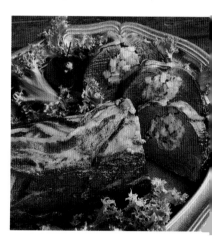

Prep: **20 min.**
Bake: **1 hour + standing**
Yield: **10-12 servings**

- 1 medium onion, chopped
- 1/2 cup diced celery
- 1 can (4 ounces) chopped mushrooms, drained
- 1/4 cup butter, cubed
- 2 cups soft bread crumbs (about 3 slices)
- 1/2 to 1 teaspoon salt
- 1/4 teaspoon dried basil *or* 1 teaspoon fresh basil
- 1/4 teaspoon dried parsley flakes *or* 1 teaspoon chopped fresh parsley
- 1/8 teaspoon pepper
- 1 beef tenderloin (about 3 pounds), trimmed
- 4 bacon strips

In a large skillet, saute the onion, celery and mushrooms in butter until vegetables are tender. Meanwhile, in a large bowl, combine the bread crumbs, salt, basil, parsley and pepper. Add onion mixture and mix well.

Make a lengthwise cut 3/4 of the way through the tenderloin. Lightly place the stuffing in the pocket; close with toothpicks. Place the bacon strips diagonally across the top, covering the toothpicks and pocket.

Place meat bacon side up on a rack in a shallow roasting pan. Bake, uncovered, at 350° until meat reaches desired doneness (for medium-rare, a meat thermometer should read 145°; medium, 160°; well-done ,170°). Remove from oven; let stand for 15 minutes. Remove toothpicks before slicing.

Deli-Style Pasta Salad

—Jill Evely, Wilmore, Kentucky

When I'm having weekend guests, I make this salad the day before they arrive. The flavors blend wonderfully when it is chilled overnight, and it keeps well for several days. It's also a great dish to take along to a picnic or potluck.

1 package (16 ounces) tricolor spiral pasta

2 medium plum tomatoes, seeded and julienned

8 ounces sliced salami, julienned

8 ounces provolone cheese, julienned

1 small red onion, thinly sliced and separated into rings

1 jar (5-3/4 ounces) pimiento-stuffed olives, drained

1 can (2-1/4 ounces) sliced ripe olives, drained

1/4 cup grated Parmesan cheese

1 bottle (8 ounces) Italian salad dressing

Cook pasta according to package directions; drain and rinse in cold water. In a large bowl, combine the pasta, tomatoes, salami, cheese, onion, olives and Parmesan cheese. Add dressing; toss to coat. Cover and refrigerate for several hours or overnight.

Prep: 15 min. + chilling
Yield: 12 servings

Sweet 'n' Moist Ham

*—Daun Hembd
Whitehall, Wisconsin*

We served 75 pounds of ham fixed this way. It could not be simpler, and it's moist and delightfully sweet.

1 sliced boneless fully cooked ham (about 6 pounds), tied

1 can (12 ounces) lemon-lime soda

Place ham on a rack in a shallow roasting pan. Pour soda over ham. Cover and bake at 325° for 2 hours or until a meat thermometer reads 140° and ham is heated through.

Prep: 5 min.
Bake: 2 hours
Yield: 18-20 servings

Delicate shrimp picks up fabulous flavor when it's sauteed in chicken broth mixed with red chili pepper, garlic and ripe olives. If you prefer a little less zip, remove the seeds from the chili pepper.

Zippy Shrimp
—Taste of Home Test Kitchen
Greendale, Wisconsin

1-1/4 cups chicken *or* vegetable broth

10 medium pitted ripe olives, finely chopped

1 red chili pepper, finely chopped

2 tablespoons lemon juice

1 tablespoon minced fresh rosemary *or* 1 teaspoon dried rosemary, crushed

4 garlic cloves, minced

2 teaspoons Worcestershire sauce

1 teaspoon paprika

1/2 teaspoon salt

1/4 to 1/2 teaspoon pepper

2 pounds uncooked medium shrimp, peeled and deveined

In a large nonstick skillet, combine the first 10 ingredients. Bring to a boil; cook until mixture is reduced by half. Add shrimp. Simmer, uncovered, for 3-4 minutes or until shrimp turn pink, stirring occasionally.

Editor's Note: When cutting or seeding hot peppers, use plastic gloves to protect your hands. Avoid touching your face.

Prep/Total Time: **20 min.**
Yield: **8 servings**

My zesty combination of pepperoni, pasta and peppers adds a little kick to your dinner lineup.

Spicy Pepper Penne
—Candace Greene
Columbiana, Ohio

1 package (16 ounces) penne

1/2 teaspoon minced fresh rosemary *or* 1/8 teaspoon dried rosemary, crushed

2 packages (3-1/2 ounces *each*) sliced pepperoni, halved

1/2 cup sliced pepperoncinis

1 jar (7 ounces) roasted sweet red peppers, drained and chopped

3-1/2 cups boiling water

1/2 cup heavy whipping cream

1/2 cup grated Parmesan cheese

In a large skillet, layer the pasta, rosemary, pepperoni, pepperoncinis and red peppers. Add water; bring to a boil. Reduce heat; cover and simmer for 12 minutes or until pasta is tender. Add cream and Parmesan cheese; toss to coat.

Editor's Note: Look for pepperoncinis (pickled peppers) in the pickle and olive section of your grocery store.

Prep/Total Time: **30 min.**
Yield: **8 servings**

Classic Cobb Salad

—Patty Kile
Greentown, Pennsylvania

Prep/Total Time: 15 min.
Yield: 12 servings

This classic recipe is easy to modify to suit your tastes. Try different meats or vegetables and enjoy!

6 cups torn lettuce

2 medium tomatoes, chopped

1 medium ripe avocado, peeled and chopped

3/4 cup diced fully cooked ham

2 hard-cooked eggs, chopped

3/4 cup diced cooked turkey

1-1/4 cups sliced fresh mushrooms

1/2 cup crumbled blue cheese

Red onion rings, lemon wedges and sliced ripe olives, optional

Salad dressing of your choice

Arrange lettuce in a large bowl. Place tomatoes across the center, dividing the bowl in half. On one half, arrange the avocado, ham and eggs in sections. On the other half, arrange the turkey, mushrooms and blue cheese. Garnish with onion, lemon and olives if desired. Serve with salad dressing.

Crispy Fried Chicken

—Jeanne Schnitzler
Lima, Montana

Prep: 10 min.
Cook: 10 min. per batch
Yield: 8 servings

Always a picnic favorite, this chicken is sensational hot or cold. Serve it with your family's favorite version of coleslaw, bean salad or potato salad.

4 cups all-purpose flour, *divided*

2 tablespoons garlic salt

1 tablespoon paprika

3 teaspoons pepper, *divided*

2-1/2 teaspoons poultry seasoning

2 eggs

1-1/2 cups water

1 teaspoon salt

2 broiler/fryer chickens (3-1/2 to 4 pounds *each*), cut up

Oil for deep-fat frying

In a large resealable plastic bag, combine 2-2/3 cups flour, garlic salt, paprika, 2-1/2 teaspoons pepper and poultry seasoning. In a shallow bowl, beat eggs and water; add salt and remaining flour and pepper. Dip chicken in egg mixture, then place in the bag, a few pieces at a time, and shake until coated.

In a deep-fat fryer, heat oil to 375°. Fry chicken, several pieces at a time, for 5-6 minutes on each side or until golden brown and crispy and juices run clear. Drain on paper towels.

This is a recipe that I adapted from an old Italian cookbook and offers a flavorful dish from my heritage. The sauce is chock-full of appetizing ingredients, such as eggplant, olives and fresh herbs. The fish adds a unique twist to the sauce. My family loves it with garlic bread.

Snappy Eggplant Spaghetti

—Brett Russo
Waterboro, South Carolina

1 medium onion, chopped

1 garlic clove, minced

2 tablespoons olive oil

3-1/2 cups tomato juice

1 small eggplant, peeled and cubed

1 medium green pepper, chopped

16 large pitted ripe olives, finely chopped

1/4 cup minced fresh parsley

2 tablespoons minced fresh basil *or* 2 teaspoons dried basil

1 teaspoon salt

1/4 teaspoon crushed red pepper flakes

1 package (1 pound) spaghetti

1 pound red snapper *or* grouper fillets, cut into 1-inch cubes

In a large saucepan or Dutch oven, saute onion and garlic in oil until tender. Add tomato juice; bring to a boil. Reduce heat; cover and simmer for 10 minutes. Add the eggplant, green pepper, olives, parsley, basil, salt and red pepper flakes. Cover and simmer for 20 minutes.

Meanwhile, cook spaghetti according to package directions. Add fish to eggplant mixture; cover and simmer 10 minutes longer. Drain spaghetti; top with fish mixture.

Prep: **10 min.**
Cook: **45 min.**
Yield: **8 servings**

Marinated Italian Pasta Salad

—Gail Buss
Westminster, Maryland

Prep: 15 min. + chilling
Yield: 12-16 servings

When I have guests coming over or a busy day ahead, I like to make this salad because it can be prepared the day before.

1 package (16 ounces) medium pasta shells

1/4 pound hard salami, cubed

1/4 pound sliced pepperoni, halved

1 block (4 ounces) provolone cheese, cubed

4 medium tomatoes, seeded and chopped

4 celery ribs, chopped

1 medium green pepper, chopped

1/2 cup sliced pimiento-stuffed olives

1/2 cup sliced ripe olives

1 bottle (8 ounces) Italian salad dressing

2 teaspoons dried oregano

1/2 teaspoon pepper

Cook pasta according to package directions; rinse in cold water and drain. Place in a large bowl; add the salami, pepperoni, cheese, vegetables and olives. Add the salad dressing, oregano and pepper; toss to coat. Cover and refrigerate overnight.

Crunchy Chicken Salad

—Diane Hixon, Niceville, Florida

Prep: 15 min. + chilling
Yield: 10 servings

To save time when entertaining, you can cook the chicken and prepare the dressing the day before. Then the day of the party, combine the salad. Just before serving, shake the dressing well and pour over the salad.

4 cups shredded cooked chicken

2 cups shredded lettuce

1 cup julienned carrots

1 cup julienned cucumber

2/3 cup green onion strips, cut into 2-inch pieces

1 cup canned bean sprouts, rinsed and drained

Dressing:

2 tablespoons vegetable oil

2 tablespoons lemon juice

2 tablespoons sesame seeds, toasted

1-1/2 teaspoons soy sauce

1/2 teaspoon salt, optional

1/4 teaspoon pepper

1/4 teaspoon ground mustard

Hot pepper sauce to taste

In a large salad bowl, toss the chicken, lettuce, carrots, cucumber, green onions and bean sprouts. Cover and refrigerate.

In a jar with a tight-filling lid, combine the dressing ingredients; shake well. Refrigerate. Just before serving, pour dressing over salad and toss gently.

This rich shrimp dish is wonderful over golden egg noodles, but you can also serve it with hot cooked rice.

2 tablespoons butter, melted

1/3 cup all-purpose flour

1-1/2 cups chicken broth

4 garlic cloves, minced

1 cup heavy whipping cream

1/2 cup minced fresh parsley

2 teaspoons paprika

Salt and pepper to taste

2 pounds large uncooked shrimp, peeled and deveined

Hot cooked noodles *or* rice

Shrimp in Cream Sauce

—Jane Birch
Edison, New Jersey

In a small saucepan, melt butter; stir in flour until smooth. Gradually add broth and garlic. Bring to a boil; cook and stir for 2 minutes or until thickened. Remove from the heat. Stir in the cream, parsley, paprika, salt and pepper.

Butterfly shrimp by cutting lengthwise almost in half, but leaving shrimp attached at opposite side. Spread to butterfly. Place cut side down in a greased 13-in. x 9-in. x 2-in. baking dish.

Pour cream sauce over shrimp. Bake, uncovered, at 400° for 15-18 minutes or until shrimp turn pink. Serve over noodles or rice.

Prep/Total Time: **30 min.**
Yield: **8 servings**

Butterflying Shrimp

After the shrimp is deveined, cut the slit deeper into the shrimp but not all the way through, leaving shrimp attached at the bottom.

Juicy Roast Turkey

—Terrie Herman
North Myrtle Beach,
South Carolina

I can't wait to serve his juicy turkey at Thanksgiving—so I make it several times a year. A whole roasted turkey makes such a nice presentation on the table, and turkey is well liked by most people. The aroma that wafts through the house during baking is almost as mouth-watering as the turkey dinner itself. Plus, while it's baking, I have plenty of time to mingle with my guests.

1/4 cup ground mustard

2 tablespoons Worcestershire sauce

2 tablespoons olive oil

1/2 teaspoon white vinegar

1 teaspoon salt

1/8 teaspoon pepper

1 turkey (10 to 12 pounds)

1 medium onion, quartered

2 celery ribs, quartered lengthwise

Fresh parsley sprigs

2 bacon strips

1/4 cup butter, softened

Additional olive oil

2 cups chicken broth

1 cup water

Prep: **20 min.** + chilling
Bake: **3-1/2 hours** + standing
Yield: **10-12 servings**

Combine the first six ingredients in a small bowl; stir to form a smooth paste. Brush over inside and outside of turkey. Cover or place in a 2-gallon resealable plastic bag; refrigerate for 1 to 24 hours.

Uncover turkey or remove from bag. Place turkey on a rack in a large roasting pan. Place the onion, celery and parsley inside turkey cavity. Lay the bacon across breast. Spread butter between legs and body. Tie drumsticks together. Brush the turkey with oil. Pour broth and water into pan.

Bake, uncovered, at 325° for 3-1/2 to 4 hours or until a meat thermometer reads 180°, basting frequently. Remove from oven; discard bacon. Let stand for 20 minutes before carving. Thicken pan juices for gravy if desired.

Baked Salmon

—Emily Chaney
Blue Hill, Maine

Prep/Total Time: **30 min.**
Yield: **8 servings**

I often make this very moist and flavorful salmon for company because I can have it ready in less than half an hour. I like to serve it with rice, or a green vegetable and a tossed salad.

- 1 salmon fillet (2 pounds)
- 2 tablespoons butter, softened
- 1/4 cup white wine *or* chicken broth
- 2 tablespoons lemon juice
- 1/2 teaspoon pepper
- 1/2 teaspoon dried tarragon

Pat salmon dry. Place in a greased 13-in. x 9-in. x 2-in. baking dish. Brush with butter. Combine remaining ingredients; pour over salmon. Bake, uncovered, at 425° for 20-25 minutes or until fish flakes easily with a fork.

Poor Man's Filet Mignon

—Gayle Mollenkamp
Russell Springs, Kansas

Even if you're on a budget, you can serve a delicious meal to guests. I find this recipe fits the bill—it's very tasty and looks special.

- 4 slices bread, crumbled
- 2 eggs, beaten
- 1/2 cup milk
- 2 teaspoons salt
- 1 tablespoon minced onion
- 2 teaspoons dried celery flakes
- 1/2 teaspoon chili powder
- 1 bottle (18 ounces) hickory smoke-flavored barbecue sauce, *divided*
- 2 pounds lean ground beef
- 12 slices uncooked bacon

In a large bowl, combine the first seven ingredients and 2 tablespoons barbecue sauce. Crumble beef over mixture and mix well. Form into 12 thick patties. Wrap a bacon slice around the sides of each patty and secure with a toothpick.

Bake on a rack at 350° for 50-60 minutes or until meat is no longer pink and a meat thermometer reads 160°. Baste frequently with remaining barbecue sauce during the last 30 minutes.

Prep: **20 min.**
Bake: **50 min.**
Yield: **12 servings**

Crunchy Baked Chicken

—Essie Malatt
Converse, Indiana

Prep: 10 min.
Bake: 35 min.
Yield: 8 servings

One bite of tender chicken in a crunchy golden coating explains why I give this recipe such a workout. Besides serving it at home for the two of us, I make a big batch for our senior group at church.

3/4 cup Western salad dressing
1/2 teaspoon chili powder
1/4 teaspoon salt
8 bone-in chicken breast halves (10 ounces *each*), skin removed
2-1/2 cups crushed cornflakes

Dipping Sauce:
1/4 cup chopped green pepper
1/4 cup chopped onion
3/4 cup Western salad dressing
1/2 teaspoon chili powder
1/4 teaspoon salt

In a shallow bowl, combine the salad dressing, chili powder and salt. Dip chicken in the mixture, then roll in cornflakes. Place in a 15-in. x 10-in. x 1-in. baking pan coated with nonstick cooking spray. Bake, uncovered, at 350° for 35-40 minutes or until the chicken juices run clear.

Meanwhile, for sauce, combine green pepper and onion in a microwave-safe bowl. Microwave on high for 1-1/2 minutes. Stir in remaining ingredients. Cover and cook 30-60 seconds longer or until heated through. Serve with chicken.

Shrimp Pasta Salad

—Sherri Gentry, Dallas, Oregon

Prep: 15 min. + chilling
Yield: 10 servings

When I'm planning a special luncheon, this pasta salad is sure to appear on the menu. The refreshing salad stirs up quickly, yet looks elegant, so it's an easy way to impress guests.

12 ounces spiral pasta, cooked and drained
1 package (10 ounces) frozen cooked shrimp, thawed
1/4 cup sliced green onions
1/4 cup Parmesan cheese
1/3 cup vegetable oil
1/3 cup red wine vinegar
2-1/2 teaspoons dill weed
2 teaspoons salt
3/4 teaspoon garlic powder
1/2 teaspoon pepper

In a large bowl, combine the pasta, shrimp, onions and the Parmesan cheese. In a small bowl, whisk the remaining ingredients until blended. Pour over pasta mixture; toss to coat. Cover and chill for 1-2 hours.

While experimenting in my kitchen, I created this wonderful herb and lemon rub. It takes only a few minutes to mix together, but when people taste the sensational flavor it gives to this tender cut of pork, they'll think you really fussed. Even my husband, who is a chef, thinks this dish is special enough for company.

Lemon-Rosemary Pork Tenderloin

—Carol Birkemeier
Nashville, Indiana

- 1 medium onion, finely chopped
- 2 tablespoons olive oil
- 1 tablespoon lemon juice
- 1 teaspoon minced fresh rosemary *or* 1/4 teaspoon dried rosemary, crushed
- 1 teaspoon minced fresh thyme *or* 1/4 teaspoon dried thyme
- 1 teaspoon grated lemon peel
- 1 garlic clove, minced
- 1/2 teaspoon salt
- 1/2 teaspoon pepper
- 2 pork tenderloins (1 pound *each*)

In a small bowl, combine the first nine ingredients; rub over tenderloins. Place on a rack in a shallow roasting pan.

Bake, uncovered, at 400° for 25-35 minutes or until a meat thermometer reads 160°. Cover with foil; let stand for 10 minutes before slicing.

Prep: **10 min.**
Bake: **25 min. + standing**
Yield: **8 servings**

Party Perfect Pork

Pork tenderloin is a terrific cut of meat for weeknight get-togethers. Because it is long and thin, this tender cut can be roasted to perfection in 30 minutes or less.

Chicken Fajitas

—Betty Foss
San Marcos, California

I was born and raised on a farm in Iowa but have been a California resident for many years. Southwestern recipes like these tasty chicken fajitas soon became family favorites. I like to serve them with salsa and guacamole.

3/4 cup lime juice

1/2 cup olive oil

3 garlic cloves, minced

2 teaspoons dried oregano

1 teaspoon ground cumin

1/2 teaspoon pepper

1-1/2 pounds boneless skinless chicken breasts, cut into thin strips

3 small zucchini, julienned

2 small yellow summer squash, julienned

2 medium green peppers, julienned

2 medium sweet red peppers, julienned

12 flour tortillas (10 inches), warmed

Prep: **15 min.** + marinating
Cook: **10 min.**
Yield: **12 servings**

In a small bowl, combine the first six ingredients; divide the mixture between two large resealable plastic bags. Add chicken to one and vegetables to the other. Seal bags and turn to coat; refrigerate for 2-4 hours, turning bags occasionally.

Drain and discard marinade from chicken and vegetables. In a large skillet, cook chicken over medium heat for 6-7 minutes or until juices run clear; drain. Remove chicken and keep warm. In the same skillet, saute vegetables for 3-4 minutes or until crisp-tender; drain.

Spoon chicken and vegetables onto tortillas; fold in sides. Serve immediately.

A taste-tempting sauce that combines orange juice, brown sugar and spices gives a wonderful flavor to this ham. It uses convenient ham steaks, so cooking time is less than half an hour.

Special Ham Slices
—Taste of Home Test Kitchen
Greendale, Wisconsin

Prep/Total Time: **25 min.**

Yield: **12 servings**

12 boneless ham steaks
(about 3 pounds)

1 cup orange juice

3/4 cup packed brown sugar

2 teaspoons grated orange
peel

1 teaspoon ground mustard

1/4 teaspoon ground cloves

Place ham in an ungreased 13-in. x 9-in. x 2-in. baking dish. Combine remaining ingredients; pour over ham. Bake, uncovered, at 325° for 20-25 minutes or until heated through, basting occasionally.

When you're cooking for a crowd that really savors the flavor of beef, this peppery, tempting tenderloin is perfect! It's no fuss since it comes together quickly. It's important to let it rest for a few minutes before carving to allow the juices to work through the meat.

Peppered Beef Tenderloin
—Margaret Ninneman
La Crosse, Wisconsin

1 teaspoon salt

1 teaspoon dried oregano

1 teaspoon dried thyme

1 teaspoon paprika

1/2 teaspoon garlic powder

1/2 teaspoon onion powder

1/2 teaspoon white pepper

1/2 teaspoon pepper

1/8 to 1/4 teaspoon cayenne
pepper

1 beef tenderloin
(3 pounds)

Combine the seasonings and rub over entire tenderloin. Place on a rack in a roasting pan. Bake, uncovered, at 425° until the meat reaches desired doneness (for medium-rare, a meat thermometer should read 145°; medium, 160°; well-done, 170°). Let stand for 10 minutes before carving.

Prep: **5 min.**

Bake: **65 min. + standing**

Yield: **8-10 servings**

Savory Roasted Chicken

—Taste of Home Test Kitchen
Greendale, Wisconsin

Prep: **10 min.**
Bake: **1-1/2 hours + standing**
Yield: **10 servings**

When you want an impressive centerpiece for Sunday dinner or a special-occasion meal, you can't go wrong with this golden chicken. The moist, tender meat is enhanced with a hint of orange, savory and thyme.

- 1 roasting chicken (6 to 7 pounds)
- 1 teaspoon onion salt
- 1/2 teaspoon dried thyme
- 1/2 teaspoon dried savory
- 1/4 teaspoon grated orange peel
- 1/4 teaspoon pepper
- 1 teaspoon vegetable oil

Place the chicken on a rack in a shallow roasting pan. Carefully loosen the skin above the breast meat. Combine the onion salt, thyme, savory, orange peel and pepper; rub half of the herb mixture under the loosened skin. Rub chicken skin with oil; sprinkle with remaining herb mixture.

Bake at 375° for 1-1/2 to 2 hours or until a meat thermometer reads 180°. Let stand for 10-15 minutes. Remove skin before carving if desired. Skim fat and thicken pan juices for gravy if desired.

Baked Seafood Avocados

—Marian Platt
Sequim, Washington

Prep: **15 min.**
Bake: **25 min.**
Yield: **8 servings**

Everyone who tastes this wonderful luncheon dish is surprised that the avocados are baked.

- 1 cup mayonnaise
- 3/4 cup chopped celery
- 1/2 cup thinly sliced green onions
- 1/8 teaspoon salt, optional
- 1/8 teaspoon pepper
- 1 can (4-1/2 ounces) crabmeat, drained, flaked and cartilage removed
- 1 can (4 ounces) medium shrimp, rinsed and drained
- 4 large ripe avocados, halved and pitted
- 1 to 2 tablespoons lemon juice
- 1/4 cup crushed potato chips, optional

In a large bowl, combine the mayonnaise, celery, onions, salt if desired and pepper. Add crab and shrimp; mix well. Peel avocados if desired. Sprinkle avocados with lemon juice; fill with seafood mixture. Sprinkle with potato chips if desired.

Place in an ungreased 13-in. x 9-in. x 2-in. baking dish. Bake, uncovered, at 350° for 25-30 minutes or until bubbly.

My mother-in-law made this delectable salad for a shower she was hosting and shared it with me. This makes a great party recipe since so many of the steps can be done the day before. Just make the dressing and refrigerate. Then cut or chop all the other ingredients, except the lettuce, and cover and refrigerate them individually.

Club Sandwich Salad

—Karen Dolan
Kunkletown, Pennsylvania

1 cup mayonnaise

1/4 cup ketchup

1 tablespoon chopped green onion

Salt and pepper to taste

1 large head iceberg lettuce, torn

2 large tomatoes, cut into wedges

2 hard-cooked eggs, chopped

10 bacon strips, cooked and crumbled

2 cups cubed cooked turkey *or* chicken

Croutons, optional

In a small bowl, combine the mayonnaise, ketchup, onion, salt and pepper. Cover and refrigerate.

Just before serving, toss the lettuce, tomatoes, eggs, bacon and turkey in a large bowl. Add croutons if desired. Serve with dressing.

Prep/Total Time: **20 min.**

Yield: **8-10 servings**

Herb-Crusted Roast Beef

—*Teri Lindquist, Gurnee, Illinois*

Prep: **20 min.**
Bake: **1-3/4 hours + standing**
Yield: **10-12 servings**

I'm married to a man who loves beef. For a long time, though, I was reluctant to cook a roast for fear of ruining it. Finally, I started buying roasts on sale and experimenting. This recipe was the result...now, my husband doesn't want a roast any other way.

1 boneless beef rump roast (4-1/2 to 5 pounds)

2 garlic cloves, minced

2 tablespoons Dijon mustard

2 tablespoons lemon juice

2 tablespoons olive oil

2 tablespoons Worcestershire sauce

1 tablespoon dried parsley flakes

1 teaspoon dried basil

1 teaspoon salt

1 teaspoon coarsely ground pepper

1/2 teaspoon dried tarragon

1/2 teaspoon dried thyme

1/4 to 1/3 cup all-purpose flour

2 teaspoons beef bouillon granules

2-1/3 cups water, *divided*

Place roast with fat side up in ungreased roasting pan. Combine the next five ingredients; pour over roast. Combine parsley, basil, salt, pepper, tarragon and thyme; rub over roast.

Bake, uncovered, at 325° for 1-3/4 to 2-1/4 hours or until meat reaches desired doneness (for medium-rare, a meat thermometer should read 145°; medium, 160°; well-done, 170°). Remove to a warm serving platter. Let stand for 10-15 minutes.

Pour drippings and loosened brown bits into a measuring cup. Skim fat, reserving 2 tablespoons. In a large saucepan, combine the flour, bouillon and 1 cup water until smooth. Gradually stir in the drippings, reserved fat and remaining water. Bring to a boil; cook and stir for 2 minutes or until thickened. Slice roast; serve with gravy.

Slicing the Roast

After the rump roast has stood for 10-15 minutes, use a carving knife and cut the roast across the grain into thin slices.

From the Grill

Oriental Pork Burgers

—Deborah Messerly
Steamboat Rock, Iowa

Prep: **15 min.** + chilling
Grill: **10 min.**
Yield: **8 servings**

My home state of Iowa is a leader in pork production. This recipe is a truly delicious and nutritious way to use ground pork.

1 cup soft bread crumbs

1/3 cup finely chopped green onions

1/3 cup finely chopped green pepper

1 can (8 ounces) water chestnuts, drained and chopped

1 egg, lightly beaten

2 tablespoons soy sauce

1 garlic clove, minced

1 teaspoon salt

1/8 teaspoon ground ginger

2 pounds ground pork

Sauce:

1 can (8 ounces) crushed pineapple, drained

2/3 cup ketchup

1/4 cup white vinegar

1/4 cup orange marmalade

2 tablespoons prepared mustard

8 hamburger buns, split and toasted

In a large bowl, combine the first nine ingredients. Crumble pork over mixture and mix well. Shape into eight patties. Cover and refrigerate for 1 hour.

Meanwhile, in a saucepan, combine the pineapple, ketchup, vinegar, marmalade and mustard. Cook and stir for 5 minutes or until marmalade is melted. Remove from the heat; set aside.

Grill patties, covered, over medium heat for 4-6 minutes on each side or until a meat thermometer reads 160°. Spoon 1 tablespoon of sauce onto each burger during the last 2 minutes of grilling. Serve on buns with remaining sauce.

Zesty Grilled Ham

—Mary Ann Lien, Tyler, Texas

Prep/Total Time: **30 min.**
Yield: **4 servings**

This is my children's first choice for ham dishes. The mixture of sweet and tangy flavors is mouth-watering on a grilled piece of ham. Even the small ones eat adult-sized portions, so be sure to make plenty.

1 cup packed brown sugar

1/3 cup prepared horseradish

1/4 cup lemon juice

1 fully cooked ham steak (1 to 1-1/2 pounds and 1 inch thick)

In a small saucepan, bring the brown sugar, horseradish and lemon juice to a boil. Brush over both sides of ham. Grill over medium-hot heat for 10-12 minutes on each side or until heated through and well glazed.

Editor's Note: Double this recipe when cooking for crowd.

I first prepared these splendid skewers at a birthday party...they were an instant success! I especially enjoy serving them for casual weekend meals with friends.

Supreme Kabobs

—*Karla Gleason, Waterville, Ohio*

3/4 cup vegetable oil

1/3 cup soy sauce

1/4 cup red wine vinegar

1/4 cup lemon juice

2 tablespoons Worcestershire sauce

2 teaspoons ground mustard

1 teaspoon pepper

1 teaspoon dried parsley flakes

2 pounds boneless skinless chicken breasts, cut into 1-inch cubes

12 ounces small fresh mushrooms

1 medium green *or* sweet red pepper, cut into 1-inch pieces

2 small onions, cut into 1-inch pieces

1 can (8 ounces) pineapple chunks, drained

In a bowl, combine the first eight ingredients. Divide the marinade evenly between two large reseal-able plastic bags. Add chicken to one bag and the mushrooms, pepper and onions to the second bag. Seal bags and turn to coat; refrigerate for at least 6 hours.

Drain and discard marinade. Thread chicken, vegetables and pineapple alternately on metal or soaked wooden skewers. Grill, covered, over medium-low heat, turning frequently, for 16-20 minutes or until chicken juices run clear.

Prep: **5 min.**
Grill: **20 min.**
Yield: **8 servings**

Basil-Stuffed Steak

—Linda Gronewaller
Hutchinson, Kansas

Prep: **15 min.**
Grill: **35 min.**
Yield: **6-8 servings**

This is a recipe I developed. We love beef, and grilling is an easy way to add variety to our meals.

1 boneless beef top sirloin steak (2 to 2-1/2 pounds and about 1-1/2 inches thick)
1/2 teaspoon salt
1/4 teaspoon pepper
1/4 teaspoon dried parsley flakes
1-1/2 cups lightly packed fresh basil leaves, coarsely chopped
1/4 cup finely chopped onion
4 garlic cloves, minced
1-1/2 teaspoons minced fresh rosemary *or* 1/2 teaspoon dried rosemary, crushed
1/8 teaspoon minced fresh thyme *or* dash dried thyme
1 teaspoon olive oil

With a sharp knife, make five lengthwise cuts three-fourths of the way through the steak. Combine the salt, pepper and parsley; rub over steak.

In a small bowl, combine the basil, onion, garlic, rosemary and thyme. Stuff into pockets in steak. Using kitchen string, tie the steak at 2-in. intervals, closing the pockets. Drizzle with oil.

Prepare grill for indirect heat, using a drip pan. Place meat over drip pan; grill, covered, over indirect medium heat for 35-45 minutes or until the meat reaches desired doneness (for medium-rare, a meat thermometer should read 145°; medium, 160°; well-done, 170°). Cover and let stand for 5-10 minutes. Remove string before slicing.

Editor's Note: Steak can also be baked, uncovered, at 400° for 45 minutes or until meat reaches desired doneness.

Spicy Pork Tenderloin

—Diana Steger, Prospect, Kentucky

Prep: **5 min. + standing**
Grill: **15 min.**
Yield: **8 servings**

A friend shared this recipe for marvelously flavorful pork years ago. It really sparks up a barbecue and has been a hit when I served it.

1 to 3 tablespoon chili powder
1 teaspoon salt
1/4 teaspoon ground ginger
1/4 teaspoon ground thyme
1/4 teaspoon pepper
2 pork tenderloins (about 1 pound *each*)

Combine the first five ingredients; rub over tenderloins. Cover and refrigerate for 2-4 hours.

Prepare grill for indirect heat, using a drip pan. Place pork over drip pan; grill, covered, over indirect medium-hot heat for 25-40 minutes or until meat thermometer reads 160°. Let stand for 5 minutes before slicing.

Kentucky Grilled Chicken

—Jill Evely
Wilmore, Kentucky

This chicken is perfect for an outdoor summer meal, and my family thinks it's fantastic. It takes about an hour on the grill but is worth the wait. I use a new large brush to "mop" on the basting sauce.

1 cup cider vinegar

1/2 cup vegetable oil

5 teaspoons Worcestershire sauce

4 teaspoons hot pepper sauce

2 teaspoons salt

10 bone-in chicken breast halves (10 ounces *each*)

In a small bowl, combine the first five ingredients. Pour 1 cup marinade into a large resealable plastic bag; add the chicken. Seal bag and turn to coat; refrigerate for at least 4 hours. Cover and refrigerate the remaining marinade for basting.

Coat grill rack with nonstick cooking spray before preparing the grill for indirect heat, using a drip pan. Drain and discard marinade from chicken. Grill bone side down, covered, over indirect medium heat for 20 minutes. Turn; grill 20-30 minutes longer or until the juices run clear, basting occasionally with the reserved marinade.

Prep: **5 min. + marinating**
Grill: **40 min.**
Yield: **10 servings**

Potluck Spareribs

—Sheri Kirkman
Lancaster, New York

These ribs are guaranteed pleasers at potlucks. I always bring home an empty dish.

6 pounds pork spareribs

1-1/2 cups ketchup

3/4 cup packed brown sugar

1/2 cup white vinegar

1/2 cup honey

1/3 cup soy sauce

1-1/2 teaspoons ground ginger

1 teaspoon salt

3/4 teaspoon ground mustard

1/2 teaspoon garlic powder

1/4 teaspoon pepper

Cut ribs into serving-size pieces; place with the meaty side up on racks in two greased 13-in. x 9-in. x 2-in. baking pans. Cover tightly with foil. Bake at 350° for 1-1/4 hours or until meat is tender.

Drain; remove racks and return ribs to pans. Combine remaining ingredients; pour over ribs. Grill over medium heat for 35 minutes or until sauce coats ribs, basting occasionally.

Editor's Note: Ribs can also be finished in the oven. Bake, uncovered, at 350° for 35 minute or until sauce coats ribs, basting occasionally.

Prep: **10 min.**
Bake: **1 hour 35 min.**
Yield: **12 servings**

Orange Vegetable Kabobs

—*Laurie Whitney*
Bradford, Massachusetts

Prep: 20 min. + marinating
Grill: 10 min.
Yield: 8 kabobs

I created this recipe to add some zip to grilled vegetables. Their color, crispness and taste are tempting to all ages.

1 large sweet onion
1 large unpeeled navel orange
1 medium sweet red pepper, cut into 1-inch pieces
1 medium sweet yellow pepper, cut into 1-inch pieces
8 medium fresh mushrooms
8 cherry tomatoes
2 small yellow summer squash, cut into 1-inch slices

Marinade:
  1/2 cup olive oil
  1/3 cup lemon juice
1-1/2 teaspoons sugar
  1 teaspoon salt, optional

1/4 teaspoon garlic powder
1/4 teaspoon pepper
  2 tablespoons orange juice

Cut the onion and orange into eight wedges; halve each wedge. Alternately thread vegetables and orange pieces onto eight metal or soaked wooden skewers. Place in a shallow oblong dish.

In a small bowl, whisk oil, lemon juice, sugar, salt if desired, garlic powder and pepper. Pour over skewers. Marinate for 15 minutes, turning and basting frequently.

Grill, covered, over indirect heat for 10-15 minutes or until vegetables are crisp-tender. Brush with orange juice just before serving.

Teriyaki Tuna Steaks

—*Michelle Dennis*
Clarks Hill, Indiana

Prep: 5 min. + marinating
Grill: 15 min.
Yield: 4 servings

After sampling some wonderful tuna at a Japanese restaurant, I decided to try my hand at coming up with the recipe. It took a little trial and error, but I was pleased with the results.

1/4 cup reduced-sodium soy sauce
3 tablespoons brown sugar
3 tablespoons olive oil
2 tablespoons white vinegar
2 tablespoons sherry *or* chicken broth
2 tablespoons unsweetened pineapple juice
2 garlic cloves, minced
1-1/2 teaspoons ground ginger
4 tuna steaks (6 ounces *each*)

In a small bowl, combine the first eight ingredients. Remove 1/3 cup for basting; cover and refrigerate. Pour remaining marinade into a large resealable plastic bag; add tuna. Seal bag and turn to coat; refrigerate for up to 1 hour.

Coat grill rack with nonstick cooking spray before starting the grill. Drain and discard marinade from tuna. Grill tuna, uncovered, over medium heat for 5-6 minutes on each side or until fish flakes easily with a fork, basting frequently with reserved marinade.

Editor's Note: Double this recipe when cooking for crowd.

Grilling is a hobby of mine that I really enjoy. This flavorful dish is one of my family's favorites. The marinade adds a wonderful taste to the meat. Try it with baked potatoes and garden-fresh veggies, or serve with a pasta salad and steamed broccoli.

Herbed Beef Tenderloin

—Paul Verner, Wooster, Ohio

- 1/2 cup olive oil
- 2 green onions, finely chopped
- 2 garlic cloves, minced
- 1 tablespoon *each* dried basil, thyme and rosemary, crushed
- 1 tablespoon balsamic vinegar
- 1 tablespoon Dijon mustard
- 1 teaspoon salt
- 1 teaspoon pepper
- 1 beef tenderloin (4 to 5 pounds)

Place the oil, green onions and seasonings in a large resealable plastic bag; add beef. Seal bag and turn to coat; refrigerate overnight.

Prepare grill for indirect heat, using a drip pan. Drain and discard marinade from beef. Place beef over the direct heat. Grill, covered, over medium-hot heat for 10-15 minutes or until beef is browned, turning frequently.

Move beef to indirect side of the grill. Cover and grill for 20-25 minutes longer or until meat reaches desired doneness (for medium-rare, a meat thermometer should read 145°; medium, 160°; well-done, 170°). Let stand for 10 minutes before slicing.

Prep: **5 min. + marinating**
Grill: **30 min. + standing**
Yield: **12 servings**

Tropical Island Chicken

—Sharon Hanson
Franklin, Tennessee

Prep: **10 min. + marinating**
Grill: **45 min.**
Yield: **8 servings**

The marinade makes a savory statement in this all-time-favorite chicken recipe that I served at our son's pirate-theme birthday party. It smelled so good on the grill that guests could hardly wait to try a piece!

1/2 cup soy sauce
1/3 cup vegetable oil
1/4 cup water
2 tablespoons dried minced onion
2 tablespoons sesame seeds
1 tablespoon sugar
4 garlic cloves, minced
1 teaspoon ground ginger
3/4 teaspoon salt
1/8 teaspoon cayenne pepper
2 broiler/fryer chickens (3 to 4 pounds *each*), quartered

In a bowl, combine the first 10 ingredients. Remove 1/3 cup for basting; cover and refrigerate. Pour remaining marinade in a large resealable plastic bag; add chicken. Seal bag and turn to coat; refrigerate for 8 hours or overnight.

Drain and discard marinade from chicken. Grill chicken, covered, over medium-hot heat for 45-60 minutes or until juices run clear and a meat thermometer reads 180°, turning and basting often with reserved marinade.

Brats with Onions

—Gunnard Stark
Englewood, Florida

Prep: **20 min.**
Cook: **20 min.**
Yield: **15 servings**

After years of eating plain old brats, I came up with this great-tasting version slathered in zippy onions. Enjoy juicy bratwurst for dinner with plenty left over for meals later in the week.

3 cans (12 ounces *each*) beer *or* 4-1/2 cups water
3 large onions, thinly sliced and separated into rings
6 garlic cloves, minced
1 tablespoon hot pepper sauce
2 to 3 teaspoons celery salt
2 to 3 teaspoons pepper
1 teaspoon chili powder
15 fresh bratwurst links (3-1/2 to 4 pounds)

15 hot dog buns, split *or* brat buns

In a Dutch oven, combine the beer or water, onion, garlic, pepper sauce, celery salt, pepper and chili powder. Bring to a boil. Add bratwurst. Reduce heat; simmer, uncovered, for 20-25 minutes or until bratwurst is firm and cooked. Drain, reserving onions.

Grill brats over medium heat or broil 4 in. from heat for 4-5 minutes or until browned, turning once. Serve on buns with reserved onions.

Angling for a healthy way to prepare seafood, our Test Kitchen came up with a recipe for halibut with a tropical twist. Grilled to tender perfection, the fillets stay moist with a light coating of lemon and oil. They're topped with a fruity salsa of emerald kiwifruit, golden mango and red peppers for an eye-catching presentation.

Halibut with Kiwi Salsa

—Taste of Home Test Kitchen
Greendale, Wisconsin

Prep/Total Time: **20 min.**
Yield: **4 servings**

2 medium mangoes *or* 4 medium peaches, peeled and cubed (about 1-1/3 cups)

4 kiwifruit, peeled and cubed (about 1 cup)

1/2 cup diced sweet red pepper

1/2 cup diced onion

1 jalapeno pepper, seeded and minced

2 tablespoons lemon juice, *divided*

1 tablespoon lime juice

2 teaspoons minced fresh mint *or* 3/4 teaspoon dried mint

1 teaspoon honey

1/2 teaspoon salt, *divided*

1 tablespoon olive oil

4 halibut fillets *or* tuna steaks (6 ounces *each*)

1/4 teaspoon chili powder

For salsa, in a large bowl, combine the mangoes, kiwi, red pepper, onion, jalapeno, 1 tablespoon lemon juice, lime juice, mint, honey and 1/4 teaspoon salt. Cover and refrigerate until serving.

In a small bowl, combine the oil and remaining lemon juice; brush over both sides of fish. Sprinkle with chili powder and remaining salt.

If grilling the fish, coat grill rack with nonstick cooking spray before starting the grill. Grill fillets, covered, over medium heat or broil 6 in. from the heat for 5-7 minutes on each side or until fish flakes easily with a fork. Serve with salsa.

Editor's Note: When cutting or seeding hot peppers, use rubber or plastic gloves to protect your hands. Avoid touching your face. Double this recipe when cooking for crowd.

Purchasing Fish

You should purchase fresh fish only 1 or 2 days before you plan on cooking it. Choose fillets or steaks that have firm, elastic and moist-looking flesh. The fish should have a mild smell. Pass on any that have a strong fish odor, bruised flesh or flesh with drying edges.

Grilled Chops With Rosemary Lemon Marinade

—Peggy Gwillim
Strasbourg, Saskatchewan

Prep: **10 min. + marinating**
Grill: **15 min.**
Yield: **4 servings**

I discovered this mouth-watering marinade in a poultry cookbook and decided to try it with pork chops. My family's glad—it's become a favorite! Don't be bashful about basting a pork roast or ribs with the marinade, either...I did, and I discovered two more family-favorite taste treats.

2 garlic cloves, minced
1/2 cup lemon juice
2 teaspoons grated lemon peel
2 tablespoons olive oil
1 tablespoon chopped fresh rosemary *or* 1 teaspoon dried rosemary, crushed
1/8 teaspoon dried basil
1/8 teaspoon lemon-pepper seasoning
4 pork chops (1 inch thick)

In a small bowl, whisk the garlic, lemon juice, peel, oil, rosemary, basil and pepper. Pour 1/3 cup marinade into a large resealable plastic bag; add the pork. Seal bag and turn to coat; refrigerate for at least 2 hours or overnight, turning occasionally. Cover and refrigerate remaining marinade.

Drain and discard marinade from pork. Grill chops, covered, over medium heat about 6 minutes per side or until juices run clear, brushing occasionally with the reserved marinade.

Editor's Note: Double this recipe when cooking for crowd.

Garlic Grilled Steaks

—Taste of Home Test Kitchen
Greendale, Wisconsin

Prep/Total Time: **20 min.**
Yield: **4 servings**

For a mouth-watering change of taste at your next barbecue, take steak to new flavor heights by basting your choice of cuts with a great garlic blend that requires minutes to fix.

10 garlic cloves
1-1/2 teaspoons salt
1/2 teaspoon pepper
2 tablespoons olive oil
1 tablespoon lemon juice
2 teaspoons Worcestershire sauce
4 New York strip steak *or* 4 boneless beef rib eye steaks (1-1/4 inches thick and 8 ounces *each*)

With a mortar and pestle, combine the garlic, salt and pepper. Add the oil, lemon juice and mix to form a paste.

Grill steaks, covered, over medium heat for 6-8 minutes on each side or until meat reaches desired doneness (for medium-rare, a meat thermometer should read 145°; medium 160°; well-done 170°). Brush with garlic mixture during the last few minutes of grilling. Let stand for 3-5 minutes before serving.

Editor's Note: Double this recipe when cooking for crowd.

Fresh lime juice helps you bring a taste of Mexico to the dinner table. The chicken, green and red sweet peppers, and onions are all cooked on the grill for these colorful fajitas. Plus, I find that the fresh flavors appeal to everyone. For an added touch, serve with homemade guacamole (see recipe on page 28).

Grilled Chicken Fajitas

—Melinda Ewbank
Fairfield, Ohio

- 2 tablespoons white wine vinegar
- 2 tablespoons fresh lime juice
- 2 tablespoons vegetable oil, *divided*
- 1 tablespoon Worcestershire sauce
- 1 tablespoon chopped onion
- 1 garlic clove, minced
- 1/2 teaspoon salt, optional
- 1/2 teaspoon dried oregano
- 1/4 teaspoon ground cumin
- 1 pound boneless skinless chicken breasts
- 1 medium green pepper, halved and seeded
- 1 medium sweet red pepper, halved and seeded
- 1 medium sweet onion, sliced
- 6 flour tortillas (8 inches), warmed

Salsa

Guacamole, sour cream and shredded cheddar cheese, optional

In a large resealable plastic bag, combine the vinegar, lime juice, 1 tablespoon oil, Worcestershire sauce, onion, garlic, salt if desired, oregano and cumin; add chicken.

Seal the bag and turn to coat; refrigerate at least 4 hours.

Coat grill rack with nonstick cooking spray before starting the grill. Drain and discard marinade from chicken. Lightly brush vegetables with remaining oil. Grill the vegetables and chicken, covered, over medium heat for 12-15 minutes or until the vegetables begin to soften and chicken juices run clear.

Quickly slice chicken and peppers into strips and separate onion slices into rings. Spoon the chicken and vegetables down the center of tortillas; fold in sides. Garnish as desired with the salsa, guacamole, sour cream and cheese.

Editor's Note: Double this recipe when cooking for crowd.

Prep: **15 min. + marinating**
Grill: **15 min.**
Yield: **6 servings**

Dressed-Up Bacon Burgers

—Carol Mizell
Ruston, Louisiana

Prep: **10 min.**
Grill: **30 min.**
Yield: **8 servings**

The tangy homemade sauce that tops these mouth-watering burgers helps them stand out from the rest. This recipe is a cinch to throw together. Because the bacon cooks on the grill alongside the burgers, cleanup is a breeze, too.

3/4 cup mayonnaise
  3 tablespoons sweet pickle relish
  3 tablespoons ketchup
  1 tablespoon sugar
  1 tablespoon dried minced onion
  1 tablespoon Worcestershire sauce
1/2 teaspoon salt
1/4 teaspoon garlic powder
1/4 teaspoon pepper
  2 pounds ground beef
  8 bacon strips
  8 slices cheddar cheese
  8 hamburger buns, split and toasted

Lettuce leaves

In a small bowl, whisk the mayonnaise, pickle relish, ketchup, sugar and onion until well blended. Cover and refrigerate. In a large bowl, combine the Worcestershire sauce, salt, garlic powder and pepper. Crumble beef over mixture; mix well. Shape into eight patties.

Place bacon on a piece of heavy-duty foil on one side of the grill. Grill, covered, over medium-hot heat for 10 minutes on each side or until bacon is crisp. Place the patties on the other side of the grill. Grill covered for 4-5 minutes on each side or until meat is no longer pink and meat thermometer reads 160°.

Drain bacon on paper towels. Place a cheese slice on each patty; cover and grill until cheese is melted. Serve on buns with the lettuce, bacon and mayonnaise mixture.

Dressed-Up Mayonnaise

Here are two other kinds of flavored mayonnaise that will taste great in the Dressed-Up Bacon Burger recipe above. **Italian-Style Mayonnaise:** Combine 3/4 cup mayonnaise with 2-1/4 teaspoons tomato paste and 1/4 teaspoon dried basil. **Horseradish Mayonnaise:** Combine 3/4 cup mayonnaise with 4-1/2 teaspoons *each* chopped green onions and horseradish.

Turkey is a great alternative for those of us who have to watch our cholesterol. This recipe featuring tenderloins is a favorite of my family.

Marinated Turkey Tenderloins

—Beth Wynne
Kill Devil Hills, North Carolina

1 cup lemon-lime soda

1/4 cup soy sauce

2 tablespoons lemon juice

2 garlic cloves, minced

1 teaspoon prepared horseradish

1/2 teaspoon lemon-pepper seasoning

1/4 teaspoon curry powder

1/4 teaspoon ground ginger

1/4 teaspoon paprika

1/4 teaspoon crushed red pepper flakes

2 pounds turkey breast tenderloins

In a large bowl, combine the first 10 ingredients. Pour 1 cup into a large resealable plastic bag; add turkey. Seal bag and turn to coat; refrigerate 8 hours or overnight, turning occasionally. Cover and refrigerate remaining marinade for serving.

Drain and discard marinade from turkey. Grill, covered, over medium-hot heat for 20-25 minutes or until a meat thermometer reads 170°, turning every 6 minutes. Serve with reserved marinade.

Prep: 10 min. + marinating
Grill: 20 min.
Yield: 8 servings

Spiedis (pronounced "speedeez") are a type of grilled meat sandwich considered a local specialty. This recipe is my own, but there are many variations in our area. In nearby Binghamton, Spiedi-Fest is held in August, featuring this delicious dish made of all different kinds of meat.

Pork Spiedis

—Beatrice Riddell
Chenango Bridge, New York

2 cups tomato juice

2 large onions, finely chopped

4 to 5 garlic cloves, minced

2 tablespoons Worcestershire sauce

2 teaspoons chopped fresh basil *or* 1 teaspoon dried basil

Pepper to taste

4 pounds pork tenderloin, cut into 1-inch cubes

12 slices Italian bread

In a large resealable plastic bag, combine the first six ingredients; add the pork. Seal bag and turn to coat; refrigerate overnight.

Drain and discard marinade. Thread pork on small metal or soaked wooden skewers. Grill over medium heat or broil 4 in. from the heat for 15 to 20 minutes, turning occasionally, until the meat is no longer pink.

To serve, wrap a slice of bread around about five pork cubes and pull off skewer.

Prep: 15 min. + marinating
Grill: 15 min.
Yield: 12 servings

Peppered Steaks With Salsa

—*Robin Hyde*
Lincoln, Nebraska

Prep: **25 min.**
Grill: **15 min.**
Yield: **4 servings**

We really enjoy these steaks paired with the refreshing from-scratch salsa. The simple marinade makes the steaks very juicy.

1/2 cup red wine vinegar

2 tablespoons lime juice

2 tablespoons olive oil

2 teaspoons chili powder

1 garlic clove, minced

1 to 2 teaspoons crushed red pepper flakes

1 teaspoon salt

1/2 teaspoon pepper

4 beef round tip sandwich steaks (8 ounces *each*)

Salsa:

1 large tomato, seeded and chopped

1 medium ripe avocado, chopped

2 green onions, thinly sliced

1 tablespoon lime juice

1 tablespoon minced fresh cilantro

1 garlic clove, minced

1/4 to 1/2 teaspoon salt

1/4 teaspoon pepper

In a small bowl combine the first eight ingredients. Pour 1/2 cup into a large resealable plastic bag; add steaks. Seal bag and turn to coat; refrigerate 8 hours or overnight. Cover and refrigerate remaining marinade for basting. Meanwhile, combine salsa ingredients; cover and chill.

Drain and discard marinade from steaks. Grill, covered, over medium heat for 7-8 minutes on each side, basting with reserved marinade, or until meat reaches desired doneness (for medium-rare, a meat thermometer should read 145°; medium, 160°; well-done, 170°). Serve with salsa.

Editor's Note: Double this recipe when cooking for crowd.

This hearty potato dish is my no-fuss favorite. And because everything is wrapped in foil and cooked on the grill, cleanup in a snap. The combination of red and sweet potatoes, plus zucchini, yellow summer squash, pepper and mushrooms makes this an eye-appealing side dish.

Grilled Vegetable Medley

—*Susan Hase, Larsen, Wisconsin*

12 small red potatoes, halved

1 medium sweet potato, peeled and cut into chunks

4 tablespoons butter, melted, *divided*

4 to 6 garlic cloves, minced, *divided*

2 tablespoons minced fresh parsley, *divided*

1-1/2 teaspoons salt, *divided*

1/2 teaspoon lemon-pepper seasoning, *divided*

3/4 pound whole fresh mushrooms

1 large onion, sliced

1 medium green pepper, cut into 1/4-inch slices

1 small zucchini, cut into chunks

1 medium yellow summer squash, cut into chunks

1 cup (4 ounces) shredded part-skim mozzarella cheese *or* shredded Swiss cheese

Sour cream, optional

Place potatoes and sweet potato on an 18-in. x 15-in. piece of heavy-duty foil. Drizzle with half of the butter and sprinkle with half of the garlic, parsley, salt and lemon-pepper. Seal foil packet tightly. Grill, covered, over indirect medium-hot heat for 20 minutes on each side.

Meanwhile, place the mushrooms, onion, green pepper, zucchini and summer squash on a 20-in. x 18-in. piece of heavy-duty foil. Drizzle with remaining butter; sprinkle with remaining seasonings. Seal packet tightly. Grill, covered, over medium-hot heat for 10 minutes on each side or until the vegetables are crisp-tender.

Combine the contents of both packets in a serving bowl; sprinkle with cheese. Serve with sour cream if desired.

Prep: **10 min.**
Grill: **40 min.**
Yield: **8-10 servings**

Grilled Corn On the Cob

—Kara De la Vega
Suisun City, California

Seasoned with cilantro, this easy-to-prepare corn on the cob is sure to be a standout at your next party. Wrapping the corn in foil helps lock in the flavors.

12 medium ears sweet corn
1/2 cup butter, melted
1/4 cup sugar
1 cup minced fresh cilantro
Salt and pepper to taste

Soak corn in cold water for 1 hour. Drain and pat dry.

In a small mixing bowl, beat the butter and sugar; spread over corn. On a shallow plate, combine the cilantro, salt and pepper. Roll corn in mixture until lightly coated. Wrap each ear in heavy-duty foil.

Grill, covered, over medium heat for 25-30 minutes or until tender, turning occasionally.

Prep: 10 min. + soaking
Grill: 25 min.
Yield: 12 servings

Marinated Flank Steak

—Debbie Bonczek
Tariffville, Connecticut

I copied this recipe from a friend's collection 15 years ago. Since then I've gotten married and had two children. Now when we make steak on the grill, this is the recipe we usually use. It's also a tempting dish to serve when entertaining. It's earned me many compliments.

3 tablespoons ketchup
1 tablespoon vegetable oil
1 tablespoon chopped onion
1 teaspoon brown sugar
1 teaspoon Worcestershire sauce
1 garlic clove, minced
1/8 teaspoon pepper
1 beef flank steak (about 2 pounds)

In a large resealable plastic bag, combine the first seven ingredients; add beef. Seal bag and turn to coat; refrigerate for at least 4 hours.

Drain meat and discard marinade. Grill, covered, over medium heat for 6-8 minutes per side or until meat reaches desired doneness (for medium-rare, a meat thermometer should read 145°; medium, 160°; well-done, 170°). Let stand for 5 minutes before slicing across the grain into thin strips.

Prep: 5 min. + marinating
Grill: 10 min.
Yield: 8 servings

Shrimp and scallops together make this a special dish for company. I serve these appealing kabobs over pasta with a green salad and garlic bread.

Tangy Shrimp and Scallops

—Lauren Llewellyn
Raleigh, North Carolina

28 uncooked large shrimp (1-1/2 pounds), peeled and deveined

28 sea scallops (about 1/2 pound)

1/2 cup butter, cubed

7 tablespoons lemon juice

5 tablespoons Worcestershire sauce

1 to 2 teaspoons garlic powder

1 teaspoon paprika

Place shrimp and scallops in a large resealable plastic bag; set aside.

In a microwave-safe bowl, combine the butter, lemon juice, Worcestershire sauce, garlic powder and paprika. Microwave at 50% power for 1-1/2 minutes or until butter is melted. Stir to blend; set aside 1/3 cup for basting. Cool remaining marinade to room temperature, then pour over shrimp and scallops. Seal bag and turn to coat; refrigerate for 1 hour, turning occasionally.

Drain and discard any liquid marinade from seafood. Alternately thread shrimp and scallops on metal or soaked wooden skewers. Grill, uncovered, over medium-hot heat for 6 minutes, turning once. Brush with reserved marinade. Grill 8-10 minutes longer or until shrimp turn pink and scallops are opaque.

Editor's Note: Double this recipe when cooking for crowd.

Prep: **15 min.** + marinating
Grill: **15 min.**
Yield: **4 servings**

What screams summer more than grilled hot dogs! I place hot dogs in buns before topping them with a zesty cheese sauce and grilling them in a double layer of foil.

Hot Dogs with The Works

—Maria Regakis
Somerville, Massachusetts

Prep/Total Time: **15 min.**
Yield: **8 servings**

1-1/2 cups (6 ounces) pepper Jack cheese

3/4 cup chopped seeded tomatoes

3 tablespoons chopped onion

2 tablespoons sweet pickle relish

8 hot dogs

8 hot dog buns

In a large bowl, combine the cheese, tomatoes, onion and relish. Place hot dogs in buns; top with cheese mixture.

Wrap hot dogs in a double layer of heavy-duty foil (about 12 in. x 10 in.). Grill, uncovered, over medium-hot heat for 8-10 minutes or until heated through and cheese is melted.

Barbecued Picnic Chicken

—Priscilla Weaver
Hagerstown, Maryland

Prep: 15 min.
Grill: 45 min.
Yield: 8 servings

When we entertain friends for a picnic at our cabin, I like to serve this savory chicken. Cooked on a covered grill, the poultry stays so tender and juicy. Everyone loves the zesty, slightly sweet homemade barbecue sauce—and it's so easy to make.

2 garlic cloves, minced
2 teaspoons butter
1 cup ketchup
1/4 cup packed brown sugar
1/4 cup chili sauce
2 tablespoons Worcestershire sauce
1 tablespoon celery seed
1 tablespoon prepared mustard
1/2 teaspoon salt
2 dashes hot pepper sauce

2 broiler/fryer chickens (3-1/2 to 4 pounds *each*), quartered

In a large saucepan, saute garlic in butter until tender. Add ketchup, sugar, chili sauce, Worcestershire sauce, celery seed, mustard, salt and hot pepper sauce. Bring to a boil, stirring constantly. Remove from the heat; set aside.

Grill chicken, covered, over medium heat for 30 minutes, turning occasionally. Baste with sauce. Grill 15 minutes longer or until juices run clear, basting and turning several times.

Grilled Herbed Pork Roast

—Marie Daley, Charles City, Iowa

Prep: 5 min.
Grill: 1-1/2 hours + standing
Yield: 10-12 servings

During the summer, we enjoy cooking outdoors on our gas grill, and this is one of our favorite ways to prepare pork.

2 tablespoons dill seed, crushed
1 tablespoon fennel seed, crushed
1 teaspoon dried oregano
1 teaspoon lemon-pepper seasoning
1/2 teaspoon garlic powder
1/4 teaspoon onion powder
1 boneless whole pork loin roast (3-1/2 to 4 pounds)

In a small bowl, combine the seasonings; rub over pork roast.

Prepare grill for indirect heat, using a drip pan. Place roast over drip pan; grill, covered, over indirect medium heat for 1-1/2 to 2 hours or until a meat thermometer reads 160°. Let stand for 10 minutes before slicing.

Make a party memorable by serving this golden-brown turkey. Marinated in apple cider, kosher salt and spices, the turkey can be grilled or roasted.

Cider Marinated Turkey

—*Taste of Home Test Kitchen*
Greendale, Wisconsin

8 cups apple cider *or* unsweetened apple juice

1/2 cup kosher salt

2 bay leaves

2 sprigs fresh thyme

8 whole cloves

5 garlic cloves

1 teaspoon whole allspice, crushed

2 medium navel oranges, quartered

3 quarts cold water

1 turkey (12 pounds)

1 medium onion, quartered

2 medium carrots, halved and quartered

2 sprigs fresh sage *or* 1 tablespoon rubbed sage

1 tablespoon canola oil

In a large kettle, combine the cider and seasonings. Bring to a boil. Cook and stir until salt is dissolved. Stir in oranges. Remove from the heat. Add water; cool to room temperature.

Remove giblets from turkey; discard. Place a turkey-size oven roasting bag inside a second roasting bag; add turkey. Place in a roasting pan. Carefully pour cooled marinade into bag. Squeeze out as much air as possible; seal bag and turn to coat. Refrigerate for 12-14 hours; turn several times.

Coat grill rack with nonstick cooking spray. Prepare grill for indirect heat, using a drip pan. Drain and discard marinade. Rinse turkey under cold water; pat dry. Place onion, carrots and sage in cavity. Rub oil over skin. Skewer turkey openings; tie drumsticks together.

Place turkey over drip pan; grill, covered, over indirect medium heat for 2 to 3 hours or until a meat thermometer reads 180° in the thigh, tenting turkey with foil after about 1 hour. Cover and let stand for 15 minutes.

If desired, thicken pan juices for gravy. Remove and discard skin and vegetables in cavity before carving turkey. Serve with gravy.

Editor's Note: It is best not to use a prebasted turkey for this recipe. However, if you do, omit the salt in the recipe.

To bake the turkey, place breast side up on a rack in a roasting pan. Bake, uncovered, at 325° for about 3 hours or until a meat thermometer reads 180° in the thigh.

Prep: 20 min. + marinating
Grill: 2 hours
Yield: 12 servings plus leftovers

Grilled Burgers

—Jesse & Anne Foust
Bluefield, West Virginia

Prep/Total Time: **20 min.**
Yield: **10 servings**

Sour cream makes these burgers delightfully moist, and thyme and black pepper give them zip. These sandwiches are a terrific taste of summer served with tall glasses of lemonade or iced tea.

1/4 cup sour cream

2 teaspoons dried parsley flakes

1 teaspoon dried thyme

1 teaspoon salt

1/2 teaspoon pepper

2-1/2 pounds ground beef

10 hamburger buns, split

Lettuce leaves, sliced tomato and onion, optional

In a large bowl, combine the first five ingredients; crumble beef over mixture and mix gently. Shape into 10 patties.

Grill, uncovered, over medium heat for 4-5 minutes on each side or until meat is no longer pink and a meat thermometer reads, 160°. Serve on buns with the lettuce, tomato and onion if desired.

Barbecued Lamb Kabobs

—Gloria Jarrett, Loveland, Ohio

Prep: **20 min.** + marinating
Grill: **15 min.**
Yield: **8-10 servings**

I like to pair these kabobs with some warm bread. It's nice to serve at parties because it can be made the day before.

1/2 tablespoon dried parsley flakes

1/2 tablespoon dried minced onion

1 teaspoon salt

1/2 teaspoon black pepper

1/2 cup lemon juice

1/2 cup white wine *or* broth of choice

2 tablespoons soy sauce

2-1/2 pounds boneless leg of lamb, cut into 1-inch cubes

Dipping Sauce:
1 large onion, chopped

2 garlic cloves, minced

Salt to taste

Pepper to taste

1/2 cup vegetable oil

1/2 cup lemon juice

Hot peppers to taste, chopped

Combine the first seven ingredients in resealable plastic bag; add lamb. Seal the bag and turn to coat; refrigerate for at least 5 hours or overnight, turning bag occasionally.

Drain and discard marinade. Thread lamb on skewers. Grill over medium-hot heat for 7-8 minutes on each side or until meat reaches desired doneness (for medium-rare, a meat thermometer should read 145°; medium, 160°; well-done, 170°).

For the dipping sauce, in a blender, add all the sauce ingredients. Cover and process on high until smooth. Serve with lamb.

Flaky grilled salmon, lettuce, tomatoes and homemade garlic croutons star in this attractive salad. A Caesar-style dressing, seasoned with lemon juice and grated Parmesan cheese, coats the colorful concoction. You can also make this salad with grilled chicken breasts.

Grilled Salmon Caesar Salad

—*Clara Barrett, Madison, Florida*

2 salmon fillets (1 pound *each*)

3 cups cubed French bread

1 tablespoon olive oil

1/4 teaspoon garlic powder

1 bunch romaine, torn

2 cups small cherry tomatoes

Dressing:

3 tablespoons olive oil

2 tablespoons lemon juice

4-1/2 teaspoons mayonnaise

2-1/4 teaspoons sugar

2 garlic cloves, minced

1/2 teaspoon salt

1/8 teaspoon pepper

1 tablespoon grated Parmesan cheese

Coat grill rack with nonstick cooking spray before starting the grill. Place salmon skin side down on grill. Grill, covered, over medium-hot heat for 15-20 minutes or until fish flakes easily with a fork. Cool.

For croutons, toss the bread cubes, oil and garlic powder in a bowl. In a nonstick skillet, saute bread cubes for 5-6 minutes or until golden brown, stirring occasionally. Remove from the heat; set aside.

Flake salmon into chunks. In a large bowl, combine the romaine and tomatoes. In a small bowl, combine the oil, lemon juice, mayonnaise, sugar, garlic, salt and pepper. Pour over salad and toss to coat. Add the salmon, croutons and Parmesan cheese; toss gently.

Editor's Note: Double this recipe when cooking for crowd.

Prep: **20 min.**
Grill: **15 min. + cooling**
Yield: **6 servings**

Grilled Steak Fajitas

—Pamela Pogue, Quitman, Texas

This tasty main dish is as quick and easy to assemble as tacos. Marinating the meat overnight makes it very tender. We like the hearty and flavorful steak slices. I serve the fajitas with Spanish rice, refried beans and a gelatin dessert.

Prep: **10 min.** + marinating
Grill: **20 min.**
Yield: **6 servings**

1 beef flank steak
  (1-1/2 pounds)

1 large onion, cut into
  wedges

1 medium green pepper,
  julienned

1 can (4 ounces) chopped
  green chilies

1/2 cup lemon juice

1/2 cup cider vinegar

1/2 cup vegetable oil

4 garlic cloves, minced

1 tablespoon
  Worcestershire sauce

1 teaspoon dried oregano

1/2 teaspoon salt

1/2 teaspoon pepper

12 flour tortillas (6 inches),
  warmed

1 medium avocado, peeled
  and sliced, optional

Sour cream, optional

Place beef in a large resealable plastic bag. In another large resealable plastic bag, add the onion and green pepper.

In a small bowl, combine the chilies, lemon juice, vinegar, oil, garlic, Worcestershire sauce, oregano, salt and pepper. Pour 1-1/2 cups marinade over meat. Pour remaining marinade over vegetables. Seal both bags and turn to coat; refrigerate overnight.

Drain meat and vegetables, discarding marinade. Grill steak, covered, over medium-hot heat for 10 minutes on each side or until meat reaches desired doneness (for medium-rare, a meat thermometer should read 145°; medium, 160°; well-done, 170°).

Meanwhile, cut two pieces of heavy-duty foil into 18-in. x 12-in. rectangles. Wrap tortillas in one piece and vegetables in the other; seal foil tightly. Grill both foil packets, covered, over indirect heat for 5-7 minutes, turning occasionally.

Cut steak into 1/8-in. slices across the grain; place on tortillas. Top with vegetables and roll up. Serve with avocado and sour cream if desired.

Editor's Note: Double this recipe when cooking for crowd.

These hearty kabobs combine beef and sausage, two of my favorite foods. Both the meat and vegetables are marinated before they're grilled, which makes this skewered meal extra flavorful.

Mixed Grill Kabobs

—Glenda Adams
Vanndale, Arkansas

3 cups pineapple juice

1 cup cider vinegar

1 cup vegetable oil

1/4 cup sugar

1/4 cup soy sauce

1 tablespoon browning sauce, optional

1/2 teaspoon garlic powder

1/4 teaspoon lemon-pepper seasoning

2 pounds beef tenderloin, cut into 1-inch cubes

1 pound smoked kielbasa *or* Polish sausage, cut into 1-inch chunks

3 to 4 medium tomatoes, quartered

3 to 4 medium green peppers, quartered

1 jar (4-1/2 ounces) whole mushrooms, drained

5 medium onions, quartered

In a large resealable plastic bag, combine the first eight ingredients. Add the meat and vegetables. Seal bag and turn to coat; refrigerate overnight.

Drain and discard marinade. Alternately thread the beef, sausage and vegetable onto metal or soaked wooden skewers. Grill, covered, over medium-hot heat for 6-8 minutes. Turn kabobs; cook 6-8 minutes longer or until beef reaches desired doneness.

Prep: **20 min.** + marinating
Grill: **15 min.**
Yield: **10-12 servings**

We love to barbecue so much that we do it all year long. This recipe is one of my favorites because it has few ingredients and, since it doesn't need marinating, can be prepared for the grill in just minutes.

Picante-Dijon Grilled Chicken

—Karen Page, St. Louis, Missouri

8 boneless skinless chicken breast halves (6 to 7 ounces *each*)

1-1/2 cups picante sauce

2 tablespoons Dijon mustard

1/4 cup packed brown sugar

Flatten chicken breasts to about 1/2-in. thickness; set aside. In a small bowl, combine picante sauce, mustard and sugar.

Place chicken over medium-hot coals; brush generously with sauce. Grill about 6-8 minutes per side or until chicken is tender and no longer pink, brushing occasionally with remaining sauce.

Prep/Total Time: **25 min.**
Yield: **8 servings**

Steak and Shrimp Kabobs

—Karen Mergener
St. Croix, Minnesota

Prep: 20 min. + marinating
Grill: 15 min.
Yield: 6-8 servings

You'll make any get-together special with these attractive kabobs. Cubes of marinated steak are skewered with shrimp, mushrooms, tomatoes, green peppers and onions, then grilled.

1 cup teriyaki sauce

1 can (6 ounces) pineapple juice

1/2 cup packed brown sugar

6 garlic cloves, minced

1/4 teaspoon Worcestershire sauce

1/8 teaspoon pepper

1 pound boneless beef sirloin steak, cut into 1-inch cubes

1 pound uncooked large shrimp, peeled and deveined

1 pound whole fresh mushrooms

2 large green peppers, cut into 1-inch pieces

2 medium onions, halved and quartered

1 pint cherry tomatoes

1-1/2 teaspoons cornstarch

In a large bowl, combine the first six ingredients. Pour half of the marinade into a large resealable plastic bag; add beef. Seal bag and turn to coat; refrigerate for 8 hours or overnight, turning occasionally. Cover and refrigerate remaining marinade.

Drain and discard marinade from beef. On metal or soaked wooden skewers, alternately thread the beef, shrimp, mushrooms, green peppers, onions and tomatoes; set aside. In a small saucepan, combine cornstarch and reserved marinade until smooth. Bring to a boil; cook and stir for 1-2 minutes or until sauce is thickened.

Prepare grill for indirect heat, using a drip pan. Place kabobs over drip pan; grill, covered, over indirect medium heat for 6 minutes, turning once. Baste with sauce. Continue turning and basting for 8-10 minutes or until shrimp turn pink and beef reaches desired doneness.

On Site Grilling

These make a special treat when you have a picnic in the park. Just assemble the kabobs at home and carry them in a large container. Cook on the park provided grill or bring along a portable grill.

Handy
Sandwiches

Chicken Cheddar Wraps

—Ruth Andrewson
Leavenworth, Washington

Prep/Total Time: **15 min.**
Yield: **12 wraps**

I keep cooked chicken in the freezer because these mildly spiced sandwiches are a snap to assemble when I'm pressed for time.

1 cup (8 ounces) sour cream
1 cup chunky salsa
2 tablespoons mayonnaise
4 cups cubed cooked chicken
2 cups (8 ounces) shredded cheddar cheese
1 cup thinly sliced fresh mushrooms
2 cups shredded lettuce
1 cup guacamole, optional
12 flour tortillas (6 inches), warmed
Tomato wedges and additional guacamole, optional

In a large bowl, combine the sour cream, salsa and mayonnaise. Stir in the chicken, cheese and mushrooms.

Divide lettuce and guacamole if desired between tortillas. Place about 1/2 cup chicken mixture on each tortilla. Fold sides over the filling. Garnish with tomato and additional guacamole if desired.

Cajun Pork Sandwiches

—Mae Kruse, Monee, Illinois

Prep: **25 min. + chilling**
Bake: **25 min. + standing**
Yield: **3 dozen**

This recipe's specially seasoned rub gives tender, juicy pork a slightly spicy flavor. You'll watch in delight as these delicious, open-faced sandwiches disappear from your buffet table!

2 pork tenderloins (1 pound *each*), trimmed
2 teaspoons vegetable oil
3 tablespoons paprika
2 teaspoons dried oregano
2 teaspoons dried thyme
1-1/2 teaspoons garlic powder
1/2 teaspoon pepper
1/2 teaspoon salt, optional
1/2 teaspoon ground cumin
1/4 teaspoon ground nutmeg
1/4 teaspoon cayenne pepper
36 French bread slices *or* mini buns
Butter *or* mayonnaise
Lettuce leaves
Thin slivers of green and sweet red pepper

Place tenderloins in a greased 13-in. x 9-in. x 2-in. baking pan. Rub each with 1 teaspoon oil.

In a large bowl, combine the paprika, oregano, thyme, garlic powder, pepper, salt if desired, cumin, nutmeg and cayenne; pat over tenderloins. Cover and refrigerate overnight.

Bake at 425° for 25-30 minutes or until a meat thermometer reads 160°. Let stand for 10 minutes; thinly slice. Spread bread or buns with butter or mayonnaise; top with lettuce, pork and green and red pepper.

BLT Tortillas

—Darla Wester, Meriden, Iowa

I first sampled these at a bridal luncheon years ago. Now I frequently make them for our weekly neighborhood dinners. Crushed red pepper flakes add some zip to every bite.

1/2 cup mayonnaise

1/2 cup sour cream

2 tablespoons ranch salad dressing mix

1/4 teaspoon crushed red pepper flakes

8 flour tortillas (8 inches), warmed

16 bacon strips, cooked and drained

2 to 3 cups shredded lettuce

2 cups chopped tomato

Green and sweet red pepper strips, optional

In a large bowl, combine the mayonnaise, sour cream, salad dressing and red pepper flakes; spread on tortillas. Layer with the bacon, lettuce and tomato. Top with peppers if desired. Roll up tortillas.

Prep/Total Time: **15 min.**
Yield: **8 servings**

Tarragon Chicken Salad Sandwiches

—Caroleah Johnson
Berry Creek, California

I became tired of traditional chicken sandwiches, so I came up with this recipe. Tarragon provides a nice subtle seasoning, while sunflower kernels add extra crunch.

1/2 cup mayonnaise

1 tablespoon lemon juice

1 teaspoon Dijon mustard

3 cups cubed cooked chicken

3/4 cup chopped celery

1 tablespoon minced fresh tarragon *or* 1 teaspoon dried tarragon

1/3 cup sunflower kernels

8 croissants *or* rolls, split

Lettuce leaves

In a large bowl, combine the first three ingredients. Stir in the chicken, celery and tarragon. Just before serving, add sunflower kernels. Line croissants with lettuce; top with 1/2 cup chicken salad.

Prep/Total Time: **15 min.**
Yield: **8 servings**

Buffet Sandwich

—*Margaret Rhodes*
Coaldale, Alberta

The first time I took this beautiful sandwich to a potluck, it disappeared so fast, I was sorry I hadn't brought two.

1 loaf unsliced French bread (1 pound, 20 inches long)

3 to 4 tablespoons mayonnaise

2 tablespoons butter, softened

1 tablespoon prepared mustard

10 lettuce leaves

5 thin slices fully cooked ham, halved

5 slices pimiento loaf, halved, optional

10 slices salami

10 slices Swiss cheese, halved

5 slices part-skim mozzarella cheese

10 thinly sliced sweet red *or* green pepper rings

Cut bread into 22 slices, leaving slices attached at the bottom. Cut off and discard end pieces. In a bowl, combine mayonnaise, butter and mustard. Spread over every other slice of bread.

Between the slices spread with the mayonnaise mixture, place a lettuce leaf, a half slice of ham, a half slice of mozzarella cheese and one pepper ring. To serve, cut completely through the bread between the plain slices.

Prep: **50 min.**
Yield: **10 servings**

Roast Beef Roll-Ups

—*Susan Scott*
Asheville, North Carolina

You can't beat these flavorful sandwiches seasoned with salsa. They're a cool addition to a buffet table and certainly offer a fun change-of-pace from traditional potluck fare. If you're making them in advance, wrap tightly in plastic wrap and refrigerate.

1/2 cup sour cream

1/4 cup mayonnaise

1/4 cup salsa

10 flour tortillas (8 inches), warmed

1 pound thinly sliced cooked roast beef

10 large lettuce leaves

Additional salsa

Combine the first three ingredients; spread over tortillas. Top with beef and lettuce. Roll up tightly and secure with toothpicks; cut in half. Serve with salsa.

Prep/Total Time: **15 min.**
Yield: **10 servings**

When we host a large family get-together, these tasty finger sandwiches score big with everyone who tries them. I like to prepare the pork ahead of time and assemble the sandwiches shortly before they're needed.

Marinated Pork Tenderloin Sandwiches

—Alice Gregory
Overland Park, Kansas

1/2 cup soy sauce

1/4 cup packed brown sugar

2 tablespoons vegetable oil

1 teaspoon ground ginger

1/2 teaspoon ground mustard

2 cloves garlic, minced

1 pound whole pork tenderloin

24 dinner rolls, warmed

In a large bowl, combine the soy sauce, brown sugar, oil, ginger, mustard and garlic. Pour 3/4 cup marinade into a large resealable plastic bag; add the pork. Seal bag and turn to coat; refrigerate for 12 hours or overnight; turning several times. Cover and refrigerate remaining marinade.

Coat grill rack with nonstick cooking spray before starting the grill. Drain and discard marinade from pork. Grill pork, uncovered, over medium heat for 7-8 minutes on each side or until a meat thermometer reaches 160°. Baste with remaining marinade during the last 7 minutes of cooking.

Let stand for 10 minutes. Carve into thin slices; serve on rolls.

Prep: **10 min.** + marinating
Grill: **15 min.**
Yield: **about 24 small sandwiches**

Pork Pointer

Stock up when your grocery store has whole pork tenderloin on sale. Ask the butcher to individually wrap the tenderloins for freezing. Then you'll be all set to thaw the pork and make Marinated Pork Tenderloin Sandwiches.

Oregon Muffuletta

—Marilou Robinson
Portland, Oregon

Prep: **20 min. + chilling**
Yield: **8-10 servings**

Traditional muffuletta is made extra special with the addition of apples, blueberries and cranberries.

1 small tart apple, chopped
1/2 cup fresh blueberries
1/2 cup thinly sliced celery
1/2 cup dried cranberries
1/2 cup thinly sliced green onions
1/2 cup orange juice
3 tablespoons vegetable oil
3 tablespoons cider vinegar
1/2 teaspoon pepper
1/8 teaspoon salt
1 round loaf (2 pounds) unsliced Italian bread
3/4 pound thinly sliced fully cooked ham, *divided*
1/2 pound thinly sliced cheddar cheese

In a large bowl, combine the first 10 ingredients; chill for at least 8 hours, stirring occasionally.

Cut a thin slice off the top of the bread; hollow out the bottom half, leaving a 1-in. shell. (Discard removed bread or save for another use.)

Drain 1/4 cup liquid from the fruit mixture; brush on inside of bread shell. In bottom of bread shell, layer half of the ham, 1-1/4 cups fruit mixture, cheese, remaining fruit mixture and remaining ham. Replace bread top and wrap tightly with plastic wrap. Refrigerate for at least 2 hours.

Remove from the refrigerator 30 minutes before serving. Cut into wedges.

I've made these sandwiches many times for family and friends. I often get asked for the recipe. The pineapple is what gives them a Hawaiian flair—we think they're a real treat.

8 submarine rolls *or* hoagie buns (8 inches)

8 slices Swiss cheese, halved

1/2 medium sweet red pepper, julienned

1/2 medium green pepper, julienned

6 to 8 green onions, sliced

2 teaspoons vegetable oil

1 pound sliced fully cooked ham, julienned

1 can (20 ounces) pineapple tidbits, drained

1 cup (4 ounces) shredded part-skim mozzarella cheese

Cut thin slices off the tops of the rolls. Hollow out bread in the center, leaving 1/4-in. shells; set aside tops and discard hollowed-out bread (or save for another use). Place rolls on a baking sheet; line the inside of each with Swiss cheese.

In a large skillet, saute peppers and onions in oil for 3 minutes. Add ham; cook for 3 minutes. Add pineapple. Remove from the heat; drain.

Spoon into rolls. Bake at 450° for 5 minutes. Sprinkle with the mozzarella cheese. Bake 1 minute longer or until cheese is melted. Replace the tops of the rolls. Serve immediately.

Hawaiian Ham Sandwiches

—Alice Lewis, Red Oak, Iowa

Prep/Total Time: **25 min.**
Yield: **8 servings**

When our office held a bridal shower, we presented the future bride with a collection of our favorite recipes. I included this one. I like serving this savory pork as an alternative to a typical ground beef barbecue.

2 boneless whole pork loin roasts (2-1/2 to 3 pounds *each*)

1 cup water

2 teaspoons salt

2 cups ketchup

2 cups diced celery

1/3 cup steak sauce

1/4 cup packed brown sugar

1/4 cup white vinegar

2 teaspoons lemon juice

20 to 25 hamburger buns

Place roasts in an 8-qt. Dutch oven; add water and salt. Cover and cook on medium-low heat for 2-1/2 hours or until meat is tender.

Remove roasts and shred with a fork; set aside. Skim fat from cooking liquid and discard. Drain all but 1 cup cooking liquid. Add the meat, ketchup, celery, steak sauce, brown sugar, vinegar and lemon juice. Cover and cook over medium-low heat for 1-1/2 hours. Serve on buns.

Barbecued Pork Sandwiches

—Karla Labby, Otsego, Michigan

Prep: **15 min.**
Cook: **4 hours**
Yield: **20-25 servings**

Tuna Cheese Spread

—Dorothy Anderson
Ottawa, Kansas

Prep/Total Time: **5 min.**
Yield: **2 cups**

The flavor of tuna is very subtle in this thick and creamy spread. It's terrific on crackers, stuffed in a tomato or used for a sandwich.

1 package (8 ounces) cream cheese, softened
1 can (6 ounces) tuna, drained and flaked
1/2 cup finely sliced green onions
1/4 cup mayonnaise
1 tablespoon lemon juice
3/4 teaspoon curry powder
Dash salt
Bread *or* crackers

In a large bowl, combine the first seven ingredients. Serve with bread or crackers.

Editor's Note: Double this recipe when cooking for a crowd.

Turkey Dill Subs

—Violet Beard, Marshall, Illinois

For a change of pace from usual sandwiches, try these dill-seasoned subs. You can use salmon or pickled herring tidbits instead of turkey to make them like a Swedish hero.

1/2 cup butter, softened
4 tablespoons snipped fresh dill *or* 4 teaspoons dill weed
8 submarine buns (about 8 inches *each*), split
Lettuce leaves
12 radishes, thinly sliced
2 cups thinly sliced zucchini *or* cucumber
2 to 3 teaspoons cider vinegar, optional
2 to 3 pounds thinly sliced deli smoked turkey

In a small bowl, combine butter and dill; spread on sub buns. Layer the lettuce, radishes and zucchini on bottom of buns. Sprinkle with vinegar if desired. Top with turkey; replace bun tops.

Prep/Total Time: **20 min.**
Yield: **8 servings**

The raspberry barbecue sauce makes these tasty grilled chicken sandwiches special. I also use this sauce on meatballs, chicken wings and pork chops.

1 cup chili sauce

3/4 cup raspberry preserves

2 tablespoons red wine vinegar

1 tablespoon Dijon mustard

6 boneless skinless chicken breast halves

2 tablespoons plus 1/2 cup olive oil, *divided*

1/2 teaspoon salt

1/4 teaspoon pepper

24 slices French bread (1/2 inch thick)

12 slices Muenster cheese, halved

Shredded lettuce

Coat grill rack with nonstick cooking spray before starting the grill. In a small saucepan, combine the first four ingredients. Bring to a boil. Reduce the heat; simmer, uncovered, for 2 minutes. Set aside 1 cup for serving and remaining sauce for basting.

Flatten the chicken breasts to 1/4-in. thickness. Cut in half widthwise; place in a large resealable plastic bag. Add 2 tablespoons oil, salt and pepper. Seal bag and turn to coat. Brush remaining oil over both sides of bread.

Grill chicken, uncovered, over medium heat for 5-7 minutes on each side or until the juices run clear, basting frequently with the remaining raspberry sauce. Remove and keep warm.

Grill bread, uncovered, for 1-2 minutes or until lightly browned on one side. Turn and top each piece of bread with a slice of cheese. Grill 1-2 minutes longer or until bottom of bread is toasted. Place a piece of chicken, lettuce and reserved raspberry sauce on half of the bread slices; top with remaining bread.

Raspberry Chicken Sandwiches

—Kelly Williams
La Porte, Indiana

Prep: **25 min.**
Grill: **15 min.**
Yield: **12 servings**

Make-Ahead Sloppy Joes

—Alyne Fuller, Odessa, Texas

Prep/Total Time: **30 min.**
Yield: **14-16 servings**

Having these zesty sandwiches in the freezer is such a time-saver when you're in a bind and need a fast dish to feed a crowd.

1 pound bulk pork sausage
1 pound ground beef
1 medium onion, chopped
14 to 16 sandwich buns, split
2 cans (8 ounces *each*) tomato sauce
2 tablespoons prepared mustard
1 teaspoon dried parsley flakes
1 teaspoon garlic powder
1 teaspoon salt
1/4 teaspoon pepper
1/4 teaspoon dried oregano

In a large skillet, cook sausage, beef and onion over medium heat until meat is no longer pink. Remove from heat; drain. Remove centers from the tops and bottoms of each bun. Tear removed bread into small pieces; add to skillet. Set buns aside.

Stir remaining ingredients into the sausage mixture. Spoon about 1/3 cupful onto the bottom of each bun; replace tops. Wrap individually in heavy-duty foil.

Place on a baking sheet. Bake at 350° for 20 minutes or until heated through or freeze for up to 3 months. Thaw frozen sandwiches in the refrigerator, then heat as directed.

Waldorf Sandwiches

*—Darlene Sutton
Arvada, Colorado*

Prep: **20 min. + chilling**
Yield: **16 servings**

The fresh fruity filling for this sandwich is a nice variation of a classic. My clan loves the cool and creamy combination.

1 can (20 ounces) crushed pineapple
3 cups cubed cooked chicken
1 medium red apple, chopped
1 medium green apple, chopped
1 cup chopped walnuts
1 cup sliced celery
1 cup mayonnaise
1 tablespoon poppy seeds
1 teaspoon sugar
1 teaspoon grated lemon peel
1/2 teaspoon vanilla extract
1/2 teaspoon salt
Rolls, croissants *or* pita bread

Drain pineapple, pressing out excess juice; discard all but 1/4 cup juice. In a large bowl, combine pineapple, chicken, apples, walnuts and celery.

In a small bowl, combine the mayonnaise, poppy seeds, sugar, lemon peel, vanilla, salt and reserved pineapple juice. Pour over chicken mixture and toss well. Chill. Serve on rolls or croissants or in pita bread.

My husband and I live on a 21-acre horse ranch and are pleased to invite friends to enjoy it with us. When entertaining, I rely on no-fuss, make-ahead entrees like this satisfying sandwich. You can vary the sandwich to suit your guests. Use turkey, salami or even carved beef for the ham or roast beef.

Sandwich For a Crowd

—Helen Hougland
Spring Hill, Kansas

- 2 loaves (1 pound *each*) unsliced Italian bread
- 1 package (8 ounces) cream cheese, softened
- 1 cup (4 ounces) shredded cheddar cheese
- 3/4 cup sliced green onions
- 1/4 cup mayonnaise
- 1 tablespoon Worcestershire sauce
- 1 pound thinly sliced fully cooked ham
- 1 pound thinly sliced roast beef
- 12 to 14 thin slices dill pickle

Cut the bread in half lengthwise. Hollow out top and bottom of loaves, leaving a 1/2-in. shell (discard removed bread or save for another use).

In a large bowl, combine the cheeses, onions, mayonnaise and Worcestershire sauce; spread over cut sides of bread. Layer ham and roast beef on bottom and top halves; place pickle slices on bottom halves. Gently press the halves together.

Wrap in plastic wrap and refrigerate for at least 2 hours. Cut into 1-1/2-in. slices.

Prep: **10 min. + chilling**
Yield: **12-14 servings**

Cream Cheese Capers

When making Sandwich for a Crowd, feel free to experiment with flavored cream cheese, including chive and onion, garlic and herbs, garden vegetable and roasted garlic.

Super Sandwich

—Patrice Barker, Tampa, Florida

Prep/Total Time: **30 min.**
Yield: **8 servings**

This big, meaty sandwich is one I've made many times when I knew I'd be feeding a hungry bunch. Everyone remarks on the tasty olive salad tucked between slices of meat and cheese. Since it can be made ahead, you're free to visit with family and friends.

1 medium cucumber, peeled, seeded and chopped

1 medium tomato, seeded and chopped

1 small onion, chopped

1/2 cup pitted ripe olives, chopped

1/2 cup pimiento-stuffed olives, chopped

1/4 cup prepared Italian salad dressing

1 round loaf (1-1/2 pounds) unsliced sourdough, white *or* whole wheat bread

1/2 pound sliced fully cooked ham

1/4 pound sliced salami

1/4 pound sliced cooked pork

1/2 pound sliced Swiss cheese

1/2 pound sliced Muenster cheese

In a large bowl, combine the cucumber, tomato, onion, olives and salad dressing; set aside.

Cut 1 in. off the top of the bread; set aside. Carefully hollow out top and bottom of loaf, leaving a 1/2-in. shell (discard removed bread or save for another use).

Layer a fourth of the ham, salami, pork and cheeses inside the shell. Top with one-third of the vegetable mixture. Repeat layers, ending with meat and cheeses, gently pressing down to flatten as needed.

Replace bread top; wrap tightly in plastic. Refrigerate until serving. Cut into slices.

A Sandwich By Any Other Name

Super Sandwich is a variation of the New Orleans' classic Muffuletta. Traditionally a round Italian bread is filled with ham, provolone and salami.

This zesty sandwich is piled high with flavor. One night instead of setting out sandwiches with antipasto on the side, I combined the two.

Antipasto Sub

—Jeanette Hios
Brooklyn, New York

Prep: 15 min. + chilling
Yield: 10-12 servings

- 1 loaf (1 pound) unsliced Italian bread
- 3 cans (2-1/2 ounces *each*) sliced ripe olives, drained
- 3 jars (6-1/2 ounces *each*) marinated artichoke hearts, drained
- 2 jars (7 ounces *each*) roasted sweet red peppers, drained
- 1/2 pound thinly sliced provolone cheese
- 3/4 pound thickly sliced salami
- 3 tablespoons olive oil
- 3 tablespoons cider vinegar
- 1/2 teaspoon garlic powder
- 1/2 teaspoon Italian seasoning
- 1/4 teaspoon salt
- 1/4 teaspoon pepper

Cut bread in half lengthwise; hollow out top, leaving a 1-1/2-in. shell. (Discard removed bread or save for another use.) Invert bread top; layer with olives, artichokes, red peppers, cheese and salami. Replace bread bottom. Wrap tightly in plastic wrap; refrigerate.

In a jar with a tight-fitting lid, combine remaining ingredients; shake well. Refrigerate. Cut sub into slices; serve with the dressing.

This stacked sandwich seems fancy with its raspberry jam surprise. Yet it's convenient because it can be assembled ahead of time and then warmed just before serving.

Sweet Club Sandwich

—Joanne Klopfenstein
North Liberty, Indiana

Prep: 20 min. + cooling
Bake: 10 min.
Yield: 8 servings

- 2 tubes (8 ounces *each*) refrigerated crescent rolls
- 2 tablespoons butter
- 4 tablespoons honey, *divided*
- 6 ounces thinly sliced deli turkey
- 6 ounces sliced Muenster *or* Monterey Jack cheese
- 6 ounces thinly sliced deli ham
- 1/3 cup raspberry preserves
- 1 tablespoon sesame seeds

Unroll each tube of crescent roll dough into two rectangles. Place 2 in. apart on ungreased baking sheets; press perforations to seal. In a small bowl, combine butter and 2 tablespoons honey. Brush over dough. Bake at 375° for 10-12 minutes or until lightly browned. Cool on pans for 15 minutes.

Carefully transfer one crust to a greased 15-in. x 10-in. x 1-in. baking pan. Layer with turkey, second crust, cheese and ham. Add third crust; spread with preserves.

Top with remaining crust; spread with remaining honey. Sprinkle with sesame seeds. Bake, uncovered, at 375° for 10-15 minutes or until the crust is golden brown and loaf is heated through. Carefully cut into slices.

Mom's Portable Beef

—Lorene Sinclair
Belleville, Ontario

Prep: 15 min.
Bake: 1 hour 30 min. + cooling
Yield: 12-14 servings

This delicious beef makes great sandwiches for a picnic, potluck or even a camping trip. The meat has a tempting from-scratch flavor that beats deli cold cuts.

1 can (14-1/2 ounces) beef broth
1 medium onion, chopped
1 cup cider vinegar
2 tablespoons minced fresh parsley
1 bay leaf
1 tablespoon mixed pickling spices
1/2 teaspoon dried marjoram
1/2 teaspoon dried savory
1/2 teaspoon salt
1/4 teaspoon pepper
1 beef eye round roast (3 pounds)
12 to 14 sandwich rolls, split
Lettuce, tomato and onion, optional

In a Dutch oven, combine the first 10 ingredients; add roast. Cover and bake at 325° for 1-1/2 hours or until the meat is tender. Remove the roast and cool completely.

Meanwhile, skim fat and strain cooking juices. Discard bay leaf. Thinly slice the beef across the grain. Serve on rolls with warmed juices and lettuce, tomato and onion if desired.

Snappy Barbecue Beef Sandwiches

—Patricia Throlson
Hawick, Minnesota

Prep: 10 min.
Bake: 5 hours
Yield: about 24 servings

The beef in these sandwiches is like an oven stew, but we'll often prepare it in a slow cooker—putting it on in the morning so we can just dish it up when we get home from work.

1 boneless beef chuck roast (4 pounds)
1 cup ketchup
1 cup barbecue sauce
4 cups chopped celery
2 cups water
1 cup chopped onion
2 tablespoons white vinegar
2 tablespoons brown sugar
2 tablespoons Worcestershire sauce

1 teaspoon chili powder
1 teaspoon garlic powder
1 teaspoon salt
Italian rolls *or* sandwich buns, split

Place beef in a Dutch oven. Combine all remaining ingredients except the rolls; pour over beef. Cover and bake at 350° for 5 hours, turning beef occasionally. Shred beef with a fork. Serve on rolls or buns.

My husband taught me how to make these fun, tasty sandwiches. Using pitas instead of regular bread makes them feel more special. They take little time to prepare, and we enjoy them all through the year. They don't last long on a buffet.

Potluck Pockets

—Debbie Jones
California, Maryland

1 pound ground beef

1/2 cup chopped onion

1/2 cup chopped green pepper

2 tablespoons Worcestershire sauce

2 tablespoons soy sauce

2 teaspoons garlic powder

1 teaspoon ground cumin

1/2 teaspoon Italian seasoning

6 pita breads, halved

2 medium tomatoes, diced

3 cups shredded lettuce

Sauce:

1/2 cup soy sauce

1/4 cup white vinegar

2 tablespoons Worcestershire sauce

1/2 teaspoon onion powder

1/2 teaspoon Italian seasoning

Dash pepper

In a large skillet, cook the beef, onion and green pepper over medium heat until the meat is no longer pink; drain. Add the Worcestershire sauce, soy sauce, garlic powder, cumin and Italian seasoning; mix well. Simmer, uncovered, for 5-10 minutes.

In a small saucepan, bring all the sauce ingredients to boil. Reduce heat; simmer, uncovered, for 5-10 minutes. Spoon meat mixture into pita halves; top with sauce, tomatoes and lettuce.

Prep/Total **Time: 30 min.**
Yield: **12 servings**

Olive-Cucumber Finger Sandwiches

—Sara Laker, Loda, Illinois

Prep: **25 min.** + standing
Yield: **3 dozen**

The crisp cucumbers on these easy-to-fix finger sandwiches get their zip from being marinated for a short time.

1 medium cucumber

1 cup water

1/2 cup cider vinegar

1 package (8 ounces) cream cheese, softened

1/4 cup mayonnaise

1/4 teaspoon garlic powder

1/4 teaspoon onion salt

1/8 teaspoon Worcestershire sauce

36 thin slices bread

Paprika

36 pimiento-stuffed olives

With a fork, score the cucumber lengthwise; cut into thin slices. Place in a bowl; add water and vinegar. Let stand for 30 minutes. Meanwhile, in a small mixing bowl, beat the cream cheese, mayonnaise, garlic powder, onion salt and Worcestershire sauce until smooth.

Cut bread into flower shapes with a 2-1/2-in. cookie cutter. Spread each with cream cheese mixture; sprinkle with paprika and top with a cucumber slice.

Remove pimientos from olives; place in center of cucumber. Cut the olives into five wedges and arrange around pimiento in a pinwheel pattern.

Super Italian Sub

—Patricia Lomp
Middleboro, Massachusetts

Prep/Total Time: **30 min.**
Yield: **10-12 servings**

I like recipes that can be made ahead of time, and this sandwich offers me that convenience.

1 loaf (1 pound) unsliced Italian bread

1/3 cup olive oil

1/4 cup cider vinegar

8 garlic cloves, minced

1 teaspoon dried oregano

1/4 teaspoon pepper

1/2 pound fully cooked ham, thinly sliced

1/2 pound thinly sliced cooked turkey

1/4 pound thinly sliced hard salami

1/4 pound sliced provolone cheese

1/4 pound sliced part-skim mozzarella cheese

1 medium green pepper, thinly sliced into rings

Cut bread in half lengthwise. Hollow out top and bottom, leaving a 1/2-in. shell (discard removed bread or save for another use).

In a small bowl, combine the oil, vinegar, garlic, oregano and pepper; brush on cut sides of bread top and bottom. On the bottom half, layer half of the meats, cheeses and green pepper. Repeat layers. Replace bread top. Wrap tightly in plastic wrap; refrigerate for up to 24 hours. Cut into slices.

Slow
& Easy

Reuben Spread

—*Rosalie Fuchs*
Paynesville, Minnesota

I received the recipe for this hearty spread from my daughter. It tastes just like a Reuben sandwich. Serve it from a slow cooker set to low so that the spread stays warm.

Prep: **5 min.**
Cook: **2 hours**
Yield: **3-1/2 cups**

1 jar (16 ounces) sauerkraut, rinsed and drained

1 package (8 ounces) cream cheese, cubed

2 cups (8 ounces) shredded Swiss cheese

1 package (3 ounces) deli corned beef, chopped

3 tablespoons prepared Thousand Island salad dressing

Snack rye bread *or* crackers

In a 1-1/2-qt. slow cooker, combine the first five ingredients. Cover and cook for 2 hours or until cheeses are melted; stir to blend. Serve warm with bread or crackers.

Cute Cutouts

Add a little pizzazz to your appetizer table when serving Reuben Spread at a party. Use assorted small cookie cutters in various shapes (like stars, circles and diamonds) to cut out fun and festive shapes in slices of snack rye bread.

I've taken this hearty, all-in-one dish to countless events, and it's popular every time. Slices of bratwurst take center stage alongside potatoes, sauerkraut, apple and onion.

Crock o' Brats

—Maryellen Boettcher
Fairchild, Wisconsin

- 5 uncooked bratwurst (1-1/4 pounds), cut into 1-inch pieces
- 5 medium potatoes, peeled and cubed
- 1 can (27 ounces) sauerkraut, rinsed and well drained
- 1 medium tart apple, chopped
- 1 small onion, chopped
- 1/4 cup packed brown sugar
- 1/2 teaspoon salt, optional

In a large skillet, brown bratwurst on all sides. In a 5-qt. slow cooker, combine the remaining ingredients. Stir in bratwurst and pan drippings. Cover and cook on high for 4-6 hours or until potatoes and apple are tender.

Editor's Note: Double this recipe and use a 6-qt. slow cooking when cooking for a crowd.

Prep: 10 min.
Cook: 4 hours
Yield: 5 servings

I work full-time and coach soccer and football, so I appreciate recipes like this one that are easy to assemble. This warm and creamy seafood appetizer is perfect for large get-togethers.

Hot Crab Dip

—Teri Rasey-Bolf
Cadillac, Michigan

- 1/2 cup milk
- 1/3 cup salsa
- 3 packages (8 ounces *each*) cream cheese, cubed
- 2 packages (8 ounces *each*) imitation crabmeat, flaked
- 1 cup thinly sliced green onions
- 1 can (4 ounces) chopped green chilies

Assorted crackers

In a small bowl, combine milk and salsa. Transfer to a greased 3-qt. slow cooker. Stir in cream cheese, crab, onions and chilies. Cover and cook on low for 3-4 hours, stirring every 30 minutes. Serve with crackers.

Prep: 5 min.
Cook: 3 hours
Yield: about 5 cups

Turkey Sloppy Joes

—Marylou LaRue
Freeland, Michigan

Prep: **15 min.**
Cook: **4 hours**
Yield: **8 servings**

This tangy sandwich filling is so easy to prepare in the slow cooker, and it goes over well at gatherings large and small. I frequently take it to potlucks, and I'm always asked for the recipe.

1 pound ground turkey breast
1 small onion, chopped
1/2 cup chopped celery
1/4 cup chopped green pepper
1 can (10-3/4 ounces) reduced-fat reduced-sodium condensed tomato soup, undiluted
1/2 cup ketchup
1 tablespoon brown sugar
2 tablespoons prepared mustard
1/4 teaspoon pepper
8 hamburger buns, split

In a large saucepan coated with nonstick cooking spray, cook the turkey, onion, celery and green pepper over medium heat until meat is no longer pink; drain if necessary. Stir in the soup, ketchup, brown sugar, mustard and pepper. Transfer to a 3-qt. slow cooker. Cover and cook on low for 4 hours. Serve on buns.

Simmered Smoked Links

—Maxine Cenker
Weirton, West Virginia

Prep: **5 min.**
Cook: **4 hours**
Yield: **16-20 servings**

A tasty, sweet-sour sauce glazes bite-size sausages in this recipe. Serve these effortless appetizers with toothpicks at parties or holiday get-togethers.

2 packages (16 ounces *each*) miniature smoked sausage links
1 cup packed brown sugar
1/2 cup ketchup
1/4 cup prepared horseradish

Place sausages in a 3-qt. slow cooker. Combine the brown sugar, ketchup and horseradish; pour over sausages. Cover and cook on low for 4 hours.

Serve this stick-to-your-ribs dish with a green salad and dessert for a complete meal. This creamy mixture is brimming with flavor.

- 4 medium red potatoes, thinly sliced
- 2 medium onions, finely chopped
- 1-1/2 cups cubed fully cooked ham
- 2 tablespoons butter
- 2 tablespoons all-purpose flour
- 1 teaspoon ground mustard
- 1/2 teaspoon salt
- 1/2 teaspoon pepper
- 1 can (10-3/4 ounces) condensed cream of celery soup, undiluted
- 1-1/3 cups water
- 1 cup (4 ounces) shredded cheddar cheese, optional

In a 3-qt. slow cooker, layer potatoes, onions and ham. In a large saucepan, melt butter. Stir in the flour, mustard, salt and pepper until smooth. Combine soup and water; gradually stir into flour mixture. Bring to a boil; cook and stir for 2 minutes or until thickened and bubbly.

Pour over ham. Cover and cook on low for 8-9 hours or until potatoes are tender. If desired, sprinkle with cheese before serving.

Editor's Note: Double this recipe and use a 5-qt. slow cooker when cooking for a crowd.

Creamy Ham And Potatoes

—Peggy Key, Grant, Alabama

Prep: 20 min.
Cook: 8 hours
Yield: 4 servings

This recipe was given to us by our daughter. My husband and I love it. Because it's made in a slow cooker, it's great for parties or busy days.

- 1 can (16 ounces) kidney beans, rinsed and drained
- 1 can (15-1/4 ounces) whole kernel corn, drained
- 1 can (15 ounces) black beans, rinsed and drained
- 1 can (14-1/2 ounces) stewed tomatoes
- 1 can (8 ounces) tomato sauce
- 1 can (4 ounces) chopped green chilies, drained
- 1 envelope taco seasoning
- 1/2 cup chopped onion
- Tortilla chips

In a 5-qt. slow cooker, combine the first eight ingredients. Cover and cook on low for 5-7 hours. Serve with tortilla chips.

Taco Joe Dip

*—Lang Secrest
Sierra Vista, Arizona*

Prep: 5 min.
Cook: 5 hours
Yield: about 7 cups

Lemony Turkey Breast

—Lynn Laux
Ballwin, Missouri

Prep: **10 min.**
Cook: **5 hours**
Yield: **14 servings**

Lemon and a hint of garlic add a lovely touch to these moist slices of slow-cooked turkey breast. I usually serve this alongside broccoli for a healthy meal.

1 bone-in turkey breast (5 pounds), halved

1 medium lemon, halved

1 teaspoon salt-free lemon-pepper seasoning

1 teaspoon garlic salt

4 teaspoons cornstarch

1/2 cup reduced-sodium chicken broth

Remove skin from turkey. Pat turkey dry with paper towels; spray turkey with nonstick cooking spray. Place breast side up in a slow cooker. Squeeze half of the lemon over turkey; sprinkle with lemon-pepper and garlic salt. Place lemon halves under turkey. Cover and cook on low for 5-7 hours or until meat is no longer pink and a meat thermometer reads 170°. Remove turkey and keep warm. Discard lemon.

For gravy, pour cooking liquid into a measuring cup; skim fat. In a saucepan, combine cornstarch and broth until smooth. Gradually stir in cooking liquid. Bring to a boil; cook and stir for 2 minutes or until thickened. Serve with turkey.

Barbecued Pork Chop Supper

—Jacqueline Jones
Round Lake Beach, Illinois

Prep: **10 min.**
Cook: **8 hours**
Yield: **8 servings**

I start this family-favorite recipe in the morning in the slow cooker and enjoy a tasty supper later without any last-minute work.

6 small red potatoes, cut into quarters

6 medium carrots, cut into 1-inch pieces

8 bone-in pork loin *or* rib chops (1/2 inch thick)

1 teaspoon salt

1/4 teaspoon pepper

1 bottle (28 ounces) barbecue sauce

1 cup ketchup

1 cup cola

2 tablespoons Worcestershire sauce

Place potatoes and carrots in a 5-qt. slow cooker. Top with pork chops. Sprinkle with salt and pepper. Combine the barbecue sauce, ketchup, cola and Worcestershire sauce; pour over chops. Cover and cook on low for 8-9 hours or until meat and vegetables are tender.

My husband always nominates me to bring a side dish when we're invited to a potluck. Canned beans cut down on prep time yet get plenty of zip from bacon, apple, red pepper and onion. I like simmering this mixture in the slow cooker because it blends the flavors, and I don't have to stand over the stove.

Slow-Simmered Kidney Beans

—Sheila Vail
Long Beach, California

- 6 bacon strips, diced
- 1/2 pound smoked Polish sausage *or* kielbasa
- 4 cans (16 ounces *each*) kidney beans, rinsed and drained
- 1 can (28 ounces) diced tomatoes, drained
- 2 medium sweet red peppers, chopped
- 1 large onion, chopped
- 1 cup ketchup
- 1/2 cup packed brown sugar
- 1/4 cup honey
- 1/4 cup molasses
- 1 tablespoon Worcestershire sauce
- 1 teaspoon salt
- 1 teaspoon ground mustard
- 2 medium unpeeled red apples, cored and cut into 1/2-inch pieces

In a large skillet, cook bacon over medium heat until crisp. Using a slotted spoon, remove to paper towels; drain, reserving 2 tablespoons drippings. Add sausage to drippings; cook and stir for 5 minutes. Drain and set aside.

In a 5-qt. slow cooker, combine the beans, tomatoes, red peppers, onion, ketchup, brown sugar, honey, molasses, Worcestershire sauce, salt and mustard. Stir in the bacon and sausage. Cover and cook on low for 4-6 hours. Stir in apples. Cover and cook 2 hours longer or until bubbly.

Prep: **15 min.**
Cook: **6 hours**
Yield: **16 servings**

Serving Suggestion

For an even heartier dish, serve Slow-Simmered Kidney Beans as a main dish over hot cooked white or brown rice.

Creamy Hash Browns

—Donna Downes
Las Vegas, Nevada

Prep: **10 min.**
Cook: **4 hours**
Yield: **14 servings**

My mother often took this comforting side dish to social dinners because it was such a hit. Now I get the same compliments when I make it. Bacon and onion jazz up a creamy mixture that takes advantage of convenient frozen hash browns and canned soups.

1 package (2 pounds) frozen cubed hash brown potatoes

2 cups (8 ounces) cubed process cheese (Velveeta)

2 cups (16 ounces) sour cream

1 can (10-3/4 ounces) condensed cream of celery soup, undiluted

1 can (10-3/4 ounces) condensed cream of chicken soup, undiluted

1 pound sliced bacon, cooked and crumbled

1 large onion, chopped

1/4 cup butter, melted

1/4 teaspoon pepper

Place potatoes in an ungreased 5-qt. slow cooker. In a large bowl, combine the remaining ingredients. Pour over potatoes and mix well. Cover and cook on low for 4-5 hours or until potatoes are tender and heated through.

This zesty salad makes a terrific side dish when served warm with crumbled bacon and fresh parsley sprinkled on top.

Hot German Potato Salad
—Marlene Muckenhirn
Delano, Minnesota

8 medium potatoes, peeled and cut into 1/4-inch slices

2 celery ribs, chopped

1 large onion, chopped

1 cup water

2/3 cup cider vinegar

1/3 cup sugar

2 tablespoons quick-cooking tapioca

1 teaspoon salt

3/4 teaspoon celery seed

1/4 teaspoon pepper

6 bacon strips, cooked and crumbled

1/4 cup minced fresh parsley

In a 3-qt. slow cooker, combine the potatoes, celery and onion. In a small bowl, combine the water, vinegar, sugar, tapioca, salt, celery seed and pepper. Pour over potatoes; stir gently to coat.

Cover and cook on high for 4-5 hours or until potatoes are tender. Just before serving, sprinkle with bacon and parsley.

Prep: **15 min.**
Cook: **4 hours**
Yield: **8-10 servings**

I often fix this delicious ham topped with a thick cherry sauce for church breakfasts. It's such a favorite that I've even served it at Easter dinners and at a friend's wedding brunch.

Ham with Cherry Sauce
—Carol Lee Jones
Taylors, South Carolina

1 boneless fully cooked ham (3 to 4 pounds)

1/2 cup apple jelly

2 teaspoons prepared mustard

2/3 cup ginger ale, *divided*

1 can (21 ounces) cherry pie filling

2 tablespoons cornstarch

Score surface of ham, making diamond shapes 1/2 in. deep. In a small bowl, combine the jelly, mustard and 1 tablespoon ginger ale; rub over scored surface of ham. Cut ham in half; place in a 5-qt. slow cooker. Cover and cook on low for 4-5 hours or until a meat thermometer reads 140° and ham is heated through. Baste with cooking juices toward end of cooking time.

For the sauce, place pie filling in a saucepan. Combine the cornstarch and remaining ginger ale; stir into the pie filling until blended. Bring to a boil; cook and stir for 2 minutes or until thickened. Serve over ham.

Prep: **15 min.**
Cook: **4 hours**
Yield: **10-12 servings**

Slow-Cooked Broccoli

—Connie Slocum
Antioch, Tennessee

Prep: 10 min.
Cook: 2 hours 40 min.
Yield: 8-10 servings

This crumb-topped side dish is quick to assemble and full of flavor. Since it simmers in a slow cooker, it frees up my oven for other things. This a great help when I'm preparing several items for a big meal.

2 packages (10 ounces *each*) frozen chopped broccoli, partially thawed

1 can (10-3/4 ounces) condensed cream of celery soup, undiluted

1-1/2 cups (6 ounces) shredded sharp cheddar cheese, *divided*

1/4 cup chopped onion

1/2 teaspoon Worcestershire sauce

1/4 teaspoon pepper

1 cup crushed butter-flavored crackers (about 25)

2 tablespoons butter

In a large bowl, combine broccoli, soup, 1 cup cheese, onion, Worcestershire sauce and pepper. Pour into a greased 3-qt. slow cooker. Sprinkle crackers on top; dot with butter. Cover and cook on high for 2-1/2 to 3 hours. Sprinkle with remaining cheese. Cook 10 minutes longer or until the cheese is melted.

French Dip Sandwiches

—Florence Robinson
Lenox, Iowa

Prep: 30 min.
Cook: 7 hours + standing
Yield: 12-14 servings

When I want to impress company, I put these satisfying sandwiches on the menu. I serve the au jus sauce in individual bowls for dipping. It's delicious.

2 large onions, cut into 1/4-inch slices

1/4 cup butter, cubed

1 beef bottom round roast (3 to 4 pounds)

5 cups water

1/2 cup soy sauce

1 envelope onion soup mix

1-1/2 teaspoons browning sauce, optional

1 garlic clove, minced

12 to 14 French rolls, split

1 cup (4 ounces) shredded Swiss cheese

In a large skillet, saute onions in butter until tender; transfer to a 5-qt. slow cooker. Cut the roast in half; place over onions. In a large bowl, combine water, soy sauce, soup mix, browning sauce if desired and garlic; pour over roast. Cover and cook on low for 7-9 hours or until the meat is tender.

Remove roast with a slotted spoon and let stand for 15 minutes. Thinly slice meat across the grain. Place on rolls; sprinkle with Swiss cheese. Broil 3 to 4 in. from the heat for 1 minute or until the cheese is melted. Skim fat from juices; strain and serve as a dipping sauce.

I enjoy fixing a sit-down meal for my husband and myself every evening, so this easy-to-prepare entree is often on the menu. It's fairly inexpensive and takes little effort to prepare. Slow cooking this tough cut of meat results in tasty, tender slices. The sweet and tangy sauce is a fantastic finishing touch.

Barbecued Beef Brisket

—Anita Keppinger
Philomath, Oregon

1 teaspoon salt
1 teaspoon chili powder
1/2 teaspoon garlic powder
1/4 teaspoon onion powder
1/4 teaspoon celery seed
1/4 teaspoon pepper
1 fresh beef brisket (2-1/2 pounds), trimmed

Sauce:
1/2 cup ketchup
1/2 cup chili sauce
1/4 cup packed brown sugar
2 tablespoons cider vinegar
2 tablespoons Worcestershire sauce
1 to 1-1/2 teaspoons Liquid Smoke, optional
1/2 teaspoon ground mustard

In a small bowl, combine the first six ingredients; rub over brisket. Place in a 3-qt. slow cooker. In a large bowl, combine the sauce ingredients. Pour half over the brisket; set the remaining sauce aside.

Cover and cook on high for 4-5 hours or until meat is tender. Serve with the reserved sauce.

Editor's Note: This is a fresh beef brisket, not corned beef. The meat comes from the first cut of the brisket.

Prep: **10 min.**
Cook: **4 hours**
Yield: **8 servings**

Sweet 'n' Sour Ribs

—Dorothy Voeltz
Champaign, Illinois

If you're looking for a change from typical barbecue ribs, you'll enjoy this recipe my mom always prepared on birthdays and special occasions. The tender ribs have a slight sweet-and-sour taste that my family loves. I usually serve them with garlic mashed potatoes and a salad or coleslaw.

Prep: **10 min.**
Cook: **8 hours**
Yield: **8 servings**

3 to 4 pounds boneless country-style pork ribs

1 can (20 ounces) pineapple tidbits, undrained

2 cans (8 ounces *each*) tomato sauce

1/2 cup thinly sliced onion

1/2 cup thinly sliced green pepper

1/2 cup packed brown sugar

1/4 cup cider vinegar

1/4 cup tomato paste

2 tablespoons Worcestershire sauce

1 garlic clove, minced

Salt and pepper to taste

Place ribs in an ungreased 5-qt. slow cooker. In a large bowl, combine the remaining ingredients; pour over the ribs. Cover and cook on low for 8-10 hours or until meat is tender. Thicken the sauce if desired.

Tip for Transporting Ribs

Ribs are great picnic fare favored by many folks. To transport hot-cooked ribs that you've prepared at home, wrap them in heavy-duty foil and then place in a brown paper bag. The ribs can remain this way for up to 1 hour.

Even those who usually don't eat much corn will ask for a second helping of this creamy, cheesy side dish. Folks love the flavor, but I love how easy it is to make with ingredients I usually have on hand.

Cheesy Creamed Corn

—Mary Ann Truitt
Wichita, Kansas

3 packages (16 ounces *each*) frozen corn

2 packages (one 8 ounces, one 3 ounces) cream cheese, cubed

1/4 cup butter, cubed

3 tablespoons water

3 tablespoons milk

2 tablespoons sugar

6 slices process American cheese, cut into small pieces

In a 3-qt. slow cooker, combine all the ingredients. Cover and cook on low for 4 hours or until heated through and the cheese is melted. Stir well before serving.

Prep: 5 min.
Cook: 4 hours
Yield: 12 servings

These sandwiches are great for large gatherings. The chicken can be cooked ahead of time, then added to the homemade barbecue sauce for simmering hours before guests arrive.

Barbecued Chicken Sandwiches

—Roberta Brown
Waupaca, Wisconsin

2 broiler/fryer chickens (3 to 3-1/2 pounds *each*), cooked and shredded

1 large onion, chopped

2 cups water

1-1/4 cups ketchup

1/4 cup packed brown sugar

1/4 cup Worcestershire sauce

1/4 cup red wine vinegar

1 teaspoon *each* salt, celery seed and chili powder

1/4 teaspoon hot pepper sauce

Hamburger buns

In a 3-qt. slow cooker or Dutch oven, combine all ingredients except buns. Cover and cook on low for 6-8 hours in the slow cooker or simmer for 1-1/2 hours on the stovetop. Serve on buns.

Prep: 5 min.
Cook: 6 hours
Yield: 8-10 servings

Italian Turkey Sandwiches

—Carol Riley, Glava, Illinois

Prep: **10 min.**
Cook: **5 hours**
Yield: **11 servings**

I hope you enjoy these tasty turkey sandwiches as much as our family does. The recipe makes plenty, so it's great for potlucks. Leftovers are just as good reheated the next day.

1 bone-in turkey breast (5-1/2 pounds), skin removed

1/2 cup chopped green pepper

1 medium onion, chopped

1/4 cup chili sauce

3 tablespoons white vinegar

2 tablespoons dried oregano *or* Italian seasoning

4 teaspoons beef bouillon granules

11 kaiser *or* hard rolls, split

Cut turkey breast in half along the bone. Place the turkey breast, green pepper and onion in a 5-qt. slow cooker coated with non-stick cooking spray. Combine the chili sauce, vinegar, oregano and bouillon; pour over turkey and vegetables. Cover and cook on low for 5-6 hours or until meat juices run clear and vegetables are tender.

Remove the turkey, reserving the cooking liquid. Shred the turkey with two forks; return to cooking juices. Spoon 1/2 cup onto each roll.

Slow-Cooked Vegetables

—Kathy Westendorf
Westgate, Iowa

Prep: **10 min.**
Cook: **7 hours**
Yield: **8 servings**

An assortment of garden-fresh vegetables is simmered into a satisfying side dish. My sister-in-law shared this recipe with me. It's a favorite at holiday gatherings and potlucks.

4 celery ribs, cut into 1-inch pieces

4 small carrots, cut into 1-inch pieces

2 medium tomatoes, cut into chunks

2 medium onions, thinly sliced

2 cups cut fresh green beans, cut into 1-inch pieces

1 medium green pepper, cut into 1-inch pieces

1/4 cup butter, melted

3 tablespoons quick-cooking tapioca

1 tablespoon sugar

2 teaspoons salt, optional

1/8 teaspoon pepper

Place the vegetables in a 3-qt. slow cooker. In a small bowl, combine the butter, tapioca, sugar, salt if desired and pepper; pour over vegetables and stir well. Cover and cook on low for 7-8 hours or until vegetables are tender. Serve with a slotted spoon.

When I know my day is going to be busy and I won't have time to devote to making dinner, this recipe is the one I reach for. It takes only a few minutes to assemble, then the slow cooker does the rest. To vary it, change the vegetables—try frozen broccoli, beans or cauliflower for the peas. My family loves this dinner.

Chicken Veggie Alfredo

—Jennifer Jordan
Hubbard, Ohio

4 boneless skinless chicken breast halves

1 tablespoon vegetable oil

1 jar (16 ounces) Alfredo sauce

1 can (15-1/4 ounces) whole kernel corn, drained

1 cup frozen peas, thawed

1 jar (4-1/2 ounces) sliced mushrooms, drained

1/2 cup chopped onion

1/2 cup water

1/2 teaspoon garlic salt

1/4 teaspoon pepper

Hot cooked linguine

In a large skillet, brown chicken in oil. Transfer to a 3-qt. slow cooker. In a large bowl, combine the Alfredo sauce, corn, peas, mushrooms, onion, water, garlic salt and pepper. Pour over the chicken. Cover and cook on low for 6-8 hours. Serve over linguine.

Editor's Note: Double this recipe and use a 5-qt. slow cooker when cooking for a crowd.

Prep: **10 min.**
Cook: **6 hours**
Yield: **4 servings**

Lemon Red Potatoes

—Tara Branham
Cedar Park, Texas

Prep: **5 min.**
Cook: **2-1/2 hours**
Yield: **6 servings**

Butter, lemon juice, parsley and chives enhance this simple side dish. I usually prepare these potatoes when I'm having company. Since they cook in the slow cooker, there's plenty of room on the stove for other dishes.

1-1/2 **pounds medium red potatoes**

1/4 **cup water**

1/4 **cup butter, melted**

1 **tablespoon lemon juice**

3 **tablespoons minced fresh parsley**

1 **tablespoon snipped fresh chives**

Salt and pepper to taste

Cut a strip of peel from around the middle of each potato. Place potatoes and water in a 3-qt. slow cooker. Cover and cook on high for 2-1/2 to 3 hours or until tender (do not overcook); drain.

In a small bowl, combine the butter, lemon juice, parsley and chives. Pour over the potatoes and toss to coat. Season with salt and pepper.

Editor's Note: Double this recipe and use a 5-qt. slow cooker when cooking for a crowd.

Marinated Chicken Wings

—Janie Botting
Sultan, Washington

Prep: **5 min. + marinating**
Cook: **3-1/2 hours**
Yield: **18-20 servings**

I've made these nicely flavored chicken wings many times for get-togethers. They're so moist and tender—I always get lots of compliments and numerous requests for the recipe.

20 **whole chicken wings (about 4 pounds)**

2 **cups soy sauce**

1/2 **cup white wine *or* chicken broth**

1/2 **cup vegetable oil**

2 to 3 **garlic cloves, minced**

2 **tablespoons sugar**

2 **teaspoons ground ginger**

Cut chicken wings into three sections; discard wing tips. In a large bowl, combine remaining ingredients. Pour half the sauce into a large resealable plastic bag. Add wings, seal and toss to coat. Refrigerate overnight. Cover and refrigerate remaining marinade.

Drain and discard the marinade. Place chicken in a 5-qt. slow cooker; top with reserved sauce. Cover and cook on low for 3-1/2 to 4 hours or until chicken juices run clear. Transfer wings to a serving dish; discard cooking juices.

Editor's Note: This recipe was prepared with the first and second sections of the chicken wings.

Turkey thighs are slowly cooked with tomato sauce, green chilies and seasonings until they're tender and flavorful. I serve this tasty turkey mixture in flour tortillas with other fresh fixings, but in a pinch the shredded meat could also be served on a bun.

Turkey Enchiladas

—*Stella Schams, Tempe, Arizona*

2 turkey thighs *or* drumsticks (about 2 pounds)

1 can (8 ounces) tomato sauce

1 can (4 ounces) chopped green chilies

1/3 cup chopped onion

2 tablespoons Worcestershire sauce

1 to 2 tablespoons chili powder

1/4 teaspoon garlic powder

8 flour tortillas (6 inches), warmed

Optional toppings: chopped green onions, sliced ripe olives, chopped tomatoes, shredded cheddar cheese, sour cream *and/or* shredded lettuce

Remove skin from turkey. Place in a 5-qt. slow cooker. In a small bowl, combine the tomato sauce, chilies, onion, Worcestershire sauce, chili powder and garlic powder; pour over turkey. Cover and cook on low for 6-8 hours or until turkey is tender.

Remove turkey; shred meat with a fork and return to the slow cooker and heat through. Discard bones.

Spoon about 1/2 cup of turkey mixture down the center of each tortilla. Fold bottom of tortilla over filling and roll up. Add toppings of your choice.

Prep: **10 min.**
Cook: **6 hours 10 min.**
Yield: **4 servings**

Melt-in-Your-Mouth Sausages

—*Ilean Schultheiss*
Cohocton, New York

Prep: **10 min.**
Cook: **5 hours**
Yield: **8 servings**

My family loves this recipe. It's such a good all-around dish, especially if you choose to eat the sausage on buns or, for a heartier meal, with spaghetti.

8 Italian sausage links
(2 pounds)

1 jar (48 ounces) spaghetti
sauce

1 can (6 ounces) tomato
paste

1 large green pepper, thinly
sliced

1 large onion, thinly sliced

1 tablespoon grated
Parmesan cheese

1 teaspoon dried parsley
flakes

1 cup water

8 brat buns, split

Additional Parmesan cheese,
optional

Place sausage in a large skillet; cover with water. Simmer 10 minutes; drain. Meanwhile, place remaining ingredients in a 5-qt. slow cooker. Add sausage. Cover and cook on low for 4 hours. Increase temperature to high; cook 1 hour longer. Serve in buns. Sprinkle with additional Parmesan cheese if desired.

Chocolate-Raspberry Fondue

—*Heather Maxwell*
Fort Riley, Kansas

Prep/Total Time: **15 min.**
Yield: **5 cups**

You don't need a fancy fondue pot to make this melt-in-your-mouth concoction. I serve the dip in my small slow cooker. Folks of all ages love the chocolate-raspberry combination.

1 package (14 ounces)
caramels

2 cups (12 ounces)
semisweet chocolate chips

1 can (12 ounces)
evaporated milk

1/2 cup butter

1/2 cup seedless raspberry
jam

Frozen pound cake, thawed

Assorted fresh fruit

In a large saucepan, combine the first five ingredients. Cook over low heat until caramels, chips and butter are melted, about 15 minutes. Stir until smooth.

Transfer to a 1-1/2-qt. slow cooker or fondue pot. Serve warm with pound cake or fruit.

Covered Dishes

Black Bean Tortilla Casserole

—Sue Briski
Appleton, Wisconsin

Prep: **20 min.**
Bake: **30 min.**
Yield: **9 servings**

A cousin gave me this recipe because she knows my family loves Southwestern fare. This is a delicious, meatless meal that we really enjoy!

2 large onions, chopped

1-1/2 cups chopped green peppers

1 can (14-1/2 ounces) diced tomatoes, drained

3/4 cup picante sauce

2 garlic cloves, minced

2 teaspoons ground cumin

2 cans (15 ounces *each*) black beans, rinsed and drained

8 corn tortillas (6 inches)

2 cups (8 ounces) shredded reduced-fat Mexican cheese blend

Toppings:

1-1/2 cups shredded lettuce

1 cup chopped fresh tomatoes

1/2 cup thinly sliced green onions

1/2 cup sliced ripe olives

In a large saucepan, combine the onions, peppers, tomatoes, picante sauce, garlic and cumin. Bring to a boil. Reduce heat; simmer, uncovered, for 10 minutes. Stir in the beans. Spread a third of the mixture in a 13-in. x 9-in. x 2-in. baking dish coated with nonstick cooking spray. Layer with four tortillas and 2/3 cup cheese. Repeat layers; top with remaining beans.

Cover and bake at 350° for 30-35 minutes or until heated through. Sprinkle with the remaining cheese. Let stand for 5 minutes or until cheese is melted. Serve with toppings.

Jalapeno Chicken Enchiladas

—Kaylin DeVries
Magna, Utah

These creamy enchiladas are likely to be as popular at your house as they are at mine. I have many requests for this recipe. For weddings, I place the recipe in a nice casserole dish to give as a gift.

2 cans (15 ounces *each*) tomato sauce, *divided*

4 cans (10-3/4 ounces *each*) condensed cream of chicken soup, undiluted

4 cups (32 ounces) sour cream

4 jalapeno peppers, seeded and chopped

1 teaspoon onion salt

1/4 teaspoon pepper

4 cups cubed cooked chicken

3 cups (12 ounces) shredded cheddar cheese, *divided*

20 flour tortillas (8 inches)

In each of two greased 13-in. x 9-in. x 2-in. baking dishes, spread 1/2 cup of tomato sauce; set aside. In a large bowl, combine soup, sour cream, jalapenos, onion salt and pepper. Stir in chicken and 2 cups cheese.

Spread about 1/2 cup chicken mixture down the center of each tortilla. Roll up and place seam side down in prepared dishes. Top with remaining tomato sauce; sprinkle with the remaining cheese. Cover and bake the casseroles at 350° for 35-45 minutes or until edges are bubbly. Or, cover and freeze casseroles for up to 1 month.

To use frozen casseroles: Thaw in the refrigerator overnight. Bake, covered, at 350° for 40-45 minutes or until edges are bubbly.

Editor's Note: When cutting or seeding hot peppers, use plastic gloves to protect your hands. Avoid touching your face.

Prep: **20 min. + freezing**
Bake: **40 min.**
Yield: **2 casseroles (5 servings each)**

Old-Fashioned Cheese Potatoes

—Martha Sue Stroud
Clarksville, Texas

When my husband and I got married in 1951, one of the first appliances we bought was an apartment-size electric range. The range came with a cookbook that included this recipe.

1/4 cup butter, cubed

1/4 cup all-purpose flour

2 teaspoons salt

1/2 teaspoon pepper

2-1/2 cups milk

1-1/2 cups (6 ounces *each*) shredded process cheese (Velveeta)

6 medium potatoes, peeled and thinly sliced

In a large saucepan, melt butter. Stir in the flour, salt and pepper until smooth; gradually add milk. Bring to a boil over medium heat; cook and stir for 2 minutes or until thickened. Reduce heat. Add cheese; stir until cheese is melted.

Place potatoes in a greased 3-in. x 9-in. x 2-in. baking dish. Pour sauce over potatoes. Bake, uncovered, at 350° for 1 hour or until potatoes are tender.

Prep: **15 min.**
Bake: **1 hour**
Yield: **8-10 servings**

French Country Casserole

—Kim Lowe
Coralville, Iowa

Prep: **10 min.**
Bake: **1 hour**
Yield: **9 servings**

This dish is a quick-to-fix version of a traditional French cassoulet that was an instant hit with my husband, who enjoys smoked sausage. Just mix everything together and bake.

1 pound smoked kielbasa *or* Polish sausage

1 can (16 ounces) kidney beans, rinsed and drained

1 can (15-1/2 ounces) great northern beans, rinsed and drained

1 can (15 ounces) black beans, rinsed and drained

1 can (15 ounces) tomato sauce

3 medium carrots, thinly sliced

2 small onions, sliced into rings

1/2 cup dry red wine *or* beef broth

2 tablespoons brown sugar

2 garlic cloves, minced

1-1/2 teaspoons dried thyme

Combine all the ingredients in a bowl; transfer to an ungreased 3-qt. baking dish. Cover and bake at 375° for 60-70 minutes or until the carrots are tender.

Breakfast Burritos

—Catherine Allan
Twin Falls, Idaho

Prep: **20 min.**
Bake: **15 min.**
Yield: **12 servings**

I discovered this different recipe at a workshop of holiday breakfasts offered at our church. It works really well when you're cooking for a crowd. I like to serve salsa or hot sauce with them.

1 bag (16 ounces) frozen Southern-style hash browns

12 eggs

1 large onion, chopped

1 green pepper, chopped

1/2 pound bulk pork sausage, cooked and drained

12 flour tortillas (10 inches), warmed

3 cups (12 ounces) shredded cheddar cheese

Salsa, optional

In a large skillet, fry hash browns according to package directions; remove and set aside.

In a large bowl, beat eggs; add onions and green pepper. Pour into the same skillet; cook and stir until eggs are set. Remove from heat. Add the hash browns and sausage; mix gently.

Place about 3/4 cup filling on each tortilla and top with about 1/4 cup cheese. Roll up and place on a greased baking sheet. Bake at 350° for 15 to 20 minutes or until heated through. Serve with salsa if desired.

This may be a basic chicken casserole, but I never bring home leftovers whenever I take it to a potluck. The stick-to-your-ribs dish has lots of broad appeal, and I especially like that the crumb topping adds a bit of crunch to each serving.

Potluck Chicken Casserole

—Faye Hintz
Springfield, Missouri

Prep: **15 min.**
Bake: **30 min.**
Yield: **10-12 servings**

- 8 cups cubed cooked chicken
- 2 cans (10-3/4 ounces *each*) condensed cream of chicken soup, undiluted
- 1 cup (8 ounces) sour cream
- 1 cup crushed butter-flavored crackers (about 25 crackers)
- 2 tablespoons butter, melted
- 1 teaspoon celery seed
- Fresh parsley and sweet red pepper rings, optional

Combine the chicken, soup and sour cream; spread into a greased 13-in. x 9-in. x 2-in. baking dish. Combine crumbs, butter and celery seed; sprinkle over chicken mixture.

Bake, uncovered, at 350° for 30-35 minutes or until bubbly. Garnish with parsley and red pepper if desired.

My sister gave me the recipe for this side dish years ago, and it's become a favorite in our household. Chock-full of colorful veggies, it's delicious and feeds a crowd.

Colorful Vegetable Bake

—Betty Brown
Buckley, Washington

- 3 cups frozen cut green beans, thawed and drained
- 2 medium green peppers, chopped
- 6 plum tomatoes, chopped and seeded
- 2 to 3 cups (8 to 12 ounces) shredded cheddar cheese
- 3 cups chopped zucchini
- 1 cup biscuit/baking mix
- 1/2 teaspoon salt
- 1/2 teaspoon cayenne pepper
- 6 eggs
- 1 cup milk

Place beans and peppers in a greased 13-in. x 9-in. x 2-in. baking dish. Top with tomatoes, cheese and zucchini. In a bowl, combine biscuit mix, salt, cayenne, eggs and milk just until moistened. Pour over vegetables.

Bake, uncovered, at 350° for 55-60 minutes or until puffed and a knife inserted near the center comes out clean. Let stand for 10 minutes before serving.

Prep: **10 min.**
Bake: **55 min. + standing**
Yield: **12 servings**

Brown Rice Vegetable Casserole

—*Gloria De Beradinis*
Greentown, Pennsylvania

Prep: **20 min.**
Bake: **1 hour 20 min.**
Yield: **8-10 servings**

One taste of this crowd-pleasing casserole brings compliments and requests for the recipe. It's been in my file for as long as I can remember. The blend of tender vegetables and rice is perfect for dish-to-pass affairs.

3 cups chicken broth
1-1/2 cups uncooked brown rice
2 cups chopped onions, *divided*
3 tablespoons soy sauce
2 tablespoons butter, melted
1/2 teaspoon dried thyme
4 cups cauliflowerets
4 cups broccoli florets
2 medium sweet red peppers, julienned
2 garlic cloves, minced
3 tablespoons olive oil
1 cup salted cashew halves
2 cups (8 ounces) shredded cheddar cheese, optional

In a greased 3-qt. baking dish, combine the broth, rice, 1 cup onion, soy sauce, butter and thyme. Cover and bake at 350° for 65-70 minutes or until rice is tender.

Meanwhile, in a large skillet, saute the cauliflower, broccoli, peppers, garlic and remaining onion in oil until crisp-tender; spoon over rice mixture. Cover and bake for 10 minutes. Uncover; sprinkle with cashews and cheese if desired. Bake 5-7 minutes longer or until the cheese is melted.

Benefits of Brown Rice

Brown rice is white rice that hasn't had the bran covering removed. One cup of brown rice has 3.5 grams of fiber while white rice has less than 1 gram.

This is a noodle casserole just like Mom used to make! Its down-home taste has great appeal at a family gathering or as a dish to pass.

Reunion Casserole

—Bernice Morris
Marshfield, Missouri

Prep: **15 min.**
Bake: **45 min.**
Yield: **8-10 servings**

1 pound ground beef

1/2 pound bulk hot sausage

1 cup chopped onion

2 cups (8 ounces) shredded cheddar cheese, *divided*

1 green pepper, chopped

1 can (11 ounces) whole kernel corn, drained

1 can (10-3/4 ounces) condensed tomato soup, undiluted

1 can (8 ounces) tomato sauce

1/3 cup sliced pimiento-stuffed olives

1 garlic clove, minced

1/2 teaspoon salt

8 ounces wide noodles, cooked and drained

In a large Dutch oven, cook the beef, sausage and onion over medium heat until meat is no longer pink; drain. Stir in 1 cup cheese, green pepper, corn, soup, tomato sauce, olives, garlic, salt and noodles.

Transfer to a 13-in. x 9-in. x 2-in. baking dish. Sprinkle with remaining cheese. Cover and bake at 350° for 35 minutes. Uncover; bake 10 minutes longer.

This cheese-and-veggie-packed pasta side dish always brings compliments. Add chicken or shrimp, and you'll have a well-balanced entree.

Cheesy Broccoli Rigatoni

—Lisa Csiki
North Windham, Connecticut

Prep: **15 min.**
Bake: **25 min.**
Yield: **10 servings**

12 ounces uncooked rigatoni pasta

3 garlic cloves, minced

1/4 cup butter, cubed

1/4 cup all-purpose flour

1 teaspoon salt

1 tablespoon olive oil

2-1/2 cups fat-free milk

5 cups fresh broccoli florets

2 cups (8 ounces) shredded part-skim mozzarella cheese, *divided*

Cook pasta according to package directions. Meanwhile, in a large saucepan, saute garlic in butter over medium heat for 2 minutes. Stir in flour and salt until blended. Gradually add milk. Bring to a boil; cook and stir for 2 minutes or until thickened. Remove from the heat; set aside. Drain pasta and toss with oil; set aside.

Add 1 in. of water to a large saucepan; add broccoli. Bring to a boil. Reduce heat; cover and simmer for 4-5 minutes or until crisp-tender. Drain and rinse with cold water.

In a 13-in. x 9-in. x 2-in. baking dish coated with nonstick cooking spray, layer 1 cup white sauce, half of the pasta and broccoli and 1/2 cup cheese. Repeat layers. Top with remaining sauce and cheese. Cover and bake at 350° for 25-30 minutes or until heated through.

Mexican Manicotti

—Lucy Shifton
Wichita, Kansas

Prep: 15 min. + chilling
Bake: 65 min. + standing
Yield: 8 servings

Serve this hearty entree with Spanish rice, homemade salsa and tortilla chips. I've also made it without ground beef, and our friends who are vegetarians requested the recipe.

1 pound lean ground beef

1 can (16 ounces) refried beans

2-1/2 teaspoons chili powder

1-1/2 teaspoons dried oregano

1 package (8 ounces) uncooked manicotti shells

2-1/2 cups water

1 jar (16 ounces) picante sauce

2 cups (16 ounces) sour cream

1 cup (4 ounces) shredded Monterey Jack *or* Mexican cheese blend

1/4 cup sliced green onions

Sliced ripe olives, optional

In a large bowl, combine the uncooked beef, beans, the chili powder and oregano. Spoon into uncooked manicotti shells; arrange in a greased 13-in. x 9-in. x 2-in. baking dish. Combine water and picante sauce; pour over shells. Cover and refrigerate overnight.

Remove from the refrigerator 30 minutes before baking. Cover and bake at 350° for 1 hour. Uncover; spoon sour cream over the top. Sprinkle with cheese, onions and olives if desired. Bake 5-10 minutes longer or until the cheese is melted.

Four-Pasta Beef Bake

—Harriet Stichter
Milford, Indiana

Prep: 15 min.
Bake: 25 min.
Yield: 2 casseroles
(8-10 servings each)

This hearty casserole looks and tastes a lot like lasagna, but it's quicker to prepare since you don't have to layer it. Served with rolls and a salad, it makes an easy and satisfying supper.

8 cups uncooked pasta (four different shapes)

2 pounds ground beef

2 medium green peppers, chopped

2 medium onions, chopped

2 cups sliced fresh mushrooms

4 jars (26 ounces *each*) meatless spaghetti sauce

2 eggs, lightly beaten

4 cups (16 ounces *each*) shredded part-skim mozzarella cheese

Cook pasta according to package directions. Meanwhile, in a large skillet, cook the beef, green peppers, the onions and mushrooms over medium heat until meat is no longer pink; drain.

Drain pasta and place in a large bowl; stir in the beef mixture, two jars of spaghetti sauce and eggs.

Transfer to two greased 13-in. x 9-in. x 2-in. baking dishes. Top with remaining sauce; sprinkle with cheese. Bake, uncovered, at 350° for 25-30 minutes or until heated through.

A great use for leftover ham, this dish has been served at countless church suppers. A puffy topping covers a mixture of sweet potatoes, ham and apples.

Apple Ham Bake

—Amanda Denton
Barre, Vermont

- 3 medium tart apples, peeled and sliced
- 2 medium sweet potatoes, peeled and thinly sliced
- 3 cups cubed fully cooked ham
- 3 tablespoons brown sugar
- 1/2 teaspoon salt
- 1/4 teaspoon pepper
- 1/4 teaspoon curry powder
- 2 tablespoons cornstarch
- 1/3 cup apple juice
- 1 cup pancake mix
- 1 cup milk
- 2 tablespoons butter, melted
- 1/2 teaspoon ground mustard

In a large skillet, combine the apples, sweet potatoes, ham, brown sugar, salt, pepper and curry. Cook over medium heat until apples are crisp-tender; drain. Combine cornstarch and apple juice until smooth; stir into apple mixture. Bring to a boil; cook and stir for 1-2 minutes or until mixture is thickened.

Transfer to a greased 2-qt. baking dish. Cover and bake at 375° for 10 minutes or until the sweet potatoes are tender. Meanwhile, in a bowl, whisk together pancake mix, milk, butter and mustard; pour over ham mixture. Bake, uncovered, for 25-30 minutes or until puffed and golden brown.

Prep: **20 min.**
Bake: **35 min.**
Yield: **8 servings**

Ham 'n' Cheese Lasagna

—Carla Specht
Annawan, Illinois

Prep: 30 min.
Bake: 45 min. + standing
Yield: 8-10 servings

This recipe came from a friend who's a wonderful cook. No-cook noodles make it a breeze to put this rich, cheesy and comforting main dish on your table in no time flat.

3 cups sliced fresh mushrooms

2 cups thinly sliced celery

2 cups chopped carrots

1 cup chopped onion

1 tablespoon olive oil

2 cups cubed fully cooked ham

1 teaspoon minced garlic

1 tablespoon all-purpose flour

2 cups heavy whipping cream

1 can (14-1/2 ounces) diced tomatoes with basil, oregano and garlic, undrained

1/4 teaspoon pepper

2 cups (8 ounces) shredded part-skim mozzarella cheese

1 package (5 ounces) shredded Swiss cheese

1 cup grated Parmesan cheese

9 no-cook lasagna noodles

In a large skillet, saute the mushrooms, celery, carrots and onion in oil for 4-5 minutes or until crisp-tender. Add ham and garlic; cook 1-2 minutes longer or until garlic is tender. In a small bowl, combine the flour and cream; stir into ham mixture. Add tomatoes and pepper. Bring to a boil; cook and stir for 2 minutes. Reduce heat; simmer, uncovered, for 8-10 minutes or until heated through (sauce will be thin).

In a small bowl, combine the cheeses. Place three noodles in a greased 13-in. x 9-in. x 2-in. baking dish; top with a third of the sauce and a third of the cheese mixture. Repeat layers twice.

Cover and bake at 350° for 30 minutes. Uncover; bake 15-20 minutes longer or until bubbly and cheese is melted. Let stand for 20 minutes before cutting.

Keep this recipe handy, because you'll certainly be asked for it when you contribute it to a potluck buffet table.

Pepperoni Pizzazz

—Marge Unger
La Porte, Indiana

8 ounces uncooked medium tube pasta

1 jar (28 ounces) spaghetti sauce, *divided*

1 package (8 ounces) sliced pepperoni

1 jar (4-1/2 ounces) sliced mushrooms, drained

1/2 cup chopped green pepper

1/2 cup chopped onion

1/2 cup grated Parmesan cheese

1/2 teaspoon garlic powder

1/2 teaspoon salt

1/8 teaspoon pepper

1/8 teaspoon crushed red pepper flakes

1 can (8 ounces) tomato sauce

2 cups (8 ounces) shredded part-skim mozzarella cheese

Cook pasta according to package directions. Meanwhile, combine 2-1/3 cups spaghetti sauce, the pepperoni, mushrooms, green pepper, onion, Parmesan cheese, garlic powder, salt, pepper and red pepper flakes in a bowl. Drain pasta; add to the sauce mixture and mix well.

Transfer to a greased 3-qt. baking dish. Combine the tomato sauce and remaining spaghetti sauce; pour over top. Cover and bake at 350° for 40-45 minutes or until bubbly. Uncover; sprinkle with mozzarella cheese. Bake 5-10 minutes longer or until cheese is melted. Let stand for 5 minutes before serving.

Prep: **10 min.**
Bake: **45 min.**
Yield: **9 servings**

I find chilies almost always improve a recipe that uses cheese. Sometimes I make this into a main dish by adding shredded cooked chicken.

Chilies Rellenos

—Irene Martin
Portales, New Mexico

Prep: **10 min.**
Bake: **50 min.**
Yield: **8 servings**

1 can (7 ounces) whole green chilies

2 cups (8 ounces) shredded Monterey Jack cheese

2 cups (8 ounces) shredded cheddar cheese

3 eggs

3 cups milk

1 cup biscuit/baking mix

Seasoned salt to taste

Salsa

Split the chilies; rinse and remove seeds. Dry on paper towels. Arrange chilies on the bottom of an 11-in. x 7-in. x 2-in. baking dish. Top with cheeses.

In a large bowl, beat eggs; add milk and biscuit mix. Pour over cheese. Sprinkle with salt. Bake at 325° for 50-55 minutes or until golden brown. Serve with salsa.

Party Potatoes

—Sharon Mensing
Greenfield, Iowa

Prep: 15 min.
Bake: 50 min.
Yield: **10-12 servings**

These creamy, tasty potatoes can be made the day before and stored in the refrigerator until you're ready to pop them in the oven. The garlic powder and chives add zip, and the shredded cheese adds color.

4 cups mashed potatoes (about 8 to 10 large) *or* prepared instant potatoes

1 cup (8 ounces) sour cream

1 package (8 ounces) cream cheese, softened

1 teaspoon minced chives

1/4 teaspoon garlic powder

1/4 cup dry bread crumbs

1 tablespoon butter, melted

1/2 cup shredded cheddar cheese

In a large bowl, combine the potatoes, sour cream, cream cheese, chives and garlic powder. Transfer to a greased 2-qt. casserole. Combine the bread crumbs and butter; sprinkle over potatoes. Bake, uncovered, at 350° for 50 to 60 minutes. Top with cheese and serve immediately.

Chicken Tetrazzini

—Kelly Heusmann
Cincinnati, Ohio

Prep: 15 min.
Bake: 30 min.
Yield: **8 servings**

My husband is not a casserole lover, but this creamy, cheesy dish is one of his favorites! Nutmeg gives it a wonderful, different taste.

2 cups sliced mushrooms

1/4 cup butter, cubed

1/4 cup all-purpose flour

2 cups chicken broth

1/4 cup half-and-half cream

1 tablespoon minced fresh parsley

1 teaspoon salt

1/8 to 1/4 teaspoon ground nutmeg

1/4 teaspoon pepper

3 tablespoons white wine *or* chicken broth, optional

3 cups cubed cooked chicken

8 ounces spaghetti, cooked and drained

3/4 cup shredded Parmesan cheese

Additional parsley

In a large skillet, cook mushrooms in butter until tender. Stir in flour until blended; gradually add the chicken broth. Bring to a boil over medium heat; cook and stir for 2 minutes or until thickened. Remove from the heat; stir in the cream, parsley, salt, nutmeg, pepper and wine if desired. Fold in the chicken and spaghetti.

Turn into a greased 11-in. x 7-in. x 2-in. baking dish; sprinkle with Parmesan cheese. Bake, uncovered, at 350° for 30 minutes or until heated through. Sprinkle with parsley.

You'll want a fork to dig into hearty squares of this beefed-up corn bread. Chock-full of ground beef, corn, cheese and jalapeno peppers, it's so filling it can be served as a main dish or cut into smaller portions and served as a side dish. If your family prefers their food on the mild side, use only two jalapeno peppers.

Beefy Jalapeno Corn Bake

—James Coleman
Charlotte, North Carolina

1 pound ground beef

2 eggs

1 can (14-3/4 ounces) cream-style corn

1 cup milk

1/2 cup vegetable oil

1 cup cornmeal

3 tablespoons all-purpose flour

1-1/2 teaspoons baking powder

3/4 teaspoon salt

4 cups (16 ounces) shredded cheddar cheese, *divided*

1 medium onion, chopped

4 jalapeno peppers, seeded and chopped

In a large skillet, cook the beef over medium heat until no longer pink; drain and set aside. In a large bowl, beat eggs, corn, milk and oil. Combine the cornmeal, flour, baking powder and salt; add to egg mixture and mix well.

Pour half of the batter into a greased 13-in. x 9-in. x 2-in. baking dish. Sprinkle with 2 cups cheese; top with the beef, onion and jalapenos. Sprinkle with remaining cheese; top with remaining batter.

Bake, uncovered, at 350° for 55-60 minutes or until a toothpick inserted into corn bread topping comes out clean. Serve warm. Refrigerate any leftovers.

Editor's Note: When cutting or seeding hot peppers, use rubber or plastic gloves to protect your hands. Avoid touching your face.

Prep: **20 min.**
Bake: **55 min.**
Yield: **12 servings**

Mexican Lasagna

—Rose Ann Buhle
Minooka, Illinois

Prep: **20 min.**
Bake: **1 hour 5 min. + standing**
Yield: **12 servings**

I collect cookbooks and recipes (this one is from my son's mother-in-law). My husband teases me that I won't live long enough to try half of the recipes in my files!

2 pounds ground beef

1 can (16 ounces) refried beans

1 can (4 ounces) chopped green chilies

1 envelope taco seasoning

2 tablespoons hot salsa

12 ounces uncooked lasagna noodles

4 cups (16 ounces) shredded Colby-Monterey Jack cheese, *divided*

1 jar (16 ounces) mild salsa

2 cups water

2 cups (16 ounces) sour cream

1 can (2-1/4 ounces) sliced ripe olives, drained

3 green onions, chopped

In a large skillet, cook beef over medium heat until no longer pink; drain. Stir in beans, chilies, taco seasoning and hot salsa.

In a greased 13-in. x 9-in. x 2-in. baking dish, layer a third of the noodles and meat mixture. Sprinkle with 1 cup of cheese. Repeat layers twice.

Combine mild salsa and water; pour over top. Cover and bake at 350° for 1 hour or until heated through. Uncover; top with sour cream, olives, onions and remaining cheese. Bake 5 minutes longer. Let stand for 10-15 minutes before cutting.

After sampling these savory beans at our local John Deere dealer's open house, I asked for the recipe. To my surprise, they had started with canned beans and easily given them a wonderful homemade taste. They went over big at our summer reunion.

Country Baked Beans

—*Jill Steiner*
Hancock, Minnesota

Prep: **10 min.**
Bake: **45 min.**
Yield: **10-12 servings**

4 cans (16 ounces *each*) baked beans, drained

1 bottle (12 ounces) chili sauce

1 large onion, chopped

1 pound sliced bacon, cooked and crumbled

1 cup packed brown sugar

In a large bowl, combine all of the ingredients. Pour into two ungreased 2-qt. baking dishes. Bake, uncovered, at 350° for 45-60 minutes or until heated through.

This colorful casserole is named after the West Coast, but it always brings appreciative oohs and aahs when I serve it to fellow Texans. It's compatible with a variety of side dishes.

California Casserole

—*Hope LaShier*
Amarillo, Texas

Prep: **20 min.**
Bake: **60 min.**
Yield: **12-16 servings**

2 pounds ground beef

1 medium green pepper, chopped

3/4 cup chopped onion

1 can (14-3/4 ounces) cream-style corn

1 can (10-3/4 ounces) condensed tomato soup, undiluted

1 can (10 ounces) tomatoes with green chilies, undrained

1 can (8 ounces) tomato sauce

1 can (4 ounces) whole mushrooms

1 jar (4 ounces) chopped pimientos, drained

1 can (2-1/4 ounces) sliced ripe olives, drained

1-1/2 teaspoons celery salt

1/2 teaspoon ground mustard

1/2 teaspoon chili powder

1/4 teaspoon pepper

8 ounces wide egg noodles, cooked and drained

2 cups (8 ounces) shredded cheddar cheese

In a large skillet, cook beef, green pepper and onion over medium heat until the meat is no longer pink and the vegetables are tender; drain. Add the next 11 ingredients; mix thoroughly. Add noodles; mix well.

Pour into a Dutch oven or large baking dish. Cover and bake at 350° for 50 minutes. Sprinkle with cheese; bake, uncovered, 10 minutes longer or until the cheese is melted.

Corn Casserole

—*Patricia Friend*
Milledgeville, Georgia

Prep: **20 min.**
Bake: **45 min.**
Yield: **10-12 servings**

Whenever I'm invited to an event that involves food, it's understood that I'll bring this tried-and-true casserole.

1 large onion, chopped

2 medium green peppers, chopped

1/2 cup butter, cubed

1/4 cup all-purpose flour

2-1/2 cups (10 ounces) shredded sharp cheddar cheese, *divided*

2 cups frozen corn

2 cups cooked long grain rice

1 can (14-1/2 ounces) diced tomatoes, undrained

4 hard-cooked eggs, chopped

2 tablespoons Worcestershire sauce

2 to 3 teaspoons hot pepper sauce

2 teaspoons salt

1 teaspoon pepper

In a large skillet, saute onion and peppers in the butter until tender. Stir in flour until blended. Remove from the heat; add 2 cups cheese, corn, rice, tomatoes, eggs, Worcestershire sauce, hot pepper sauce, salt and pepper.

Pour into a greased 2-1/2-qt. baking dish. Bake, uncovered, at 350° for 45 minutes. Top with remaining cheese; let stand for 5 minutes.

Fourth of July Bean Casserole

—*Donna Fancher*
Lawrence, Indiana

Prep: **20 min.**
Bake: **60 min.**
Yield: **12 servings**

The outstanding barbecue taste of these beans makes them a favorite for cookouts all summer and into the fall.

1/2 pound sliced bacon, diced

1/2 pound ground beef

1 cup chopped onion

1 can (28 ounces) pork and beans

1 can (16 ounces) kidney beans, rinsed and drained

1 can (15-1/4 ounces) lima beans

1/2 cup barbecue sauce

1/2 cup ketchup

1/2 cup sugar

1/2 cup packed brown sugar

2 tablespoons prepared mustard

2 tablespoons molasses

1 teaspoon salt

1/2 teaspoon chili powder

In a large skillet, cook the bacon, beef and onion over medium heat until the meat is no longer pink and onion is tender; drain.

Transfer to a greased 2-1/2-qt. baking dish; add all of the beans and mix well. In a small bowl, combine the remaining ingredients; stir into beef and bean mixture. Cover and bake at 350° for 45 minutes. Uncover; bake 15 minutes longer.

This cheesy bake is wonderful for potlucks because it goes well with any main dish. I often sprinkle a little paprika over the top for color.

Green Chili Rice Casserole

—Naomi Newkirk
Sacramento, California

4 cups cooked rice

2 cans (4 ounces *each*) chopped green chilies

1/2 teaspoon salt

3/4 pound Monterey Jack cheese, cut into 1/2-inch cubes

2 cups (16 ounces) sour cream

In a large bowl, combine all ingredients. Transfer to a greased 2-qt. baking dish. Cover and bake at 350° for 30 minutes or until heated through.

Prep: 5 min.
Bake: 30 min.
Yield: 8 servings

I concocted this recipe one day while trying to straighten up my canned goods cupboard. Friends and relatives have told me how much they like it. Many have asked for the recipe.

Company Casserole

—Marcia McCutchan
Hamilton, Ohio

8 ounces process cheese (Velveetta), cubed

1/4 cup milk

2 cans (14-1/2 ounces *each*) diced tomatoes, undrained

3/4 cup mayonnaise

1 tablespoon Worcestershire sauce

4 cups cubed fully cooked ham

4 cups cooked elbow macaroni

1 package (10 ounces) frozen chopped broccoli, thawed and drained

1 package (10 ounces) frozen peas, thawed

1 small green pepper, chopped

1 small onion, chopped

1/2 cup crushed stuffing mix

1 can (2.8 ounces) french-fried onions, chopped, optional

1 cup soft bread crumbs

1/4 cup butter, melted

In a large saucepan, cook and stir cheese and milk over low heat until cheese is melted. Stir in the tomatoes until blended. Remove from the heat; stir in the mayonnaise and Worcestershire sauce until blended. Stir in the ham, macaroni, broccoli, peas, green pepper, onion, stuffing mix and onions if desired.

Transfer to two greased 2-1/2-qt. baking dishes. Toss bread crumbs and butter; sprinkle over the top. Bake, uncovered, at 350° for 35-40 minutes or until bubbly.

Editor's Note: Reduced-fat or fat-free mayonnaise is not recommended for this recipe.

Prep: 20 min.
Bake: 35 min.
Yield: 2 casseroles
(8-10 servings each)

Creamy Hash Brown Casserole

—*Teresa Stutzman*
Adair, Oklahoma

Prep: **10 min.**
Bake: **50 min.**
Yield: **8 servings**

This versatile side dish is perfect with grilled steaks and other meats. Its creamy cheese sauce and crunchy topping are popular with my family.

1 package (32 ounces) frozen Southern-style hash brown potatoes, thawed

1 pound process cheese (Velveeta), cubed

2 cups (16 ounces) sour cream

1 can (10-3/4 ounces) condensed cream of chicken soup, undiluted

3/4 cup butter, melted, *divided*

3 tablespoons chopped onion

1/4 teaspoon paprika

2 cups cornflakes, slightly crushed

Fresh savory, optional

In a large bowl, combine the hash browns, cheese, sour cream, soup, 1/2 cup butter and onion. Spread into a greased 13-in. x 9-in. x 2-in. baking dish. Sprinkle with paprika. Combine cornflakes and remaining butter; sprinkle on top. Bake, uncovered, at 350° for 50-60 minutes or until heated through. Garnish with savory if desired.

Pineapple Casserole

—*Margaret Lindemann*
Kenvil, New Jersey

Prep: **15 min.**
Cook: **35 min.**
Yield: **12-16 servings**

My family enjoyed this dish at a church ham supper, so I asked for the recipe. I've made it for countless covered-dish meals since and have received many compliments. It really is delicious.

1/2 cup butter, softened

2 cups sugar

8 eggs

2 cans (20 ounces *each*) crushed pineapple, drained

3 tablespoons lemon juice

10 slices day-old white bread, cubed

In a large mixing bowl, cream butter and sugar. Add the eggs, one at a time, beating well after each addition. Stir in pineapple and lemon juice. Fold in the bread cubes.

Pour into a greased 13-in. x 9-in. x 2-in. baking dish. Bake, uncovered, at 325° for 35-40 minutes or until set.

Just for Kids

Trail Mix Snack

—Chris Kohler
Nelson, Wisconsin

Prep/Total Time: 5 min.
Yield: 8 cups

With only four ingredients, this recipe takes just minutes to mix. It's a crowd pleaser that appeals to young and old.

1 jar (12 ounces) dry roasted peanuts

2 cups (12 ounces) semisweet chocolate chips

1 box (9 ounces) raisins

1-3/4 cups salted sunflower kernels

Combine all ingredients in a large bowl; mix gently. Store in an airtight container.

Crispy Onion Wings

—Jonathan Hershey
Akron, Ohio

Prep: 15 min.
Bake: 30 min.
Yield: 2 dozen

My wife, daughters and I often enjoy these buttery wings on weekends. The crisp coating of french-fried potato chips is also great on the chicken tenders I make from cut-up chicken breasts.

12 whole chicken wings (about 2-1/2 pounds)

2-1/2 cups crushed potato chips

1 can (2.8 ounces) french-fried onions, crushed

1/2 cup cornmeal

2 teaspoons dried oregano

1 teaspoon onion salt

1 teaspoon garlic powder

1 teaspoon paprika

2 eggs, beaten

1/4 cup butter, melted

Line a 15-in. x 10-in. x 1-in. baking pan with foil and grease the foil; set aside. Cut chicken wings into three sections; discard wing tip section.

In a large resealable plastic bag, combine the potato chips, onions, cornmeal and seasonings; mix well. Dip the chicken wings in eggs. Place in the bag, a few at a time; shake to coat and press crumb mixture into chicken.

Place wings in prepared pan; drizzle with butter. Bake, uncovered, at 375° for 30-35 minutes or until chicken juices run clear and coating is crisp.

Editor's Note: This recipe was prepared with the first and second sections of the chicken wings.

This wonderful recipe deliciously proves you can easily prepare corn dogs at home just like those at the fair. Both kids and grown-ups will like this hearty snack. Serve with condiments like mustard and ketchup, as well as pickles and potato chips.

Corn Dogs

—Ruby Williams
Bogalusa, Louisiana

3/4 cup yellow cornmeal

3/4 cup self-rising flour

1 egg, beaten

2/3 cup milk

10 Popsicle sticks

10 hot dogs

Oil for deep-fat frying

In a large bowl, combine the cornmeal, flour and egg. Stir in milk to make a thick batter; let stand 4 minutes. Insert sticks into hot dogs; dip in batter.

Heat oil to 375°. Fry corn dogs until golden brown, about 5-6 minutes. Drain on paper towel.

Editor's Note: As a substitute for self-rising flour, place 1 tea-spoon baking powder and 1/4 teaspoon salt in a measuring cup. Add all-purpose flour to measure 3/4 cup.

Prep/Total Time: **25 min.**

Yield: **10 servings**

A layer of grape jelly between a peanut-oatmeal crust and topping gives these bars a taste of a peanut butter and jelly sandwich!

Peanut Jelly Bars

—Sonja Blow
Reeds Spring, Missouri

Prep: 20 min.
Bake: 25 min.
Yield: 2 dozen

3/4 cup butter, softened

1 cup packed brown sugar

1-1/2 cups all-purpose flour

1 teaspoon salt

1/2 teaspoon baking soda

1-1/2 cups quick-cooking oats

1/2 cup chopped salted peanuts

1 jar (12 ounces) grape jelly

In a large mixing bowl, cream butter and brown sugar. Combine the flour, salt and baking soda; gradually add to creamed mixture. Stir in oats and peanuts (mixture will be crumbly).

Press half of the mixture into a greased 13-in. x 9-in. baking pan. Spread with jelly. Cover with re-maining crumb mixture. Bake at 400° for 25 minutes or until golden brown. Cool on a wire rack. Cut into bars.

Vegetable Garden

—Barbara Wellner
Menominee, Michigan

I was planning on bringing veggies and dip to my grandson's graduation party, but I wanted to do something special. So I created a mini garden by arranging corn, cherry tomatoes and other small vegetables on a foam board. It was a big hit! You can make the radish roses the day before. Just keep them in ice water in the refrigerator.

2 bunches green onions

12 large radishes

1 bunch curly endive

1 can (15 ounces) baby corn, rinsed and drained

12 mini zucchini *or* 12 zucchini slices

12 cherry tomatoes

12 whole fresh mushrooms

12 baby carrots

Prepared vegetable dip

Prep: **50 min.**
Yield: **12 servings**

For cornstalks, trim both ends of each green onion. Using a sharp knife or scissors, cut green portion of onions lengthwise into thin strips. Fill a large bowl with ice water; add onions and refrigerate until curled.

For flowers, trim both ends of each radish. With a sharp knife, cut radishes to make flowers. Place flowers in a bowl of ice water; refrigerate until opened.

For the base, attach fencing around foam board with pins, fasteners or staples. Line top of foam board with endive. Drain onions and radishes. With toothpicks, attach the onions in rows along one short side of base. Trim

one end of each baby corn into a wedge; insert into onion tops. (Refrigerate any extra corn for another use.)

Add rows of radish flowers, zucchini, tomatoes, mushrooms and carrots. Place scarecrow in garden. Serve veggies with dip.

Editor's Note: To prepare as pictured above left, you will need wooden fencing (60 inches long x 2-1/2 inches high), 1 green foam board (17-7/8 inches x 11-7/8 inches x 15/16 inch), 16 T-shaped pins, U-shaped wire fasteners or heavy-duty staples, toothpicks and a miniature scarecrow.

This salad is great for last-minute planning because it's easy to prepare with convenient, on-hand ingredients.

1 can (11 ounces) mandarin oranges, drained

1 can (8 ounces) pineapple chunks, drained

1 cup miniature marshmallows

1 cup flaked coconut

1 cup (8 ounces) sour cream

In a large bowl, combine the oranges, pineapple, marshmallows and coconut. Add sour cream and toss to mix. Cover and refrigerate for several hours.

Editor's Note: Double this recipe when cooking for a crowd.

Ambrosia Salad

—Judi Bringegar
Liberty, North Carolina

Prep: **10 min. + chilling**
Yield: **4 servings**

This tasty, cold snack dip is one of my most-requested recipes and always pleases friends at get-togethers. People keep scooping until the platter is clean.

2 packages (8 ounces *each*) cream cheese, softened

1 bottle (12 ounces) chili sauce

1 package (6 ounces) Canadian bacon, chopped

1 small onion, chopped

1 small green pepper, chopped

3/4 cup shredded part-skim mozzarella cheese

3/4 cup shredded cheddar cheese

Corn chips

Spread cream cheese on an ungreased 12-in. pizza pan. Spread with chili sauce. Sprinkle with the Canadian bacon, onion, green pepper and cheeses. Serve with chips.

Pizza by the Scoop

—Georgene Robertson
Pikeville, Kentucky

Prep/Total Time: **10 min.**
Yield: **14-16 servings**

Pineapple Orange Slush

—Roni Goodell
Spanish Fork, Utah

Prep/Total Time: 10 min.
Yield: 2 servings

This tart, refreshing drink hits the spot, and you don't have to make a lot. And with just four ingredients whirred in a blender, it's ready in a jiffy!

1 cup orange juice
1/2 cup unsweetened pineapple juice
2 tablespoons lemon juice
2 cups crushed ice cubes

In a blender, combine all ingredients; cover and process until thick and slushy. Pour into chilled glasses; serve immediately.

Editor's Note: Double this recipe when cooking for a crowd. You'll also need to make multiple batches. If you're feeding a large group of kids, assign an adult to blender duty.

Ice Cream Cone Treats

—Mabel Nolan
Vancouver, Washington

Prep/Total Time: 15 min.
Yield: 12 servings

I came up with this recipe as a way for my grandkids to enjoy Rice Krispies Treats and not get sticky hands, since they're eating out of a cone. I've also packed the cereal mixture into paper cups and inserted a popsicle stick like a sucker.

4 cups miniature marshmallows
3 tablespoons butter
6 cups crisp rice cereal
12 ice cream cones
Colored sprinkles

In a microwave or large saucepan, melt the marshmallows and butter. Remove from the heat and stir in cereal.

Using greased hands, shape the mixture into 12 balls; pack each ball into an ice cream cone. Dip the tops in colored sprinkles.

Kids can pitch in with assembling these colorful sandwiches stacked with chicken, cheese, lettuce and tomatoes. To score with big appetites, try adding extra slices of meat or offer a few varieties of sliced cheese. Are you entertaining some finicky eaters? Set up a sandwich station and have guests assemble their own hoagies.

Home Run Hoagies

—Taste of Home Test Kitchen
Greendale, Wisconsin

3/4 cup mayonnaise

1/2 cup Italian salad dressing

12 hoagie buns, split

24 slices thinly sliced deli chicken (about 2-1/2 pounds)

12 slices cheddar cheese, halved

12 lettuce leaves

8 medium tomatoes, sliced

In a small bowl, combine mayonnaise and salad dressing. Spread on cut side of buns. On bun bottoms, layer the chicken, cheese, lettuce and tomatoes. Replace bun tops.

Prep/Total Time: **20 min.**
Yield: **12 servings**

Better Bread Idea   When making Home Run Hoagies for parties, consider using a loaf of French or Italian bread instead of the rolls. It will save you the time of wrapping them individually.

Tutti-Frutti Cups

—Holly Keithley
Lowell, Indiana

Scooping up spoonfuls of this tangy slush is a tongue-tingling treat! The convenient, single-serving cups burst with wholesome chunks of strawberries, bananas and more. Mix in diet pop instead of the regular kind to make the fruit salad cups lower in calories.

1 can (11 ounces) mandarin oranges, undrained

1 can (8 ounces) unsweetened crushed pineapple, undrained

2 medium firm bananas, thinly sliced

3/4 cup fresh *or* frozen sliced strawberries

3/4 cup fresh *or* frozen blueberries

3/4 cup lemon-lime soda

1/2 cup water

6 tablespoons frozen lemonade concentrate, thawed

1/4 cup sugar

In a large bowl, combine all ingredients. Fill 8-oz. plastic cups three-fourths full; cover and freeze for about 4 hours or until solid. Remove from the freezer 30 minutes before serving.

Prep: **10 min. + freezing**
Yield: **10 servings**

Tender Turkey Burgers

—Sherry Hulsman
Elkton, Florida

Prep/Total Time: **30 min.**
Yield: **6 servings**

These juicy, tender patties on whole wheat buns make a wholesome, satisfying sandwich. We especially like to grill them, but you could also pan-fry them.

1 egg, lightly beaten

2/3 cup soft whole wheat bread crumbs

1/2 cup finely chopped celery

1/4 cup finely chopped onion

1 tablespoon minced fresh parsley

1 teaspoon Worcestershire sauce

1 teaspoon dried oregano

1/2 teaspoon salt

1/4 teaspoon pepper

1-1/4 pounds lean ground turkey

6 whole wheat hamburger buns, split

Coat grill rack with nonstick cooking spray before starting the grill. In a bowl, combine the egg, bread crumbs, celery, onion, parsley, Worcestershire sauce and seasonings. Crumble turkey over mixture and mix well. Shape into six patties.

Grill, covered, over medium heat for 5-6 minutes on each side or until a meat thermometer reads 165° and juices run clear. Serve on buns.

Even finicky eaters love to come for tacos because they can add toppings to suit their tastes. In this recipe, chicken is coated with taco seasoning and then stir-fried, so the zesty flavor really shines through.

Chicken Tacos

—*Taste of Home Test Kitchen*
Greendale, Wisconsin

1 envelope taco seasoning

1 pound boneless skinless chicken breasts, cut into 1/2-inch cubes

3 tablespoons butter, *divided*

1/3 cup chopped onion

1/3 cup chopped green pepper

8 taco shells, warmed

Shredded lettuce and cheddar cheese

Salsa, optional

Place taco seasoning in a large re-sealable plastic bag; add chicken in batches and shake to coat.

In a large skillet, cook and stir chicken in 2 tablespoons butter for 4-5 minutes or until juices run clear. Remove chicken and keep warm. In the same skillet, saute the onion and green pepper in re-maining butter for 2-3 minutes or until crisp-tender.

Combine the chicken, onion and green pepper; spoon into taco shells. Top with lettuce and cheese. Serve with salsa if desired.

Editor's Note: Double this recipe when cooking for a crowd.

Prep/Total Time: **20 min.**
Yield: **4 servings**

Soft Taco Burgers

—Joan Hallford
North Richland Hills, Texas

Prep/Total Time: **25 min.**
Yield: **8 servings**

I love to grill these sandwiches for quick summer meals or impromptu get-togethers around the pool. They're a snap to prepare, and no one ever guesses that they're low fat.

1 cup fat-free refried beans
1 can (4 ounces) chopped green chilies, drained, *divided*
1/4 cup chopped onion
1/4 teaspoon salt
1-1/2 pounds lean ground beef
1 cup (4 ounces) shredded reduced-fat cheddar cheese
8 flour tortillas (6 inches), warmed
1 cup chopped lettuce
1 medium tomato, chopped
1/2 cup salsa

If grilling the burgers, coat grill rack with nonstick cooking spray before starting the grill. In a large bowl, combine the beans, 2 tablespoons green chilies, onion and salt. Crumble the beef over mixture and mix well. Shape into eight 5-in. patties. Top each patty with 2 tablespoons cheddar cheese; fold in half and press edges to seal, forming a half moon.

Grill burgers, uncovered, over medium heat or broil 4 in. from the heat for 7-9 minutes on each side or until meat is no longer pink and a meat thermometer reads 160°. Serve on tortillas with lettuce, tomato, salsa and remaining chilies.

These luscious kabobs are perfect as a summer appetizer, snack or side dish. The citrus glaze clings well and keeps the fruit looking fresh. These tasty kabobs encourage mingling at parties because folks can grab them and go! Pictured here are strawberries, seedless red grapes, cubed canaloupe, honeydew and pineapple, and sliced kiwifruit and star fruit.

Colorful Fruit Kabobs

—Ruth Ann Stelfox
Raymond, Alberta

Assorted fruit of your choice

- 1/3 cup sugar
- 2 tablespoons cornstarch
- 1 cup orange juice
- 2 teaspoons lemon juice

Alternately thread fruit onto skewers; set aside. In a saucepan, combine sugar, cornstarch and juices until smooth. Bring to a boil; cook and stir for 1-2 minutes or until thickened. Brush over the fruit. Refrigerate the fruit until serving.

Prep/Total Time: **15 min.**
Yield: **1 cup glaze**

We love all types of melons, so I'm always experimenting with different ways to serve them. A light dressing brings out the refreshing fruit flavors in this cool salad that's so delightful in warm weather.

Fresh 'n' Fruity Salad

—Bernice Morris
Marshfield, Missouri

Prep/Total Time: **15 min.**
Yield: **8 servings**

- 1 can (20 ounces) unsweetened pineapple chunks, drained
- 1 can (15 ounces) unsweetened dark sweet cherries, drained
- 1-1/2 cups cubed cantaloupe
- 1-1/2 cups cubed seeded watermelon
- 1-1/2 cups cubed honeydew

Dressing:
- 3 tablespoons vegetable oil
- 3 tablespoons orange juice
- 3 tablespoons lemon juice
- 2 tablespoons sugar
- 1/4 teaspoon paprika

Combine the fruit in a large bowl. In a small bowl, combine dressing ingredients; pour over fruit and toss to coat. Serve immediately with a slotted spoon.

Orange Cream Cake

—Star Pooley
Paradise, California

Kids of all ages will enjoy the old-fashioned flavor of this super-moist cake topped with a soft, light frosting. This dessert reminds me of the frozen Creamsicles I enjoyed as a child. Enlist your little ones to poke holes in the cake when it comes out of the oven and to pour the gelatin mixture over the cooled cake.

1 package (18-1/4 ounces) lemon cake mix

1 envelope unsweetened orange soft drink mix

3 eggs

1 cup water

1/3 cup vegetable oil

2 packages (3 ounces *each*) orange gelatin, *divided*

1 cup boiling water

1 cup cold water

1 cup cold milk

1 teaspoon vanilla extract

1 package (3.4 ounces) instant vanilla pudding mix

1 carton (8 ounces) frozen whipped topping, thawed

Prep: **20 min.** + chilling
Bake: **25 min.** + cooling
Yield: **12-15 servings**

In a large mixing bowl, combine cake and drink mixes, eggs, water and oil. Beat on medium speed for 2 minutes.

Pour into an ungreased 13-in. x 9-in. x 2-in. baking pan. Bake at 350° for 25-30 minutes or until a toothpick inserted near the center comes out clean. Using a meat fork, poke holes in cake. Cool on a wire rack for 30 minutes.

Meanwhile, in a large bowl, dissolve one package of gelatin in boiling water. Stir in the cold water. Pour over cake. Cover and refrigerate for 2 hours.

In a large mixing bowl, combine milk, vanilla, pudding mix and remaining gelatin; beat on low for 2 minutes. Let stand for 5 minutes; fold in whipped topping. Frost cake. Refrigerate leftovers.

These irresistible treats are simple enough for kids to make, and they sell well at bazaars. You can use different candy sprinkles to reflect holiday or party themes.

Pretzel Sparklers

—Renee Schwebach
Dumont, Minnesota

8 squares (1 ounce *each*) white baking chocolate

1 package (10 ounces) pretzel rods

Colored candy stars *or* sprinkles

Place chocolate in a microwave-safe bowl; heat until melted. Dip each pretzel rod about halfway into chocolate; sprinkle with stars. Place on waxed paper to dry.

Prep/Total Time: **30 min.**
Yield: **about 2 dozen**

This is a recipe born out of desperation. One day I couldn't think of anything to serve the kids for lunch. Rummaging through the fridge, I came across some simple ingredients and prepared individual pizzas.

Kid-Size Pizza

—Polly Coumos
Mogadore, Ohio

Prep/Total Time: **25 min.**
Yield: **20 servings**

2 tubes (10 ounces *each*) refrigerator biscuits

1 can (8 ounces) tomato sauce

1-1/2 teaspoons dried minced onion

1 teaspoon dried oregano

1 teaspoon dried basil

1/8 teaspoon garlic powder

2 cups (8 ounces) shredded part-skim mozzarella cheese

Roll or pat biscuits into 2-1/2 in. circles. Place on two greased baking sheets.

In a small bowl, combine the tomato sauce, onion, oregano, basil and garlic powder; spread over the biscuits. Sprinkle with cheese. Bake at 400° for 8-10 minutes.

Fruit on a Stick

—Faye Hintz
Springfield, Missouri

Prep/Total Time: **15 min.**
Yield: **1-1/2 cups dip**

In the summer, my family loves this fun finger food with its smooth, creamy dip.

1 package (8 ounces)
cream cheese, softened

1 jar (7 ounces)
marshmallow creme

3 to 4 tablespoons milk

Whole strawberries

Melon and kiwifruit, cut into
bite-size pieces

Mix cream cheese, marshmallow creme and milk until smooth. Thread fruit on wooden skewers. Serve with dip.

S'more Tarts

—Trish Quinn
Cheyenne, Wyoming

Prep: **10 min.**
Bake: **25 min.**
Yield: **1 dozen**

A fireside favorite is brought indoors with this taste-tempting treat. Kids of all ages will gobble up the individual graham cracker tarts filled with a fudgy brownie and golden marshmallows before asking, "Can I have s'more?"

1 package fudge brownie
mix (13-inch x 9-inch
pan size)

12 individual graham
cracker shells

1-1/2 cups miniature
marshmallows

1 cup milk chocolate chips

Prepare brownie batter according to package directions.

Place graham cracker shells on a baking sheet and fill with brownie batter. Bake at 350° for 20-25 minutes or until a toothpick inserted in the center comes out with moist crumbs. Immediately sprinkle with marshmallows and chocolate chips. Bake 3-5 minutes longer or until marshmallows are puffed and golden brown.

My mother has been making these wonderful sandwiches since she left her hometown of Boston many years ago. They're quick to prepare and travel well if tightly wrapped in plastic wrap. The recipe is great for parties.

Boston Subs

—Sue Erdos
Meriden, Connecticut

1/2 cup mayonnaise

12 submarine sandwich buns, split

1/2 cup Italian salad dressing, *divided*

1/4 pound *each* thinly sliced bologna, deli ham, hard salami, pepperoni and olive loaf

1/4 pound thinly sliced provolone cheese

1 medium onion, diced

1 medium tomato, diced

1/2 cup diced dill pickles

1 cup shredded lettuce

1 teaspoon dried oregano

Spread mayonnaise on inside of buns. Brush with half of the salad dressing. Layer deli meats and cheese on bun bottoms. Top with onion, tomato, pickles and lettuce. Sprinkle with oregano and drizzle with remaining dressing. Replace bun tops.

Prep/Total Time: **20 min.**
Yield: **12 servings**

Ice Box Sandwiches

—Sandy Armijo
Naples, Italy

My mother liked making these cool creamy treats when I was growing up in the States because they're so quick to fix. Now my three kids enjoy them. Feel free to experiment with different pudding flavors, including chocolate and banana cream. Or replace the miniature chocolate chips with chocolate jimmies or chopped walnuts.

1 package (3.4 ounces) instant vanilla pudding mix

2 cups cold milk

2 cups whipped topping

1 cup (6 ounces) miniature semisweet chocolate chips

48 graham cracker squares

Mix pudding and milk according to package directions; refrigerate until set. Fold in whipped topping and chocolate chips.

Place 24 graham crackers on a baking sheet; top each with about 3 tablespoons filling. Place another graham cracker on top. Wrap individually in plastic wrap; freeze for 1 hour or until firm. Serve sandwiches frozen.

Prep: 20 min. + freezing
Yield: 2 dozen

Ice Cream Sandwiches

If your family loves ice cream sandwiches, it's easy to make them from scratch. Simply sandwich a scoop of your family's favorite ice cream flavor between homemade or store-bought cookies. Roll the edges in miniature chocolate chips, chopped nuts or colored sprinkles. Wrap individually in plastic wrap and freeze.

Ice Cream Crunch

Settle in with a slice of this easy dessert, which is a summertime favorite in my home. It's a cool, crunchy and chewy, make-ahead treat I like to have on hand for drop-in guests.

—Carol Seybert
Willmar, Minnesota

Prep: **15 min.** + freezing
Yield: **12-16 servings**

1/2 cup butter, cubed
1/2 cup packed brown sugar
3 cups crisp rice cereal
2 cups flaked coconut
1 cup chopped mixed nuts
1/2 gallon vanilla ice cream, softened

In a large saucepan over medium heat, cook butter and brown sugar until butter is melted and sugar is dissolved.

In a large bowl, combine the cereal, coconut and nuts; add sugar mixture and stir until coated. Press half into a greased 13-in. x 9-in. x 2-in. baking pan. Spread ice cream over crust. Top with remaining cereal mixture. Freeze until firm.

Lemonade Stand Snack

You don't have to wait for a lemonade stand to mix up this sweet and savory snack featuring animal crackers, peanuts, raisins and M&Ms. With a short list of ingredients, this munchable mix is a breeze to toss together whenever your family craves it. It makes a good snack and travels well, too.

—Dot Nickerson
Cincinnati, Ohio

3 cups animal crackers
2 cups salted peanuts
2 cups raisins
2 cups milk chocolate M&M's

In a large bowl, combine all of the ingredients. Store in snack-size re-sealable plastic bags.

Prep/Total Time: **5 min.**
Yield: **9 cups**

Fruity Yogurt Ice Pops

—Taste of Home Test Kitchen
Greendale, Wisconsin

Prep: 10 min. + freezing
Yield: 10 servings

These sweet strawberry-pineapple pops are so yummy, youngsters won't even guess that they're good for them, too!

2 cups (16 ounces) reduced-fat strawberry yogurt

1 can (8 ounces) unsweetened crushed pineapple

1 tablespoon honey

2 to 3 drops red food coloring, optional

In a food processor or blender, combine the yogurt, pineapple, honey and food coloring if desired; cover and process until smooth.

Pour 1/4 cupfuls into 10 plastic molds or 3-oz. paper cups; top with holders or insert wooden sticks. Freeze until firm, about 8 hours or overnight.

Chocolate Oatmeal Cake

—Vera Schreiner
Akron, Pennsylvania

Prep: 5 min. + standing
Bake: 35 min.
Yield: 12-15 servings

I've had this recipe a long time. It's one of my family's favorite desserts, and I still make it often.

1 cup old-fashioned oats

1-1/2 cups boiling water

1/2 cup butter, softened

1-1/2 cups sugar

2 eggs

1-1/2 cups all-purpose flour

1/2 cup baking cocoa

1-1/2 teaspoons baking soda

1/2 teaspoon salt

Topping:

2/3 cup packed brown sugar

1/2 cup plus 1 tablespoon butter, melted

1-1/2 cups flaked coconut

3/4 cup chopped walnuts

6 tablespoons half-and-half cream

1-1/2 teaspoons vanilla extract

In a bowl, combine the oats and boiling water. Let stand for 15 minutes or until cooled. In a large mixing bowl, cream butter and sugar. Add eggs, one at a time, beating well after each addition. Add the oat mixture; mix well. Combine the flour, cocoa, baking soda and salt; add to creamed mixture.

Transfer to a greased 13-in. x 9-in. x 2-in. baking pan. Bake at 350° for 30-35 minutes or until a toothpick inserted near the center comes out clean.

Combine the topping ingredients; spoon over top of warm cake; broil about 4 in. from heat for 3-4 minutes or until top is lightly browned.

Party
Salads

Creamy Coleslaw

—Renee Endress
Galva, Illinois

Prep/Total Time: 10 min.
Yield: 6 servings

A package of shredded cabbage and carrots really cuts down on prep time. This coleslaw is great for potlucks or for busy weeknight dinner.

1 package (16 ounces) coleslaw mix
3/4 cup mayonnaise
1/3 cup sour cream
1/4 cup sugar
3/4 teaspoon seasoned salt
1/2 teaspoon ground mustard
1/4 teaspoon celery salt

Place coleslaw mix in a large bowl. In a small bowl, combine the remaining ingredients. Pour over coleslaw mix and toss to coat. Refrigerate until serving.

Editor's Note: Double this recipe when cooking for a crowd.

Italian Potato Salad

—Jeannette Macera
Utica, New York

Prep/Total Time: 20 min.
Yield: 12 servings

You'll want to take this simple-to-assemble potato salad to all your picnics and outings. It's always on the menu when my tomato plants yield a bumper crop. Feel free to improvise by adding other vegetables.

5 to 6 medium red potatoes, cooked and cut into 1-inch pieces
2 garlic cloves, minced
1/2 cup chopped red onion
3 to 4 plum tomatoes, quartered
1/3 cup olive oil
3 to 4 fresh basil leaves, chopped
1 jar (5-3/4 ounces) pimiento-stuffed olives, drained and halved
1 teaspoon dried oregano
1-1/2 teaspoons salt
1/4 teaspoon pepper
Lettuce leaves, optional

In a large bowl, combine the first 10 ingredients; toss to coat. Cover and refrigerate until serving. Serve salad in a lettuce-lined bowl if desired.

This salad makes a lot so it's great for a crowd. The combination of beans, sausage, cheese and pasta is a hearty complement to any entree—but it's absolutely perfect for an Italian themed meal. Using garden-fresh basil in the vinaigrette really enhances the flavor.

Antipasto Pasta Salad

—Bernadette Nelson
Arcadia, California

1 package (16 ounces) uncooked penne pasta

1 green *or* sweet red pepper, julienned

1 can (15 ounces) garbanzo beans *or* chickpeas, rinsed and drained

1 bunch green onions, sliced

4 ounces Monterey Jack cheese, julienned

4 ounces part-skim mozzarella cheese, juilenned

4 ounces brick *or* provolone cheese, julienned

4 ounces thinly sliced hard salami, julienned

3 ounces thinly sliced pepperoni

1 can (2-1/4 ounces) sliced ripe olives, drained

1 to 2 tablespoons minced fresh chives

2 plum tomatoes, sliced and halved

Basil Vinaigrette:
  2/3 cup vegetable oil
  1/3 cup red wine vinegar

3 tablespoons minced fresh basil *or* 1 tablespoon dried basil

1 garlic clove, minced

1/4 teaspoon salt

Prep: 20 min. + chilling
Yield: 18 servings

Cook the pasta according to package directions; rinse under cold water and drain. In a large bowl, combine the pasta, vegetables, cheeses, meats, olives, chives and tomatoes.

In a small bowl, whisk together the vinaigrette ingredients. Pour over salad; toss to coat. Cover and refrigerate. Toss before serving.

Barbecued Bean Salad

—Linda Ault
Newberry, Indiana

Prep: 40 min. + standing
Cook: 1-1/2 hours + chilling
Yield: 16-20 servings

This tangy salad is a refreshing dish to serve at a summertime picnic. Mild spices blend nicely with the beans and garden ingredients. Be prepared to bring home an empty bowl.

1 package (16 ounces) dried pinto beans, rinsed

1 medium onion, chopped

1 medium green pepper, diced

1 medium sweet red pepper, diced

1 can (15-1/4 ounces) whole kernel corn, drained

Dressing:
1/4 cup ketchup

1/4 cup cider vinegar

1/4 cup olive oil

3 tablespoons brown sugar

1 tablespoon Worcestershire sauce

1 tablespoon chili powder

5 teaspoons Dijon mustard

1 teaspoon ground cumin

1 teaspoon salt

1/4 teaspoon pepper

In a large kettle, cover beans with water; bring to a boil. Boil for 2 minutes. Remove from the heat and let stand 1 hour. Drain and rinse beans; return to the kettle. Cover with water again and bring to a boil. Reduce heat; cover and simmer for 1-1/2 hours or until beans are tender.

Drain and rinse beans; place in a large bowl and cool to room temperature. Add the onion, peppers and corn; toss.

In a saucepan, combine all dressing ingredients; bring to a boil. Reduce heat; simmer, uncovered, for 10 minutes. Pour over vegetables and mix well. Cover and chill.

Quick Barbecued Bean Salad

When in a hurry, you can omit the time it takes to soak and cook the dried pinto beans by using canned pinto beans instead. You'll need roughly 6 cups or about four 15-ounce cans of beans, rinsed and drained.

This hearty pasta salad is sure to please appetites of all ages...and it serves a lot of folks!

Macaroni Salad

—LaVerna Mjones
Moorhead, Minnesota

Prep: **15 min. + chilling**
Yield: **8-1/2 quarts**

2 pounds uncooked elbow macaroni

12 hard-cooked eggs, chopped

2-1/2 pounds fully cooked ham, cubed

1 package (16 ounces) frozen peas, thawed

3 cups sliced celery

1 large green pepper, chopped

1/2 cup chopped onion

1 jar (4 ounces) diced pimientos, drained

4 cups mayonnaise

Cook macaroni according to package directions. Rinse in cold water; drain and cool completely. Place in a large bowl; stir in remaining ingredients. Cover and refrigerate for at least 3 hours.

Presented in a glass bowl, this colorful layered salad looks beautiful on a buffet. Sweet mandarin oranges nicely complement the lettuce and vegetables.

Sunny Layered Salad

—Susan West
North Grafton, Massachusetts

Prep: **20 min. + chilling**
Yield: **10-12 servings**

1/4 cup sliced almonds

2 tablespoons sugar

6 cups shredded lettuce

1 can (8 ounces) sliced water chestnuts, drained

1 cup frozen peas, thawed and well drained

1/2 medium cucumber, sliced

2 medium tomatoes, cut into thin wedges

2 cups (8 ounces) shredded part-skim mozzarella cheese

1 can (15 ounces) mandarin orange, drained

Dressing:
1/4 cup vegetable oil

2 tablespoons sugar

2 tablespoons cider vinegar

1/4 teaspoon salt

1/4 teaspoon pepper

In a large skillet, cook and stir almonds and sugar over low heat until sugar is dissolved and almonds are coated. Spread the almonds on waxed paper and set aside.

In a large salad bowl, layer the lettuce, water chestnuts, peas, cucumber, tomatoes, cheese and oranges. Sprinkle with the sugared almonds. Cover and refrigerate for at least 2 hours.

In a jar with a tight-fitting lid, combine dressing ingredients; shake well. Pour over salad and serve immediately.

Three Potato Salad

—Nan Cairo
Greenwood, Delaware

Prep: 20 min. + chilling
Cook: 20 min.
Yield: 15 servings

This pretty salad—made with white, red and sweet potatoes—tastes as good as it looks. The mild dill dressing enhances the tender spuds and onion, especially if you refrigerate it overnight. Even those who don't care for sweet potatoes like this salad.

3 medium russet potatoes, peeled and cubed

3 medium unpeeled red potatoes, cubed

1 large sweet potato, peeled and cubed

1 medium onion, chopped

1 cup mayonnaise

2 tablespoons sugar

1 tablespoon white vinegar

1 teaspoon salt

3/4 teaspoon dill weed

1/2 teaspoon pepper

Place all of the potatoes in a Dutch oven; cover with water. Cover and bring to a boil. Reduce heat; cook for 20-30 minutes or until tender. Drain and cool.

Place potatoes in a large bowl; add onion. In a small bowl, combine the remaining ingredients. Pour over potato mixture and toss gently to coat. Cover and refrigerate overnight.

Cauliflower Salad

—Paula Pelis
Rocky Point, New York

Prep: 15 min. + chilling
Yield: 12 servings

Everyone who tries this salad loves it! I like to make it often when cauliflower is in season. There's nothing like fresh Long Island produce.

1 medium head cauliflower, cut into florets

1-1/2 cups diced carrots

1 cup sliced celery

3/4 cup sliced green onions

1/2 cup sliced radishes

1 carton (8 ounces) plain yogurt

2 tablespoons white vinegar

1 tablespoon sugar

1 teaspoon caraway seeds

1 teaspoon celery seed

1/2 teaspoon salt, optional

1/4 teaspoon pepper

In a large bowl, toss the cauliflower, carrots, celery, green onions and radishes. Combine all of the remaining ingredients; pour over vegetables and stir to coat. Cover and chill for several hours.

Red Grape Salad

—Lorraine Black
Barnum, Iowa

Prep/Total Time: **15 min.**
Yield: **10-12 servings**

My mother-in-law shared this recipe with me 40 years ago. She served this salad at all holiday meals, and the tradition has continued in our family. Preparation is so much easier today, thanks to red grapes without seeds! Another "updated" shortcut in the preparation is miniature marshmallows...cooks from the good old days know what "sticky fun" it was to snip regular-sized marshmallows!

- 1 can (20 ounces) pineapple tidbits
- 2 packages (3 ounces *each*) cream cheese, softened
- 2 tablespoons mayonnaise
- 3 cups miniature marshmallows
- 2 cups seedless red grapes, halved
- 1 cup heavy whipping cream, whipped

Drain the pineapple, reserving 2 tablespoons juice; set pineapple aside. In a mixing bowl, beat the juice, cream cheese and mayonnaise until fluffy. Stir in the pineapple, marshmallows and grapes. Fold in whipped cream. Serve immediately or refrigerate.

Fire and Ice Tomatoes

—Nan Rickey, Yuma, Arizona

Prep: **10 min. + chilling**
Yield: **8 servings**

You won't miss the salt in this refreshing tomato salad! It's well-seasoned with cayenne pepper, mustard seed and vinegar but not the least bit spicy. This dish is always a hit at potlucks.

- 5 large tomatoes, cut into wedges
- 1 medium onion, sliced
- 3/4 cup white vinegar
- 6 tablespoons sugar
- 1/4 cup water
- 1 tablespoon mustard seed
- 1/4 teaspoon cayenne pepper
- 1 large cucumber, sliced

In a large bowl, combine the tomatoes and onion; set aside. In a small saucepan, combine the vinegar, sugar, water, mustard seed and cayenne. Bring to a boil; boil for 1 minute.

Pour over tomatoes and onion; toss to coat. Cover and refrigerate for at least 2 hours. Add cucumber; toss to coat. Refrigerate overnight. Serve with a slotted spoon.

Fresh Cucumber Salad

—Betsy Carlson
Rockford, Illinois

Prep: **10 min.** + chilling
Yield: **10-12 servings**

Crisp, garden-fresh cukes are always in season when we hold our family reunion...and they really shine in this simple salad. The recipe can easily be expanded to make large quantities, too.

3 medium cucumbers, sliced
1 cup sugar
3/4 cup water
1/2 cup white vinegar
3 tablespoons minced fresh dill *or* parsley

Place cucumbers in a 1-1/2-qt. to 2-qt. glass container. In a jar with tight-fitting lid, combine the remaining ingredients. Pour over cucumbers. Cover and refrigerate overnight. Serve with a slotted spoon.

Watermelon Ambrosia

—Sandy Leversee
Apache Junction, Arizona

Prep: **25 min.** + chilling
Yield: **10 servings**

Colorful watermelon, pineapple, fruit cocktail, maraschino cherries and more are combined in this eye-catching fruit salad that's sure to take center stage at your next summer buffet!

1 medium watermelon
1 can (20 ounces) unsweetened pineapple tidbits, drained
1 can (15 ounces) reduced-sugar fruit cocktail, drained
1 can (15 ounces) mandarin oranges, drained
1 jar (10 ounces) maraschino cherries, well drained
1 cup miniature marshmallows
1 cup diet lemon-lime soda, chilled
1/4 cup flaked coconut

Cut watermelon into basket. Remove fruit from both sections of the top. Remove fruit from basket with a melon baller. Set aside 3 cups of melon balls (save remaining melon for another use).

In a large bowl, combine the pineapple, fruit cocktail, oranges, cherries, marshmallows and reserved watermelon balls. Add soda; gently toss to coat. Cover and refrigerate for 2 hours or until chilled. Just before serving, stir in coconut. Spoon into watermelon basket.

Popular any time of the year, this crowd-pleasing pasta salad is perfect for summer picnics. Made the day before, it has a pleasant vinaigrette dressing sparked with herbs. I set aside the Parmesan cheese and add it just before the salad is served.

Salami Pasta Salad

—*Marion Lowery*
Medford, Oregon

- 3 cups uncooked medium tube pasta
- 8 ounces hard salami, cubed
- 1/2 cup minced fresh parsley
- 4 green onions, sliced
- 1/2 cup olive oil
- 1/2 cup cider vinegar
- 4 teaspoons minced fresh oregano *or* 1 teaspoon dried oregano
- 4 teaspoons minced fresh basil *or* 1 teaspoon dried basil
- 2 garlic cloves, minced
- 1 teaspoon salt
- 1/4 teaspoon pepper
- 1/2 cup shredded Parmesan cheese

In a saucepan, cook pasta according to package directions; rinse in cold water and drain. Transfer to a large bowl; add salami, parsley and onions.

In a small bowl, whisk together the oil, vinegar and seasonings. Drizzle over pasta mixture and toss to coat. Cover and refrigerate overnight. Just before serving, stir in Parmesan cheese.

Prep: **15 min. + marinating**
Yield: **8 servings**

It's simple to put a refreshing salad on the menu when you follow this rapid recipe. Brown rice, coleslaw mix, apples and nuts make an appealing combination when coated with a sweet orange dressing.

Brown Rice Slaw

—*Mary McGeorge*
Little Rock, Arkansas

Prep/Total Time: **15 min.**
Yield: **8 servings**

- 2 cups coleslaw mix
- 2 cups cooked brown rice
- 1 medium tart apple, chopped
- 1/3 cup orange juice concentrate
- 1/3 cup fat-free mayonnaise
- 1 teaspoon sugar
- 1/4 teaspoon salt
- 1/4 cup chopped pecans, toasted

In a large bowl, combine the coleslaw mix, rice and apple. In a small bowl, combine the orange juice concentrate, mayonnaise, sugar and salt; pour over coleslaw mixture and toss to coat. Cover and refrigerate until serving. Stir in pecans.

Cherry Gelatin Squares

—Chris Rentmeister
Ripon, Wisconsin

Prep: **15 min.** + chilling
Yield: **9 servings**

I like to take advantage of gelatin mixes and pie fillings to make colorful salads that can be prepared the day before you need them. These fruity squares are great for everyday suppers yet special enough for company.

1 package (6 ounces) cherry gelatin
1-1/2 cups boiling water
1 can (21 ounces) cherry pie filling
1-1/4 cups lemon-lime soda, chilled
Whipped topping, optional

In a bowl, dissolve gelatin in water. Stir in pie filling; mix well. Slowly stir in soda (mixture will foam).

Pour into an 8-in. square dish. Cover and refrigerate until firm. Cut into squares. Garnish with whipped topping if desired.

Raspberry Tossed Salad

—Taste of Home Test Kitchen
Greendale, Wisconsin

Our home economists tossed together mixed greens, fresh raspberries, mushrooms, feta cheese and more in this pretty salad. Toasted pecan halves add fun crunch...and a homemade raspberry dressing brings a delicious tang to the mix!

Prep/Total Time: **10 min.**
Yield: **8 servings**

4 cups torn red leaf lettuce
1 package (5 ounces) spring mix salad greens
1 cup fresh raspberries
1 cup sliced fresh mushrooms
1/2 cup julienned red onion
1/4 cup crumbled feta cheese
1/4 cup pecan halves, toasted
2 tablespoons 100% raspberry fruit spread, melted

2 tablespoons raspberry vinegar
2 tablespoons vegetable oil
1/8 teaspoon salt
Dash pepper

In a large salad bowl, combine the first seven ingredients. In a jar with a tight-fitting lid, combine the fruit spread, vinegar, oil, salt and pepper; shake well. Pour over salad; toss gently to coat.

I like to serve this refreshing salad during the summer when my family craves pizza but I don't want to heat up the house by turning on the oven. It's so popular at potlucks that I always bring home an empty bowl.

Pepperoni Pizza Salad

—Cathy Riebschlager
Hordville, Nebraska

10 plum tomatoes, chopped

3 medium green peppers, cut into 1-inch pieces

2 cups (8 ounces) shredded part-skim mozzarella cheese

1 package (3-1/2 ounces) sliced pepperoni

1 can (2-1/4 ounces) sliced ripe olives, drained

1/4 cup chopped onion

1/3 cup tomato juice

1/4 cup red wine vinegar

1/4 cup olive oil

1 garlic clove, minced

1/2 teaspoon dried basil

1/4 teaspoon pepper

3/4 cup salad croutons

In a large bowl, combine the tomatoes, green peppers, cheese, pepperoni, olives and onion. In a small bowl, combine the tomato juice, vinegar, oil, garlic, basil and pepper.

Pour over tomato mixture and toss to coat. Cover and refrigerate for several hours. Just before serving, sprinkle with croutons.

Prep: 15 min. + chilling
Yield: 12-14 servings

A friend fixed this for a company outing a few years ago, and it has since become my favorite picnic salad. Jars of marinated mushrooms and artichoke hearts, along with fresh vegetables, turn prepared rice mix into something special.

Special Wild Rice Salad

—Suzanne Strocsher
Bothell, Washington

Prep: 15 min. + chilling
Cook: 25 min.
Yield: 10-12 servings

2 packages (6 ounces *each*) long grain and wild rice mix

2 to 3 ripe avocados, peeled and chopped

1 jar (8 ounces) marinated whole mushrooms, undrained

1 jar (6-1/2 ounces) marinated artichoke hearts, undrained

1 to 2 medium tomatoes, diced

2 celery ribs, chopped

2 to 3 green onions, chopped

1/2 cup Italian salad dressing

Prepare rice according to package directions. Cool; place in a large bowl. Add remaining ingredients and toss to coat. Cover and refrigerate overnight.

Layered Fruit Salad

—Page Alexander
Baldwin City, Kansas

Prep: **15 min. + chilling**
Yield: **8 servings**

Fresh fruit is layered into an eye-catching salad that's a welcome side dish all summer long.

1/2 cup orange juice

1/4 cup lemon juice

1/4 cup packed brown sugar

1/2 teaspoon grated orange peel

1/2 teaspoon grated lemon peel

1 cinnamon stick (3 inches)

2 cups fresh *or* drained canned pineapple chunks

1 cup seedless red grapes

2 medium bananas, sliced

2 medium oranges, sectioned

1 medium grapefruit, sectioned

1 pint fresh strawberries, sliced

2 medium kiwifruit, peeled and sliced

In a large saucepan, combine the juices, sugar, peels and cinnamon stick; bring to a boil. Reduce heat; simmer, uncovered, for 5 minutes. Remove from the heat; cool completely.

Meanwhile, layer fruit in a glass serving bowl. Remove cinnamon stick from the sauce; pour sauce over fruit. Cover and refrigerate for several hours.

Robust Italian Salad

—Shelley McKinney
New Castle, Indiana

Prep/Total Time: **15 min.**
Yield: **12 servings**

This is a hearty combination of lettuce, pastrami, tomatoes and mozzarella cheese. If you like, you can make homemade croutons with day-old bread, some oil, herbs and seasonings.

1 package (16 ounces) ready-to-serve salad greens

1 package (2-1/2 ounces) sliced pastrami, cut into 1/2-inch pieces, optional

1 cup (4 ounces) shredded part-skim mozzarella cheese

4 plum tomatoes, chopped

1 teaspoon Italian seasoning

1/3 cup Italian salad dressing

1 cup salad croutons

Sliced ripe olives, optional

In a large salad bowl, combine the first five ingredients. Drizzle with the dressing; toss to coat. Top with the croutons and olives if desired.

My family enjoys hiking in the mountains. This salad is great with chicken or trout grilled over a campfire. It's perfect for backyard picnics.

Corn Relish Salad

—Claudia Poynter
Augusta, Kansas

Prep: **20 min.** + chilling
Yield: **10 servings**

- 2 cups fresh *or* frozen corn
- 3 medium tomatoes, seeded and chopped
- 1 medium green pepper, diced
- 1/2 cup chopped red onion
- 1/2 cup sliced celery
- 1 can (2-1/4 ounces) sliced ripe olives, drained
- 1 jar (6-1/2 ounces) marinated artichoke hearts, undrained
- 1/4 cup reduced-fat Italian salad dressing
- 5 fresh basil leaves, finely chopped *or* 1 teaspoon dried basil
- 1/2 teaspoon garlic powder
- 1/2 teaspoon dried oregano
- 1/4 teaspoon lemon-pepper seasoning

In a large bowl, combine the first six ingredients. In another bowl, combine the artichokes, salad dressing, basil, garlic powder, oregano and lemon-pepper. Add to corn mixture and toss gently. Cover and refrigerate for at least 6 hours before serving.

A tangy Dijon mustard vinaigrette dresses up traditional bean salad. I'm a busy home-schooling mom, so I love how easy this colorful side dish is to prepare.

Dijon Four-Bean Salad

—Karen Riordan
Fern Creek, Kentucky

- 1 package (10 ounces) frozen baby lima beans
- 1 package (10 ounces) frozen cut green beans
- 2 cans (16 ounces *each*) red kidney beans, rinsed and drained
- 1 can (15 ounces) white kidney *or* cannellini beans, rinsed and drained
- 1/3 cup white vinegar
- 1/4 cup sugar
- 3 tablespoons Dijon mustard
- 2 tablespoons vegetable oil
- 1/2 teaspoon salt

Cook lima and green beans according to package directions; drain. Place in a large serving bowl; cool. Add kidney beans.

In a jar with a tight-fitting lid, combine the vinegar, sugar, mustard, oil and salt; shake well. Pour over beans and stir gently to coat. Cover and refrigerate overnight. Serve with a slotted spoon.

Prep: **15 min.** + chilling
Yield: **10 servings**

Brunch Fruit Salad

—Millie Vickery, Lena, Illinois

This appealing fruit salad is a lovely addition to breakfast, lunch or even supper. Light and refreshing, it's perfect alongside egg bakes, sausages and other hearty staples you find on breakfast buffets.

Prep/Total Time: **30 min.**
Yield: **10 servings**

1 can (20 ounces) pineapple chunks

2 large firm bananas, cut into 1/4-inch chunks

1 cup green grapes

1 can (15 ounces) mandarin oranges, drained

1 medium red apple, sliced

1 medium green apple, sliced

1/2 cup sugar

2 tablespoons cornstarch

1/3 cup orange juice

1 tablespoon lemon juice

Drain pineapple, reserving juice. Combine pineapple, bananas, grapes, oranges and apples in a large bowl; set aside.

In a small saucepan, combine sugar and cornstarch. Add the orange juice, lemon juice and reserved pineapple juice; stir until smooth. Bring to a boil over medium heat; cook and stir for 2 minutes or until thickened. Pour over fruit; mix gently. Cover and refrigerate until serving.

Idaho Potato Salad

—Rhonda Munk, Boise, Idaho

Mom used to make this potato salad without a recipe. When I got married, she and I made it one afternoon and wrote down the ingredients so I could prepare it at home.

4 pounds potatoes, cooked and peeled

3/4 cup sliced peeled cucumber

2 hard-cooked eggs, chopped

2 green onions, sliced

4-1/2 teaspoons chopped dill pickle

1 cup mayonnaise

1-1/2 teaspoons dill pickle juice

1-1/2 teaspoons prepared mustard

3/4 cup sliced radishes

Cut potatoes into 1/4-in. thick slices; place in a large bowl. Add the cucumber, eggs, onions and pickle. In a small bowl, combine the mayonnaise, pickle juice and mustard; pour over potato mixture and toss gently to coat. Cover and refrigerate. Fold in radishes just before serving.

Prep: **20 min.** + chilling
Yield: **10-12 servings**

This colorful and tasty salad is always well received at picnics and potlucks. It's so easy to make when you start with a package of corn bread, but if you like make one from scratch. Corn bread salads have long been popular in the South but may be new to people in other regions. No matter where you live, I think you'll like this one.

Corn Bread Confetti Salad

—Jennifer Horst
Goose Creek, South Carolina

1 package (8-1/2 ounces) corn bread/muffin mix

2 cans (15-1/2 ounces *each*) whole kernel corn, drained

2 cans (15 ounces *each*) pinto beans, rinsed and drained

1 can (15 ounces) black beans, rinsed and drained

3 small tomatoes, chopped

1 medium green pepper, chopped

1 medium sweet red pepper, chopped

1/2 cup chopped green onions

10 bacon strips, cooked and crumbled

2 cups (8 ounces) shredded cheddar cheese

Dressing:
1 cup (8 ounces) sour cream

1 cup mayonnaise

1 envelope ranch salad dressing mix

Prepare the corn bread according to package directions. Cool completely; crumble. In a large bowl, combine the corn, beans, tomatoes, peppers, onions, bacon, cheese and crumbled corn bread.

In a small bowl, combine the dressing ingredients until well blended. Just before serving, pour dressing over salad and toss.

Prep: **15 min.**
Bake: **15 min. + cooling**
Yield: **20-22 servings**

Time-Saving Trick

Bake the corn bread earlier in the day or even the night before. Cool the bread completely, then store in a resealable plastic bag at room temperature. When ready to use, crumble and combine with the other ingredients.

Bow Tie Garden Pasta

—Miriam Hershberger
Holmesville, Ohio

Just-picked veggies, pleasing bow tie pasta and flavorful seasonings mix together to make a delicious dish. To top it off, it's easy and fun to fix. Our daughter likes to make the pasta on a regular basis. You can serve this as a salad or add the freshly cooked pasta to the vegetables in the skillet and heat through and serve as a side dish.

Prep/Total Time: **15 min.**
Yield: **14 servings**

1 cup fresh cauliflowerets

1 medium onion, julienned

1 small green pepper, julienned

1 small zucchini, sliced

1 yellow summer squash, sliced

3 carrots, julienned

1 can (14 ounces) water-packed artichoke hearts, rinsed, drained and quartered

4 cups cooked multicolor cheese-filled tortellini

2 cups cooked bow tie pasta

1 cup Italian salad dressing

2 tablespoons olive oil

1 cup packed fresh basil leaves

2 tablespoons grated Parmesan cheese

2 tablespoons chopped walnuts

1 tablespoon minced garlic

2 cups quartered fresh mushrooms

1 cup fresh broccoli florets

In a blender or food processor, combine the first six ingredients; cover and process until smooth. Pour 1/2 cup into a large skillet; saute all of the vegetables until crisp-tender, about 3-5 minutes. Add pasta and remaining dressing; toss to coat.

Editor's Note: Make the pasta and tortellini the night before and store in the refrigerator until needed.

Storing Fresh Basil

To keep fresh basil for up to 1 week in the refrigerator, place the stems in a cup of water and loosely cover the leaves with a plastic bag.

Peanut butter in the dressing and interesting ingredients like marshmallows and mixed nuts give this Waldorf salad a tasty twist. I've tried versions without the peanut butter, but this is my favorite.

Nutty Apple Salad

—Maryellen Hays
Fort Wayne, Texas

Prep/Total Time: **30 min.**
Yield: **12-14 servings**

- 2 cups cubed tart apples
- 2 cups thinly sliced celery
- 2 cups halved seedless grapes
- 1 cup miniature marshmallows
- 1/3 cup cold evaporated milk
- 1/2 teaspoon sugar
- 1/4 teaspoon vanilla extract
- 3 tablespoons mayonnaise
- 3 tablespoons peanut butter
- 1/2 cup mixed nuts, optional

In a large bowl, combine the apples, celery, grapes and marshmallows. In a chilled mixing bowl, beat milk until frothy. Add sugar and vanilla. Beat in mayonnaise and peanut butter.

Pour over apple mixture; stir until coated. Cover and refrigerate. Just before serving, stir in nuts if desired.

Here's a pasta salad that's sure to keep folks coming back for seconds. Tortellini, cheese, ham, turkey and a harvest of veggies make the pasta toss satisfying enough for a main meal.

Parsley Tortellini Toss

—Jacqueline Graves
Lawrenceville, Georgia

Prep/Total Time: **30 min.**
Yield: **12-15 servings**

- 1 package (16 ounces) frozen cheese tortellini
- 1-1/2 cups cubed provolone cheese
- 1-1/2 cups cubed part-skim mozzarella cheese
- 1 cup cubed fully cooked ham
- 1 cup cubed cooked turkey
- 1 cup frozen peas, thawed
- 2 medium carrots, shredded
- 1/2 medium sweet red pepper, diced
- 1/2 medium green pepper, diced
- 1 cup minced fresh parsley
- 1/2 cup olive oil
- 3 tablespoons cider vinegar
- 2 tablespoons grated Parmesan cheese
- 2 garlic cloves, minced

Cook tortellini according to package directions; rinse in cold water and drain. Place in a large bowl; add the cheeses, meats, peas, carrots and peppers.

In a jar with a tight-fitting lid, combine the remaining ingredients; shake well. Pour over salad; toss to coat. Cover and refrigerate until serving. Serve with a slotted spoon.

Blueberry Gelatin Salad

—Mildred Livingston
Phoenix, Arizona

Prep: 15 min. + chilling
Yield: 10-12 servings

I make this recipe often, because I'm regularly asked to bring it along for potlucks. This dish can be served as either a salad or a dessert. Preparing it a day ahead makes it taste even better!

1 package (6 ounces) cherry gelatin
2 cups boiling water
1 can (15 ounces) blueberries, drained
1 package (8 ounces) cream cheese, softened
1/2 cup sugar
1 teaspoon vanilla extract
1 cup (8 ounces) sour cream
1/4 cup chopped pecans

In a large bowl, dissolve gelatin in boiling water; stir in blueberries. Pour into an 11-in. x 7-in. x 2-in. dish; chill until set.

In a large mixing bowl, beat cream cheese and sugar until smooth. Add vanilla and sour cream; mix well. Spread over the gelatin layer; sprinkle with the pecans. Chill for several hours or overnight.

Southwestern Rice And Bean Salad

—Sherre Yurenko
Cypress, California

Prep: 10 min. + chilling
Yield: 8-10 servings

This salad has a definite Mexican influence with the beans and picante sauce. I've made it for many get-togethers, and it's been well received.

2 cups cold cooked long grain rice
1 can (16 ounces) kidney beans, rinsed and drained
1 can (8-3/4 ounces) whole kernel corn, drained
1/2 cup sliced green onions with tops
1/2 cup picante sauce
1/4 cup prepared Italian salad dressing
1 teaspoon ground cumin

Combine all of the ingredients in a large salad bowl. Cover and refrigerate for 2-3 hours.

Everyone loves this festive, coleslaw, which has bursts of color from shredded carrots and julienned green and red sweet pepper. It not only looks good, it tastes great, too. Crisp vegetables covered with a light creamy dressing make a refreshing side dish you'll be proud to serve.

Picnic Slaw

—Jesse & Anne Foust
Bluefield, West Virginia

1 medium head cabbage, shredded

1 large carrot, shredded

1 medium green pepper, julienned

1 medium sweet red pepper, julienned

1 medium onion, finely chopped

1/3 cup sliced green onions

1/4 cup minced fresh parsley

Dressing:

1/4 cup milk

1/4 cup buttermilk

1/2 cup mayonnaise

1/3 cup sugar

2 tablespoons lemon juice

1 tablespoon white vinegar

1/2 teaspoon salt

1/2 teaspoon celery seed

Dash pepper

In a large bowl, combine the first seven ingredients. Combine the dressing ingredients in a blender; cover and process until smooth. Pour over vegetables; toss to coat. Cover and refrigerate overnight. Stir before serving.

Prep: **15 min.** + chilling
Yield: **12-16 servings**

Shredding Cabbage

To easily shred a cabbage head for coleslaw, cut the cabbage into wedges and core. Place cut side down on a cutting board. Cut into thin slices with a large, sharp knife.

Sunny Vegetable Salad

—Char Holm
Goodhue, Minnesota

Prep: **15 min.** + chilling
Yield: **12-16 servings**

A terrific mixture of crisp and chewy, fresh and sweet and savory ingredients makes this salad taste as good as it looks. A nutritious vegetable like broccoli is a lot more palatable dressed up this way.

5 cups fresh broccoli florets
5 cups fresh cauliflowerets
2 cups (8 ounces) shredded cheddar cheese
2/3 cup chopped onion
1/2 cup raisins
1 cup mayonnaise
1/2 cup sugar
2 tablespoons cider vinegar
6 bacon strips, cooked and crumbled
1/4 cup sunflower kernels

In a large bowl, toss broccoli, cauliflower, cheese, onion and raisins. In a small bowl, combine mayonnaise, sugar and vinegar. Pour over salad; toss to coat. Cover and refrigerate for 1 hour. Sprinkle with the bacon and sunflower kernels.

Make-Ahead Vegetable Medley

—Ramona Hook Wysong
Barlow, Kentucky

Prep: **10 min.** + chilling
Yield: **16-18 servings**

I like experimenting with different combinations and this is one of my most popular creations. I make it often for potlucks and seldom is there any left over.

1 can (16 ounces) kidney beans, rinsed and drained
1 can (15-3/4 ounces) lima beans, rinsed and drained
1 can (15 ounces) garbanzo beans, rinsed and drained
1 can (14-1/2 ounces) wax beans, drained
1 can (14-1/2 ounces) green beans, drained
1 can (15 ounces) small peas, drained
1 can (11 ounces) white shoepeg corn, drained
1-1/2 cups chopped onion
1/2 cup chopped green pepper
1 large cucumber, chopped
1 jar (2 ounces) diced pimientos, drained
2 cups cider vinegar
1-1/2 cups sugar
2/3 cup vegetable oil
1/2 teaspoon seasoned salt
1/2 teaspoon pepper
1/4 teaspoon garlic powder

In a large bowl, combine all of the beans, peas, corn, onion, green pepper, cucumber and pimientos. Combine the remaining ingredients; pour over vegetables and toss to coat. Cover and refrigerate overnight.

This refreshing salad is excellent for a summer cookout. Since you mix it ahead, the flavors have time to blend and there's no last-minute fussing. My friends ask me to bring it every time we get together for a meal.

Zesty Gazpacho Salad

—Teresa Fischer
Munster, Indiana

2 medium zucchini

2 medium tomatoes, chopped

1 small ripe avocado, chopped

1 cup fresh *or* frozen corn, thawed

1/2 cup thinly sliced green onions

1/2 cup picante sauce

2 tablespoons minced fresh parsley

2 tablespoons lemon juice

1 tablespoon vegetable oil

3/4 teaspoon garlic salt

1/4 teaspoon ground cumin

In a bowl, combine the first five ingredients. In a small bowl, combine remaining ingredients; mix well. Pour over zucchini mixture; toss to coat. Cover and refrigerate for at least 4 hours.

Prep: **10 min. + chilling**
Yield: **8-10 servings**

This medley of strawberries, melon and pineapple gets its rich, sweet taste from a creamy banana dressing. It's an eye-appealing salad that's perfect for breakfast or brunch.

Melon Fruit Bowl

—Edie DeSpain, Logan, Utah

Prep/Total Time: **15 min.**
Yield: **12 servings**

1 medium cantaloupe, cut into chunks

1 medium honeydew, cut into chunks

3 cups fresh pineapple chunks

1 cup halved strawberries

Banana Dressing:

1 medium ripe banana, cut into chunks

1/2 cup sour cream

2 tablespoons brown sugar

1-1/2 teaspoons lemon juice

In a large bowl, combine the melons, pineapple and strawberries; set aside. Place the dressing ingredients in a blender; cover and process until smooth. Serve with fruit salad.

Citrus Spinach Salad

—Pauline Taylor
Spokane, Washington

Prep/Total Time: **15 min.**
Yield: **12 servings**

Grapefruit and orange segments add zest to this delightful salad that's tossed with a pleasant honey-lime dressing. It's perfect for a springtime luncheon or shower.

3 tablespoons honey

2 tablespoons lime juice

1 teaspoon grated lime peel

1/8 to 1/4 teaspoon ground nutmeg

1/3 cup vegetable oil

10 cups torn fresh spinach

3 medium navel oranges, peeled and sectioned

2 medium pink grapefruit, peeled and sectioned

1 medium red onion, sliced and separated into rings

In a blender, combine the honey, lime juice, lime peel and nutmeg; cover and process until blended. While processing, gradually add oil in a steady stream until dressing is thickened.

In a large salad bowl, combine the spinach, oranges and grapefruit. Drizzle with dressing; toss to coat. Top with the onion. Serve immediately.

Marinated Tomatoes

—Myrtle Matthews
Marietta, Georgia

Prep: **10 min. + marinating**
Yield: **8 servings**

My niece introduced me to this colorful recipe some time ago. I now make it when I have buffets or large gatherings because it can be prepared hours ahead. This is a great way to use a bumper crop of tomatoes.

3 large fresh tomatoes, thickly sliced

1/3 cup olive oil

1/4 cup red wine vinegar

1 teaspoon salt, optional

1/4 teaspoon pepper

1/2 garlic clove, minced

2 tablespoons chopped onion

1 tablespoon chopped fresh parsley

1 tablespoon minced fresh basil *or* 1 teaspoon dried basil

Arrange tomatoes in a large shallow dish. Combine remaining ingredients in a jar with a tight-fitting lid and shake well. Pour over tomato slices. Cover and refrigerate for several hours.

Crowd-Pleasing
Sides

Sauerkraut Hot Dog Topping

—Erlene Cornelius
Spring City, Tennessee

Prep/Total Time: **10 min.**
Yield: **2 cups**

You'll relish this zesty condiment. For years, I stirred this up "by guess and by golly" before finally figuring out the proper measure of ingredients so I could share the recipe. It's great to have on hand anytime that you grill hot dogs or smoked sausages.

1 can (15 ounces) sauerkraut, rinsed and drained

1/4 cup sweet pickle relish

2 tablespoons brown sugar

1 tablespoon prepared mustard

1/2 teaspoon caraway seed

Combine all the ingredients in a saucepan; cook on low heat until heated through. Serve over hot dogs.

Garlic Potato Wedges

—Amy Werner
Grand Ledge, Michigan

Prep: **15 min.**
Bake: **25 min.**
Yield: **8 servings**

Looking for a change from run-of-the-mill potatoes? Try these tender wedges that are generously seasoned with garlic, rosemary and other flavorful ingredients. They complement any meal.

4 pounds small red potatoes, cut into wedges

1/3 cup olive oil, *divided*

16 unpeeled garlic cloves

2 tablespoons minced fresh rosemary *or* 2 teaspoons dried rosemary, crushed

1 teaspoon salt

1/3 cup white vinegar

4 teaspoons Dijon mustard

3 teaspoons sugar

1/4 teaspoon pepper

1/3 cup chopped green onions

In a large bowl, combine the potatoes, 1 tablespoon of oil, garlic, rosemary and salt. Pour into two 15-in. x 10-in. x 1-in. baking pans coated with nonstick cooking spray. Bake, uncovered, at 450° for 25-30 minutes or until potatoes are tender, stirring every 10 minutes.

In a small bowl, combine the vinegar, mustard, sugar, pepper and remaining oil until smooth. Squeeze roasted garlic into vinegar mixture (discard skins). Pour over potatoes and toss to coat. Sprinkle with onions.

Well received at parties and picnics, this colorful, tasty dish adds zest to the menu. I also make it as accompaniment for luncheons or dinners at home.

Pickled Peppers

—Heather Prendergast
Sundre, Alberta

- 2 *each* medium green, sweet red and yellow peppers, cut into 1-inch pieces
- 1 large red onion, halved and thinly sliced
- 1 cup cider vinegar
- 1 cup sugar
- 1/3 cup water
- 2 teaspoons mixed pickling spices
- 1/2 teaspoon celery seed

In a large glass bowl, combine peppers and onion; set aside. In a saucepan, combine the vinegar, sugar and water. Place the pickling spices and celery seed in a double thickness of cheesecloth; bring up the corners of cloth and tie with string to form a bag. Add to saucepan. Bring to a boil; boil for 1 minute.

Transfer spice bag to pepper mixture. Pour the vinegar mixture over all. Cover and refrigerate for 24 hours, stirring occasionally.

Discard spice bag. Peppers may be stored in the refrigerator for up to 1 month.

Prep: **20 min. + chilling**
Yield: **4 cups**

Making a Spice Bag

To keep spices together so they can be removed from a saucepan or kettle, place them on several thicknesses of cotton cheesecloth that has been cut into 3-in. squares. Tie with kitchen string to form a bag.

Copper Pennies

—*Agnes Circello*
Belle Rose, Louisiana

Prep: 20 min. + chilling
Yield: 8 cups

This recipe has become such a reliable standby for me that it's expected and welcomed by my friends. This dish can be served chilled for a salad or warm for a side dish. Either way it's always a hit. This can be prepare and kept in the refrigerator for a few days.

2 pounds carrots, peeled and sliced into 1/4-inch pieces

1/2 cup vegetable oil

1 cup sugar

1 large onion, diced

1 large green pepper, diced

1 can (5-1/2 ounces) tomato juice

3/4 cup red wine vinegar

1 teaspoon prepared mustard

1 teaspoon Worcestershire sauce

1 teaspoon salt

1/4 teaspoon pepper

Cook the carrots just until crisp-tender; drain. Combine all of the remaining ingredients in a large bowl. Add carrots and stir until well mixed. Cover and refrigerate at least 3-4 hours.

Serve cold as a salad, or warm it and use as a side dish. Store in the refrigerator for up to 2 weeks.

Garlic Green and Wax Beans

—*Marilou Robinson*
Portland, Oregon

Prep: 5 min.
Cook: 10 min. + chilling
Yield: 12 servings

This make-ahead vegetable dish showcases summer beans. A sprinkling of cheese and parsley before serving is a nice finishing touch. Even nongarlic lovers like this fresh-tasting dish.

1-1/2 pounds fresh green beans

1-1/2 pounds fresh wax beans

7 garlic cloves, minced, *divided*

1/4 cup reduced-fat sour cream

1/4 cup fat-free milk

1 teaspoon white wine vinegar

1 teaspoon olive oil

1/2 teaspoon salt

1/8 teaspoon pepper

1 cup shredded part-skim mozzarella cheese

Minced fresh parsley

Place beans and 6 garlic cloves in a steamer basket. Place in a large saucepan over 1 in. of water; bring to a boil. Cover and steam for 8-10 minutes or until beans are crisp-tender. Transfer to a large bowl; set aside.

In a small bowl, combine the sour cream, milk and vinegar; let stand for 1 minute. Whisk in the oil, salt, pepper and remaining garlic. Pour over beans and toss. Cover and refrigerate for at least 2 hours. Just before serving, sprinkle with cheese and parsley.

This cool and crunchy asparagus gets a flavor boost from soy sauce. It's a nice accompaniment to chicken, roast beef or ham.

Chilled Marinated Asparagus

—Nicole LeCroy
Nashville, Tennessee

Prep: 20 min. + marinating
Yield: 8 servings

2/3 cup packed brown sugar
2/3 cup cider vinegar
2/3 cup soy sauce
2/3 cup vegetable oil
4 teaspoons lemon juice
1 teaspoon garlic powder
2 pounds fresh asparagus, trimmed
1 cup chopped pecans, toasted

In a saucepan, combine brown sugar, vinegar, soy sauce, oil, lemon juice and garlic powder. Bring to a boil. Reduce heat; simmer, uncovered, for 5 minutes. Refrigerate until cool.

Meanwhile, in a large skillet, bring 1/2 in. of water to a boil. Add asparagus. Reduce heat; cover and simmer for 3-5 minutes or until crisp-tender. Drain and rinse in cold water.

Place asparagus in a large resealable plastic bag; add the marinade. Seal bag and turn to coat; refrigerate for 2 hours or overnight, turning occasionally. Drain and discard marinade. Place asparagus on a serving plate; sprinkle with pecans.

My family can never get enough of these sweet cucumber slices in the summer. They're crunchy, delicious and simple to make. At picnics or potlucks, I bring a big batch—folks tend to come back for more.

Refrigerator Cucumber Slices

—Denise Baumert
Jameson, Missouri

Prep: 15 min. + marinating
Yield: about 2-1/2 quarts

4 pounds cucumbers (about 6 large), cut into 1/4-inch slices
3 medium onions, cut into 1/8-inch slices
3 cups sugar
3 cups cider vinegar
4 teaspoons canning/pickling salt
1-1/2 teaspoons mustard seed
1/2 teaspoon alum

In a large container, combine cucumbers and onions. In a large bowl, combine the remaining ingredients, stirring until sugar is dissolved.

Pour over cucumber mixture; mix well. Cover and refrigerate overnight. May be refrigerated for up to 2 weeks.

Freezer Salsa

—Deanna Richter
Elmore, Minnesota

Prep: 25 min. + freezing
Cook: 45 min. + cooling
Yield: 10 cups

Kids in the home economics class at the school where I teach were making this salsa, and it smelled so good that I got the recipe.

8 cups diced seeded peeled tomatoes (about 10 large)

2 medium green peppers, chopped

2 large onions, chopped

2 jalapeno peppers, seeded and finely chopped

3/4 cup tomato paste

2/3 cup condensed tomato soup, undiluted

1/2 cup white vinegar

2 tablespoons sugar

2 tablespoons salt

4-1/2 teaspoons garlic powder

1 tablespoon cayenne pepper

In a Dutch oven or large saucepan, combine all ingredients. Bring to a boil. Reduce heat; simmer, uncovered, for 45 minutes, stirring often.

Pour into small freezer containers. Cool to room temperature, about 1 hour. Cover and freeze for up to 3 months. Stir before serving.

Editor's Note: When cutting or seeding hot peppers, use rubber or plastic gloves to protect your hands. Avoid touching your face.

Southwestern Rice

—Michelle Dennis
Clarks Hill, Indiana

Prep/Total Time: 30 min.
Yield: 8 servings

I created this zippy side dish after eating something similar at a restaurant. It makes a delicious side to any Tex-Mex meal.

1 medium green pepper, diced

1 medium onion, chopped

2 garlic cloves, minced

1 tablespoon olive oil

1 can (14-1/2 ounces) reduced-sodium chicken broth

1 cup uncooked long grain rice

1/2 teaspoon ground cumin

1/8 teaspoon ground turmeric

1 can (15 ounces) black beans, rinsed and drained

1 can (10 ounces) diced tomatoes and green chilies, undrained

1 package (10 ounces) frozen corn, thawed

In a large nonstick skillet, saute the green pepper, onion and garlic in oil for 3 minutes. Stir in the broth, rice, cumin and turmeric; bring to a boil. Reduce heat; cover and simmer for 15 minutes or until rice is tender. Add the beans, tomatoes and corn; heat through.

Dipping whole tomatoes into boiling water makes them easier to peel for this garden-fresh recipe. Parmesan or Romano cheese makes a great topper. This pleasing pasta complements any entree. You can also serve it as a meatless meal alongside a green salad. Or, for a heartier main course, toss in cubes of grilled chicken breast.

Fresh Tomato Pasta Toss

—Cheryl Travagliante
Independence, Ohio

- 3 pounds ripe fresh tomatoes
- 1 package (16 ounces) uncooked penne pasta *or* pasta of your choice
- 2 garlic cloves, minced
- 1 tablespoon vegetable oil
- 1 tablespoon minced fresh parsley *or* 1 teaspoon dried parsley flakes
- 1 tablespoon minced fresh basil *or* 1 teaspoon dried basil
- 2 teaspoons minced fresh oregano *or* 3/4 teaspoon dried oregano
- 1 teaspoon salt
- 1/4 teaspoon sugar
- 1/8 teaspoon pepper
- 1/4 cup heavy whipping cream
- 1/4 cup shredded Parmesan *or* Romano cheese

To remove peels from tomatoes, fill a large saucepan with water and bring to a boil. Place tomatoes, one at a time, in boiling water for 30 seconds. Immediately plunge in ice water. Peel skins with a sharp paring knife and discard. Chop pulp; set aside.

Cook pasta according to package directions. In a large skillet, cook garlic in oil over medium heat until golden. Add the parsley, basil, oregano, salt, sugar, pepper and reserved tomato pulp; mix well. Bring to a boil; reduce heat. Add cream; heat through.

Drain pasta and transfer to a serving bowl. Pour tomato sauce over pasta and toss to coat. Sprinkle with cheese.

Prep/Total Time: **30 min.**
Yield: **8 servings**

Tex-Mex Corn On the Cob

—Helen Jacobs
Euless, Texas

Prep/Total Time: **15 min.**
Yield: **12 servings**

It's a snap to add zippy flavor to fresh corn on the cob. The tender ears get a special treatment when seasoned with chili powder, cilantro and lime.

12 small ears fresh corn on the cob (about 6 inches)

3 tablespoons minced fresh cilantro

1-1/2 teaspoons chili powder

1-1/2 teaspoons grated lime peel

3/4 teaspoon salt

3/4 teaspoon ground cumin

1/4 teaspoon garlic powder

Refrigerated butter-flavored spray

Place corn in a Dutch oven; cover with water. Bring to a boil. Reduce heat; cover and cook for 3-5 minutes or until tender.

Meanwhile, in a small bowl, combine the cilantro, chili powder, lime peel, salt, cumin and garlic powder. Drain the corn. Spritz with butter-flavored spray; brush or pat seasoning over corn.

Cukes and Carrots

—Karla Hecht
Plymouth, Minnesota

Prep: **15 min. + chilling**
Yield: **12 servings**

Carrots and green peppers bring extra color and crunch to this refreshing cucumber salad. The sweet dressing is a lovely match for the crisp summer produce.

5 medium cucumbers, thinly sliced

4 medium carrots, thinly sliced

1 medium onion, halved and thinly sliced

1 small green pepper, chopped

2 teaspoons canning salt

1-1/2 cups sugar

1/2 cup white vinegar

In a large bowl, combine the cucumbers, carrots, onion and green pepper. Sprinkle with salt; toss to coat. Cover and refrigerate for 2 hours. Combine sugar and vinegar. Pour over vegetables; toss to coat. Cover and refrigerate for at least 1 hour. Serve with a slotted spoon.

When the weather turns chilly, our daughter, who is an inventive cook, transforms her favorite cold pasta salad into this warm, hearty side dish. I love recipes like this one that bring compliments and don't keep me in the kitchen too long. It seems as soon as I set out this dish at gatherings, it disappears!

Bacon 'n' Veggie Pasta

—Muriel Hollenbeck
Sedalia, Colorado

2 cans (14-1/2 ounces *each*) stewed tomatoes

2 cups fresh broccoli florets

2 medium carrots, thinly sliced

1/2 teaspoon salt

1/2 teaspoon Italian seasoning

1/2 teaspoon dried oregano

1/4 teaspoon dried basil

4 bacon strips, diced

1/2 pound fresh mushrooms, sliced

1/3 cup chopped green pepper

1/4 cup chopped onion

2 garlic cloves, minced

16 ounces uncooked medium shell pasta

1/4 cup shredded Parmesan cheese

In a large saucepan, combine the first seven ingredients. Bring to a boil. Reduce heat; cover and simmer for 25-30 minutes or until broccoli and carrots are tender.

In a large skillet, cook bacon over medium heat until crisp. Using a slotted spoon, remove to paper towels; drain, reserving 1 tablespoon drippings. In the drippings, saute the mushrooms, green pepper, onion and garlic until tender; add to tomato mixture and heat through.

Meanwhile, cook the pasta according to package directions. Drain and place in a serving bowl; top with vegetable mixture. Sprinkle with bacon and Parmesan cheese.

Prep: **10 min.**
Cook: **35 min.**
Yield: **13 servings**

Hot Vegetable Plate

—Julie Polakowski
West Allis, Wisconsin

Prep/Total Time: 30 min.
Yield: 8 servings

A creamy mustard sauce adds spark to an interesting lineup of vegetables in this fall side dish. You'll always receive compliments with this special presentation.

1 medium kohlrabi

1 medium turnip

1 small rutabaga

4 medium carrots, halved crosswise

4 medium leeks (white portion only), sliced

12 fresh cauliflowerets

Mustard Sauce:
1/4 cup butter, cubed

2 tablespoons all-purpose flour

1/4 teaspoon salt, optional

Pinch pepper

1 cup milk

1 to 2 teaspoons Dijon mustard

Peel kohlrabi, turnip and rutabaga; cut into 1/4-in. slices. Halve the kohlrabi and turnip slices; quarter the rutabaga slices. Place all vegetables in a large saucepan and cover with water; cook until crisp-tender, about 8-10 minutes.

Meanwhile, melt the butter in a small saucepan. Stir in flour, salt if desired and pepper; gradually add milk. Bring to a boil over medium heat; cook and stir for 2 minutes or until thickened. Remove from heat; stir in mustard.

Drain the vegetables; serve with warm mustard sauce.

South Liberty Hall Relish

—Melinda Winchell
Las Vegas, Nevada

Prep: 10 min. + chilling
Yield: 2 cups

My grandparents originated this recipe that's been treasured in our family for four generations. It's named after a dance hall they ran in rural Iowa. Whenever I bite into a hot dog or hamburger dressed up with this taste bud-tingling relish, I think of them and their delicious country cooking.

1 jar (16 ounces) whole dill pickles, drained

1/4 cup chopped onion

2 to 3 tablespoons sugar

1/2 cup yellow mustard

Place the pickles and onion in a food processor; cover and process until finely chopped. Transfer to a bowl; stir in sugar and mustard. Store in the refrigerator for up to 1 week.

If you're looking for a tasty change from plain buttered noodles, serve this pleasing pasta toss as a streamlined side dish.

Spinach Parmesan Linguine

—Mary Curran
Sandwich, Illinois

Prep/Total Time: **30 min.**
Yield: **10 servings**

1 package (16 ounces) linguine
1 cup chicken broth
1 small onion, chopped
2 garlic cloves, minced
1 package (10 ounces) frozen chopped spinach, thawed and well drained
1/3 cup milk
2 tablespoons cream cheese
Salt and pepper to taste
1 cup (4 ounces) shredded Parmesan cheese
1/2 cup shredded part-skim mozzarella cheese

Cook linguine according to package directions. Meanwhile, in a saucepan over medium-high heat, bring broth to a boil. Add onion and garlic. Reduce heat; cook, uncovered, for 5 minutes. Stir in spinach; cook for 2 minutes.

Add the milk, cream cheese, salt and pepper; stir until cheese is melted. Drain linguine and place in a serving bowl. Add sauce and toss to coat. Sprinkle with Parmesan and mozzarella cheeses; toss to coat.

Living in the Willamette Valley of Oregon, we always have fresh vegetables from the garden, and this recipe allows me to use many of them.

Summer Stuffed Peppers

—Pat Whitaker
Lebanon, Oregon

Prep: **20 min.**
Cook: **30 min.**
Yield: **8 servings**

8 medium yellow, green *or* sweet red peppers
1-1/2 pounds lean ground beef
1/2 garlic clove, minced
1 medium onion, minced
1/2 cup finely chopped cabbage
1 medium carrot, shredded
1/2 cup shredded zucchini
1 can (28 ounces) diced tomatoes, undrained
1/2 cup uncooked long-grain rice
1 tablespoon brown sugar
1/4 teaspoon dried basil
Pepper to taste

Cut the tops off each pepper and reserve. Cook peppers in boiling water until crisp-tender, about 2-3 minutes. Remove from water and rinse with cold water. Remove stems from pepper tops and chop enough of the tops to make 1/3 cup.

In a large skillet, cook beef over medium heat until no longer pink. Add the garlic, onion, cabbage, carrot, zucchini and reserved chopped peppers. Saute until vegetables are tender. Add the tomatoes, rice, sugar, basil and pepper. Cover and reduce heat to simmer. Cook until the rice is tender, about 20 minutes.

Stuff hot meat mixture into peppers. Serve immediately.

German Red Cabbage

—Jeannette Heim
Concord, California

Prep: **10 min.**
Cook: **1 hour 5 minutes**
Yield: **10 servings**

Sunday afternoons were a time for family gatherings when I was a child. While the uncles played cards, the aunts prepared wonderful German fare such as this traditional red cabbage.

1 medium onion, sliced

1 unpeeled apple, cored and sliced

1 medium red cabbage, shredded

1/3 cup sugar

1/3 cup white vinegar

3/4 teaspoon salt, optional

1/4 teaspoon pepper

In a Dutch oven coated with non-stick cooking spray, saute onion and apple until tender. Add all remaining ingredients. Cover and cook until tender, about 1 hour. Serve hot or cold.

Mixed Vegetables

—Anna Beiler
Strasburg, Pennsylvania

Prep: **10 min.**
Cook: **30 min.**
Yield: **11 servings**

This comforting skillet side dish has been a huge hit with my family from the first time I served it. Using reduced-fat and reduced-sodium ingredients makes it even more nutritious.

1 cup sliced celery

1/2 cup chopped onion

2 garlic cloves, minced

3 tablespoons reduced-fat butter

1-1/2 cups reduced-sodium chicken broth

4 cups cubed peeled potatoes

1 cup julienned carrots

1/4 teaspoon pepper

1 tablespoon chopped fresh parsley

In a large skillet, saute the celery, onion and garlic in butter until tender. Add the broth, potatoes, carrots and pepper; bring to a boil. Reduce heat; cover and simmer for 15-20 minutes or until potatoes are tender.

Uncover; simmer 5 minutes longer or until broth has thickened slightly, stirring occasionally. Sprinkle with parsley; serve with a slotted spoon.

Editor's Note: This recipe was tested with Land O' Lakes light stick butter.

A fun and tasty alternative to potatoes, this savory rice is popular at gatherings. I especially like its mild soy sauce flavor and flecks of green onions and toasted slivered almonds.

Potluck Rice Pilaf

—Annette Rodgers
Rosston, Arkansas

- 1/2 cup butter, cubed
- 4 cups uncooked long grain rice
- 16 cups water
- 2 tablespoons chicken bouillon granules
- 10 green onions, thinly sliced
- 2/3 cup soy sauce
- 1 cup slivered almonds, toasted

In a Dutch oven, melt butter. Add rice; cook and stir for 3-5 minutes or until rice is lightly browned. Add water and bouillon; bring to a boil. Reduce heat; cover and simmer for 15-20 minutes or until rice is tender and liquid is absorbed.

Remove from the heat; stir in the onions and soy sauce. Cover and let stand for 5 minutes. Stir in almonds.

Prep: **25 min.**
Cook: **15 min.**
Yield: **20-22 servings**

Cashew Rice Pilaf

—Tina Coburn
Tucson, Arizona

Prep: **5 min.**
Cook: **35 min.**
Yield: **12 servings**

This hearty dish will add pizzazz to your plate, thanks to its beautiful blend of flavors and colors. I also serve it as a main course.

1-1/2 cups uncooked long grain rice
1 cup chopped onion
1 cup diced carrots
1 cup golden raisins
1/4 cup butter, cubed
3 cups chicken broth
1 teaspoon onion salt
2 cups frozen peas
1-1/2 cups cooked wild rice
1 cup salted cashews
1/4 cup thinly sliced green onions, optional

In a Dutch oven, saute the long grain rice, onion, carrots and raisins in butter until onion is tender. Add the broth and onion salt; bring to a boil. Reduce heat; cover and simmer for 20 minutes or until liquid is absorbed and rice is tender. Stir in peas, wild rice and cashews; heat through. Sprinkle with the green onions if desired.

Pickled Mushrooms

—Linda Keiper-Quinn
Hazelton, Pennsylvania

Prep: **5 min.** + chilling
Yield: **about 2-1/2 cups**

Pennsylvania is known for its mushrooms, and they are featured in this recipe. They taste great alongside grilled foods.

1/2 cup red wine vinegar
1/2 cup water
2 bay leaves
2 tablespoons sugar
1-1/2 teaspoons salt
1 garlic clove, minced
1 pound fresh mushrooms, quartered

In a saucepan over medium heat, combine the vinegar, water, bay leaves, sugar, salt and garlic. Add mushrooms. Bring to a boil; boil for 2 minutes.

Cool slightly. Transfer to a bowl; cover and refrigerate for 8 hours or overnight. Discard bay leaves before serving.

Need a tasty side dish or a fun appetizer? Look no further. These potato skins are sure to fill the bill! Potato shells are topped with Canadian bacon, chopped tomato and reduced-fat cheese. They are popular with adults, teens and children. Make plenty because they go fast!

Canadian Bacon Potato Skins

—Mary Plummer
De Soto, Kansas

- 6 large baking potatoes (12 ounces *each*)
- 2 teaspoons canola oil
- 1/8 teaspoon hot pepper sauce
- 1 teaspoon chili powder
- 1 medium tomato, seeded and finely chopped
- 2/3 cup chopped Canadian bacon
- 2 tablespoons finely chopped green onion
- 1 cup (4 ounces) shredded reduced-fat cheddar cheese
- 1/2 cup reduced-fat sour cream

Place potatoes on a microwave-safe plate; prick with a fork. Microwave, uncovered, on high for 14-17 minutes or until tender but firm, turning once. Let stand for 5 minutes. Cut each potato in half lengthwise. Scoop out pulp, leaving a 1/4-in. shell (discard pulp or save for another use).

Combine oil and hot pepper sauce; brush over potato shells. Sprinkle with chili powder. Cut each potato shell in half lengthwise. Place on baking sheets coated with nonstick cooking spray. Sprinkle with the tomato, bacon, onion and cheese. Bake at 450° for 12-14 minutes or until heated through and cheese is melted. Serve with sour cream.

Editor's Note: This recipe was tested in a 1,100-watt microwave.

Prep: **30 min. + standing**
Bake: **15 min.**
Yield: **8 servings**

Potato Skin Topping Ideas

It's easy to vary the flavor of Canadian Bacon Potato Skins. Simply substitute cooked, crumbled bacon for the Canadian Bacon, or get creative and use your favorite taco or pizza toppings.

Old-Fashioned Corn Relish

—Jean Peterson
Mulliken, Michigan

Prep/Total Time: 30 min.
Yield: 6-1/2 cups

This was the first recipe I received after moving away from the city—a farm wife neighbor shared it. I've made a few additions to it and gotten many compliments. It's wonderful made with garden-fresh ingredients. Serve it with any grilled entree.

2 cups fresh *or* frozen corn
2 cups chopped onions
2 cups chopped tomatoes
2 cups chopped seeded cucumber
1 large green pepper, chopped
1 cup sugar
1 cup cider vinegar
1-1/2 teaspoons celery seed
1-1/2 teaspoons mustard seed
1 teaspoon salt
1/2 teaspoon ground turmeric

In a large saucepan, combine all of the ingredients. Bring to a boil. Reduce heat; simmer, uncovered, for 20-30 minutes or until thickened. Store in the refrigerator for up to 3 weeks.

Beans with Cherry Tomatoes

—Betty Brown
Buckley, Washington

Prep/Total Time: 25 min.
Yield: 8 servings

This recipe is a favorite of my family. We love this dressed-up version of garden green beans. It's great with any meat.

4 bacon strips, diced
1-1/2 pounds fresh green beans, cut into 2-inch pieces
4 garlic cloves, thinly sliced
1-1/2 cups halved cherry tomatoes
1/2 teaspoon salt
1/4 cup slivered almonds, toasted

In a large skillet, cook bacon over medium heat until crisp. Using a slotted spoon, remove to paper towels to drain. In the drippings, saute beans for 12-14 minutes or until crisp-tender. Add garlic; cook 2-3 minutes longer. Stir in tomatoes and salt; heat through. Sprinkle with bacon and almonds. Serve immediately.

Sweet
Endings

Chocolate Mint Ice Cream

—Frann Skaff
Egg Harbor, Wisconsin

When the weather gets hot, my family really enjoys this cool combination of chocolate and mint. It doesn't require an ice cream maker—all that you need is an ordinary freezer. My ice cream's versatile, too. We've used crushed Heath bars, Oreo cookies and miniature chocolate chips in place of the Andes candies.

1 can (14 ounces) sweetened condensed milk
1/2 cup chocolate syrup
2 cups heavy whipping cream
1 package (4.67 ounces) mint Andes candies (28 pieces), chopped

In a small bowl, combine the milk and chocolate syrup; set aside. In a mixing bowl, beat cream until stiff peaks form. Fold in chocolate mixture and candies.

Transfer to a freezer-proof container; cover and freeze for 5 hours or until firm. Remove from freezer 10 minutes before serving.

Prep: 10 min. + freezing
Yield: 1-1/2 quarts

Rocky Road Brownies

—Rita Lenes, Kent, Washington

Anyone who likes rocky road ice cream will like these moist, fudgy brownies loaded with goodies. They're great for children's parties.

3/4 cup butter, cubed
4 squares (1 ounce *each*) unsweetened chocolate
4 eggs
2 cups sugar
1 teaspoon vanilla extract
1 cup all-purpose flour
2 cups miniature marshmallows
1 cup (6 ounces) semisweet chocolate chips
1 cup chopped walnuts

In a large saucepan over low heat, melt butter and chocolate; cool for 10 minutes.

In a large mixing bowl, beat the eggs, sugar and vanilla. Stir in chocolate mixture. Add flour and mix well.

Spread into a greased 13-in. x 9-in. x 2-in. baking pan. Bake at 350° for 25-30 minutes or until a toothpick inserted near the center comes out clean. Sprinkle with the marshmallows, chocolate chips and walnuts; bake 4 minutes longer. Cool on a wire rack.

Prep: 20 min.
Bake: 30 min.
Yield: 2 dozen

I've been making these treats for many years. I don't remember where the recipe came from. But one thing is certain, they're always a hit at family get-togethers. The secret to tasty banana desserts is the ripeness of the bananas—the riper, the better. The orange butter frosting is a tasty change from ordinary cream cheese frosting.

Banana Orange Bars

—Mary Sturgis
Hingham, Massachusetts

2 cups mashed ripe bananas (3 to 4 bananas)

1-2/3 cups sugar

1 cup vegetable oil

4 eggs

2 cups all-purpose flour

2 teaspoons ground cinnamon

1 teaspoon salt

1 teaspoon baking powder

1/2 teaspoon baking soda

Orange Butter Frosting:
5 tablespoons butter, softened

4-1/2 cups confectioners' sugar

5 tablespoons orange juice

1/2 teaspoon grated orange peel

In a large mixing bowl, beat the bananas, sugar, oil and eggs until well blended. Combine dry ingredients; fold into the banana mixture until blended.

Pour into a greased 15-in. x 10-in. x 1-in. baking pan. Bake at 350° for 25-30 minutes or until a toothpick inserted near the center comes out clean. Cool on a wire rack.

For frosting, in a mixing bowl, beat butter, sugar, orange juice and peel until smooth. Spread over cooled bars.

Prep: **15 min.**
Bake: **25 min. + cooling**
Yield: **3 dozen**

Ripe Bananas

To ripen bananas, place in a brown paper bag with an apple. To store overripe bananas for future baking, place them whole, with the peel on, in a resealable plastic bag in the freezer.

Picnic Bars

—*Frank Bee, Eugene, Oregon*

You'll score points with a crowd when you stir together these delicious, fudge-like treats. They're very moist and rich. The chocolate chips and walnuts make a pretty topping.

1-3/4 cups all-purpose flour

    1 cup sugar

1/4 cup baking cocoa

1/2 cup cold butter, cubed

    2 eggs

    1 can (14 ounces) sweetened condensed milk

    2 cups (12 ounces) semisweet chocolate chips, *divided*

    1 cup chopped walnuts

Prep: **10 min.**
Bake: **25 min.**
Yield: **3 dozen**

In a large bowl, combine the flour, sugar and cocoa; cut in butter until mixture resembles coarse crumbs. Stir in eggs. Set aside 1-1/2 cups for topping.

Press remaining crumb mixture into a greased 13-in. x 9-in. x 2-in. baking pan. Bake at 350° for 6-8 minutes or until set.

Meanwhile, in a saucepan, combine milk and 1 cup of chocolate chips; cook and stir over low heat until melted. Carefully spread over crust. Combine reserved crumb mixture with nuts and remaining chips. Sprinkle over chocolate layer.

Bake for 15-20 minutes or until top is set (chips will not look melted). Cool before cutting.

Here's the scoop on a sensational sauce! It has fresh-fruit flavor and is delicious with angel food cake, too.

Blueberry Ice Cream Topping

—Betty Leibnitz
Hallock, Minnesota

2 cups fresh *or* frozen blueberries

1 tablespoon water

2 tablespoons sugar

Pinch salt

1/2 teaspoon cornstarch

1 teaspoon cold water

1-1/2 teaspoons lemon juice

1/4 teaspoon vanilla extract

1/8 teaspoon ground cinnamon

Ice cream

In a saucepan, combine the blueberries, water, sugar and salt; cook and stir over low heat until sugar is dissolved. Bring to a boil. Reduce heat; simmer, uncovered, for 7 minutes or until the berries burst.

Combine cornstarch and cold water until smooth; stir into hot blueberry mixture. Bring to a boil; cook and stir for 2 minutes or until thickened. Remove from the heat; stir in the lemon juice, vanilla and cinnamon. Serve over ice cream.

Prep/Total Time: **20 min.**

Yield: **1-1/4 cups**

When I serve this dessert to company, they often think it has ice cream in it. It does have a smooth texture like an ice cream pie. I've been making this recipe for years—it's a refreshing end to a meal anytime!

Frozen Chocolate Pie

—Bonnie Scott
McLouth, Kansas

1 package (3 ounces) cream cheese, softened

1/2 cup sugar

1 teaspoon vanilla extract

1/3 cup baking cocoa

1/3 cup milk

1 carton (8 ounces) frozen whipped topping, thawed

1 pie pastry (9 inches), baked

Chocolate curls *or* chips, optional

In a large mixing bowl, beat the cream cheese, sugar and vanilla until smooth. Add cocoa alternately with milk; mix well. Fold in whipped topping.

Pour into pie shell. Freeze for 8 hours or overnight. Sprinkle with chocolate curls or chips if desired. Serve directly from the freezer (pie does not need to be thawed to cut).

Prep: **10 min.** + freezing
Yield: **6-8 servings**

Frosty Freezer Pie

—Sue Blow, Lititz, Pennsylvania

Prep: **10 min.** + freezing
Yield: **8-10 servings**

This pretty pie can be whipped up in no time. But it tastes so sweet and creamy, people will think you fussed.

1 package (8 ounces)
    cream cheese, softened

1 jar (7 ounces)
    marshmallow creme

2 cups raspberry, orange *or*
    lime sherbet, softened

2 to 3 cups whipped topping

1 graham cracker crust
    (9 or 10 inches)

In a large mixing bowl, beat the cream cheese and marshmallow creme until smooth. Stir in sherbet. Fold in whipped topping.

Pour into crust. Freeze until firm. Remove from the freezer 10 minutes before serving. The pie may be frozen for up to 3 months.

Cranberry Chip Cookies

—Betty Albee, Buhl, Idaho

Prep: **10 min.**
Prep: **15 min. per batch**
Yield: **about 6 dozen**

Chock-full of cranberries, chocolate chips and nuts, these cookies offer a change of pace from traditional Christmas cookies...but don't wait until December to make them. My family requests them year-round.

1 cup butter, softened

1 cup sugar

2 egg yolks

1 teaspoon vanilla extract

2-1/4 cups all-purpose flour

1/2 teaspoon baking powder

1/4 teaspoon salt

1-1/2 cups (9 ounces)
    semisweet chocolate chips

1-1/2 cups dried cranberries

3/4 cup chopped pecans

1/2 cup English toffee bits *or*
    almond brickle chips,
    optional

In a large mixing bowl, cream butter and sugar. Add egg yolks and vanilla; mix well. Combine the flour, baking powder and salt; gradually add to the creamed mixture and mix well. Stir in the chocolate chips, cranberries, pecans and toffee bits if desired (dough will be stiff).

Drop by rounded tablespoonfuls 2 in. apart onto ungreased baking sheets. Flatten slightly. Bake at 350° for 11-14 minutes or until set and edges are lightly browned. Cool for 2 minutes before removing to wire racks.

Apples are plentiful this time of year, and this cake is one of my favorite recipes using this delicious and nutritious fruit.

Apple Walnut Cake

—Judy Dennis
Brown City, Michigan

3 eggs, beaten

2 cups sugar

1/2 cup vegetable oil

2 teaspoons vanilla extract

2 cups all-purpose flour

2 teaspoons baking soda

2 teaspoons ground cinnamon

1/2 teaspoon ground nutmeg

1/4 teaspoon salt

4 cups diced unpeeled apples

1 cup coarsely chopped walnuts

Cream Cheese Frosting:
  2 packages (3 ounces *each*) cream cheese, softened

1/4 cup butter, softened

1-1/2 cups confectioners' sugar

1/2 teaspoon vanilla extract

In a large mixing bowl, beat together the eggs, sugar, oil and vanilla. Combine the flour, baking soda, cinnamon, nutmeg and salt; mix into the batter. Fold in apples and nuts.

Spread into a 13-in. x 9-in. x 2-in. baking pan. Bake at 325° for 50-60 minutes or until toothpick inserted near the center comes out clean. Cool on a wire rack.

For the frosting, combine all ingredients in a small mixing bowl. Beat until smooth and spread over cooled cake.

Prep: **20 min.**
Bake: **50 min.**
Yield: **12-15 servings**

A traditional cooked custard base is the key to this creamy ice cream with rich vanilla flavor. It is a family favorite.

Creamy Vanilla Ice Cream

—Mary Thompson
Minneapolis, Minnesota

Prep: **15 min. + chilling**
Freeze: **30 min.**
Yield: **about 1-1/2 quarts**

2 eggs

1 cup sugar

1/4 teaspoon salt

2-1/2 cups heavy whipping cream

2 cups half-and-half cream

2-1/4 teaspoons vanilla extract

In a heavy saucepan, combine the first five ingredients. Cook over medium-low heat, stirring constantly, until the mixture is thick enough to coat a metal spoon and reaches at least 160°. Remove from the heat; cool quickly by setting pan in ice and stirring the mixture.

Cover and refrigerate overnight or freeze immediately. When ready to freeze, pour custard and vanilla into the cylinder of an ice cream freezer. Freeze according to the manufacturer's directions.

Toffee Mocha Dessert

—Jean Ecos, Waukesha, Wisconsin

Prep: **15 min.** + chilling
Yield: **16-20 servings**

Angel food cake takes on richness and bold flavor in this special treat. Coffee and chocolate are perfect partners.

1 angel food cake
   (8 inches), cut into
   1-inch cubes
3/4 cup brewed coffee, cooled
1 package (8 ounces)
   cream cheese, softened
1/2 cup chocolate syrup
2 to 4 tablespoons sugar
2 cups whipped topping
2 Heath bars (1.4 ounces
   each), crushed
Additional Heath bars, optional

Place cake cubes in an ungreased 13-in. x 9-in. x 2-in. dish. Add coffee and toss lightly.

In a large mixing bowl, combine the cream cheese, chocolate syrup and sugar until blended. Fold in whipped topping. Spread over cake. Sprinkle with crushed Heath bars.

Cover and refrigerate for at least 1 hour. Garnish with additional Heath bars if desired.

Triple Fruit Pie

—Jeanne Freybler
Grand Rapids, Michigan

My goal is to create pies as good as my mother's. I came up with this recipe as a way to use fruit in my freezer. The first time I made it, my family begged for seconds.

1-1/4 cups *each* fresh
   blueberries, raspberries
   and chopped rhubarb
1/2 teaspoon almond extract
1-1/4 cups sugar
1/4 cup quick-cooking tapioca
1/4 teaspoon ground nutmeg
1/4 teaspoon salt
1 tablespoon lemon juice
Pastry for double-crust pie
   (9 inches)

In a large bowl, combine fruits and extract; toss to coat. In another bowl, combine the sugar, tapioca, nutmeg and salt. Add to fruit; stir gently. Let stand for 15 minutes.

Line a 9-in. pie plate with bottom crust; trim pastry even with edge. Stir the lemon juice into fruit mixture; spoon into the crust. Roll out remaining pastry; make a lattice crust. Seal and flute edges.

Bake at 400° for 20 minutes. Reduce heat to 350°; bake 30 minutes longer or until the crust is golden brown and the filling is bubbly.

Prep: **15 min.**
Bake: **50 min.**
Yield: **6-8 servings**

My father-in-law introduced this recipe to the family. The fudgy sauce has a nice flavor and is a special favorite of our four children. Use whatever ice cream flavor your family prefers.

Fudge Sundaes

—*Tammy Mackie*
Seward, Nebraska

2 cups (12 ounces) semisweet chocolate chips

2 squares (1 ounce *each*) unsweetened chocolate

1 cup heavy whipping cream

1/4 cup cold brewed coffee

Dash salt

1 teaspoon vanilla extract

Ice cream

Maraschino cherries, optional

In a large saucepan, combine the first five ingredients. Heat on low, stirring constantly, until chocolate is melted. Remove from the heat; stir in vanilla. Serve over ice cream. Top with a cherry if desired.

Prep/Total Time: **10 min.**

Yield: **2-1/2 cups topping**

Instant pudding mix and cake mix cut the preparation time for this delicious cake that is loaded with chocolate. I often make it for weekend guests and work luncheons. It always goes over well.

Chocolate Chip Snack Cake

—*Karen Walker*
Sterling, Virginia

1 package (18-1/4 ounces) yellow cake mix

1 package (3.4 ounces) instant vanilla pudding mix

4 eggs

1 cup water

1/2 cup vegetable oil

1 package (12 ounces) miniature semisweet chocolate chips

1 package (4 ounces) German sweet chocolate, grated, *divided*

Confectioners' sugar

In a large mixing bowl, combine the first five ingredients; beat for 5 minutes. Stir in chocolate chips and half of the grated chocolate.

Pour into a greased 13-in. x 9-in. x 2-in. baking pan. Bake at 350° for 45-50 minutes or until a toothpick inserted near the center comes out clean. Sprinkle with remaining grated chocolate while slightly warm. Cool completely on a wire rack. Dust with confectioners' sugar.

Prep: **15 min.**

Bake: **45 min. + cooling**

Yield: **12-15 servings**

Broadway Brownie Bars

—Anne Frederick
New Hartford, New York

Prep: **20 min.** + chilling
Bake: **30 min.**
Yield: **30 bars**

I named these dessert bars for Broadway because they're a hit every time I serve them. I especially like to make these for the holidays or for hostess gifts. They're always sure to please any sweet tooth!

Filling:
   6 ounces cream cheese, softened
   1/2 cup sugar
   1/4 cup butter, softened
   2 tablespoons flour
   1 egg, lightly beaten
   1/2 teaspoon vanilla extract

Brownie:
   1/2 cup butter
   1 square (1 ounce) unsweetened chocolate
   2 eggs, lightly beaten
   1 teaspoon vanilla extract
   1 cup sugar
   1 cup all-purpose flour
   1 teaspoon baking powder
   1 cup chopped walnuts

Topping:
   1 cup (6 ounces) semisweet chocolate chips
   1/4 cup chopped walnuts
   2 cups miniature marshmallows

Frosting:
   1/4 cup butter
   1/4 cup milk
   2 ounces cream cheese
   1 square (1 ounce) unsweetened chocolate
   3 cups confectioners' sugar
   1 teaspoon vanilla extract

In small mixing bowl, combine the first six ingredients until smooth; set aside.

In a medium saucepan, over medium heat, melt butter and chocolate. Remove from the heat and cool. Stir in the eggs and vanilla. Add the sugar, flour, baking powder and nuts, stirring until blended.

Spread batter in a 13-in. x 9-in. x 2-in. pan coated with nonstick cooking spray. Spread filling over batter. For topping, in small bowl, combine the chocolate chips and nuts; sprinkle over filling.

Bake at 350° for about 28 minutes or until almost set. Sprinkle with marshmallows; bake 2 minutes longer.

For frosting, in a medium saucepan, heat butter, milk, cream cheese and chocolate until melted, stirring until smooth. Remove from heat; stir in confectioners' sugar and vanilla. Immediately drizzle over marshmallows. Chill well; cut into bars.

If you like pecan pie, you're sure to love these bars. They don't last very long at my house.

Pecan Pie Bars

—Karlen Dentinger
Louisville, Kentucky

Prep: **10 min.**
Bake: **1 hour + cooling**
Yield: **20 servings**

1/2 cup butter, softened

3 tablespoons confectioners' sugar

1 cup all-purpose flour

3 eggs

3/4 cup packed brown sugar

3/4 cup corn syrup

Dash salt

3/4 cup chopped pecans

In a small mixing bowl, cream butter and confectioners' sugar. Gradually add flour, mixing until blended. Pat into an ungreased 9-in. square baking pan. Bake at 350° for 20-22 minutes or until golden.

In another small mixing bowl, beat the eggs, brown sugar, corn syrup and salt until smooth. Pour over crust; sprinkle with pecans. Bake 40-45 minutes longer or until set. Cool on a wire rack. Cut into bars.

I've made this ice cream often, and it comes out smooth and creamy every time. Our state produces of lot of strawberries, and they are so good!

Strawberry Ice Cream

—Leone Mayne
Frostproof, Florida

2 eggs

2 cups milk

1-1/4 cups sugar

1 cup miniature marshmallows

2 cups pureed unsweetened strawberries

1 cup half-and-half cream

1/2 cup heavy whipping cream

1 teaspoon vanilla extract

In a large heavy saucepan, combine eggs and milk; stir in sugar. Cook and stir over medium-low heat until mixture is thick enough to coat a metal spoon and a thermometer reads at least 160°, about 14 minutes. Remove from the heat; stir in the marshmallows until melted.

Set saucepan in ice and stir the mixture for 5-10 minutes or until cool. Stir in the remaining ingredients. Cover and refrigerate overnight.

Pour into the cylinder of an ice cream freezer and freeze according to manufacturer's directions.

Prep: **20 min. + chilling**
Freeze: **30 min.**
Yield: **about 2 quarts**

Cherry Pineapple Pie

—Carolyn Bartley
Curtice, Ohio

Prep: 15 min.
Bake: 50 min.
Yield: 6-8 servings

My husband never liked cherry pie, until one day when I added some crushed pineapple. Now he loves it!

1 cup sugar
1/3 cup all-purpose flour
1/8 teaspoon salt
2 cans (14-1/2 ounces *each*) pitted tart cherries, well drained
2 cans (8 ounces *each*) crushed pineapple, well drained
3 drops almond extract
Pastry for double-crust pie (9 inches)
2 tablespoons butter
1 tablespoon milk
Additional sugar

In a large bowl, combine the sugar, flour and salt. Stir in the cherries, pineapple and extract.

Line a 9-in. pie plate with the bottom crust. Trim the pastry with ease. Add filling; dot with butter. Roll out remaining pastry; make a lattice crust. Seal and flute edges. Brush with milk and sprinkle with sugar. Bake at 375° for 50-60 minutes or until bubbly and golden brown.

Strawberry Oatmeal Bars

—Flo Burtnett, Gage, Oklahoma

Prep: 15 min.
Bake: 25 min.
Yield: 3 dozen

The fruity filling and fluffy coconut topping make these bars truly one of a kind. They really dress up my trays of Christmas goodies.

1-1/4 cups all-purpose flour
1-1/4 cups quick-cooking oats
1/2 cup sugar
1/2 teaspoon baking powder
1/4 teaspoon salt
3/4 cup butter, melted
2 teaspoons vanilla extract
1 cup strawberry preserves
1/2 cup flaked coconut

In a bowl, combine dry ingredients. Add butter and vanilla; stir until crumbly. Set aside 1 cup. Press remaining crumb mixture evenly into an ungreased 13-in. x 9-in. x 2-in. baking pan.

Spread preserves over the crust. Combine the coconut and reserved crumb mixture; sprinkle over the preserves. Bake at 350° for 25-30 minutes or until coconut is lightly browned. Cool in pan on a wire rack.

The line at the dessert table convinced me this cake was a winner when I served it at a party. It makes a pretty presentation, baking up nice and high. Some people are timid to try their hand at making cheesecake. But it's fairly easy to prepare. But best of all, it needs to be made ahead so there's no last-minute fuss.

White Chocolate Lime Mousse Cake

—*Margery Richmond*
Fort Collins, Colorado

2 cups crushed gingersnaps (about 38 cookies)

2 tablespoons sugar

1/3 cup butter, melted

Filling:

1 envelope unflavored gelatin

6 tablespoons lime juice

9 squares (1 ounce *each*) white baking chocolate, chopped

2-1/2 cups heavy whipping cream, *divided*

3 packages (8 ounces *each*) cream cheese, softened

1 cup sugar

1 tablespoon grated lime peel

In a large bowl, combine the gingersnaps, sugar and butter; press onto the bottom and 1 in. up the sides of a greased 9-in. springform pan. Set aside.

In a microwave-safe dish, sprinkle gelatin over lime juice. Let stand for 1 minute. Microwave on high for 10-20 seconds; stir until gelatin is dissolved. Set aside.

In a heavy saucepan or microwave, melt chocolate with 1/2 cup cream; stir until smooth. Cool slightly; stir in dissolved gelatin.

In a large mixing bowl, beat cream cheese and sugar until smooth. Gradually add chocolate mixture and lime peel; mix well. In another large mixing bowl, beat remaining cream until stiff peaks form. Gently fold into cream cheese mixture. Spoon over the crust. Cover and chill overnight. Refrigerate leftovers.

Prep: **20 min. + chilling**

Yield: **12-16 servings**

Hawaiian Dessert

—Eunice Stoen, Decorah, Iowa

Prep: 20 min.
Bake: 15 min. + chilling
Yield: 24 servings

A chilled, fluffy dessert like this one is a satisfying way to finish off a big meal. Leftovers taste just as good the next day.

1 package (18-1/4 ounces) yellow cake mix
3 packages (3.4 ounces *each*) instant vanilla pudding mix
4 cups cold milk
1-1/2 teaspoons coconut extract
1 package (8 ounces) cream cheese, softened
1 can (20 ounces) crushed pineapple, well drained
2 cups heavy whipping cream
1/3 cup confectioners' sugar
2 cups flaked coconut, toasted

Mix cake batter according to package directions. Pour into two greased 13-in. x 9-in. x 2-in. baking pans. Bake at 350° for 15 minutes or until a toothpick inserted near the center comes out clean. Cool completely in pans on wire racks.

In a large mixing bowl, combine pudding mixes, milk and coconut extract; beat for 2 minutes. Add the cream cheese and beat well. Stir in the pineapple. Spread over the cooled cakes.

In a mixing bowl, beat cream until it begins to thicken. Add confectioners' sugar; beat until stiff pearls form. Spread over top; sprinkle with coconut. Cover and refrigerate for at least 2 hours.

Amish Sugar Cookies

—Sylvia Ford, Kennett, Missouri

Prep: 10 min.
Bake: 10 min. per batch
Yield: about 5 dozen

These easy-to-make cookies simply melt in your mouth. I've passed the recipe around to many friends. After I gave the recipe to my sister, she entered the cookies in a local fair and won the best-of-show prize!

1 cup butter, softened
1 cup vegetable oil
1 cup granulated sugar
1 cup confectioners' sugar
2 eggs
1 teaspoon vanilla extract
4-1/2 cups all-purpose flour
1 teaspoon baking soda
1 teaspoon cream of tartar

In large mixing bowl, beat the butter, oil and sugars. Beat in eggs until well blended. Beat in vanilla. In separate bowl, combine the flour, baking soda and cream of tartar; add to creamed mixture, mixing well.

Drop by small teaspoonfuls on ungreased baking sheet. Bake at 375° for 8-10 minutes. Remove to wire racks to cool.

When strawberries are in season, I love to make this pleasing pie. There are fresh berries in every bite. The recipe calls for a purchased graham cracker crust. But for special occasions, I sometimes make the crust from scratch. Either way, this lovely pie is sure to impress folks at any gathering.

White Chocolate Berry Pie

—Connie Laux
Englewood, Ohio

- 5 squares (1 ounce *each*) white baking chocolate, *divided*
- 2 tablespoons milk
- 1 package (3 ounces) cream cheese, softened
- 1/3 cup confectioners' sugar
- 1 teaspoon grated orange peel
- 1 cup heavy whipping cream, whipped
- 1 graham cracker crust (9 inches)
- 2 cups sliced fresh strawberries

In a microwave or heavy saucepan, melt four squares of chocolate with the milk, stirring until smooth. Cool to room temperature.

Meanwhile, in a large mixing bowl, beat cream cheese and sugar until smooth. Beat in orange peel and melted chocolate. Fold in whipped cream.

Spread into crust. Arrange strawberries on top. Melt remaining chocolate; drizzle over berries. Refrigerate for at least 1 hour. Store in the refrigerator.

Prep: **20 min. + chilling**
Yield: **8 servings**

Carrot Cupcakes

—Doreen Kelly
Rosyln, Pennsylvania

Prep: 15 min.
Bake: 20 min.
Yield: 2 dozen

I often hide nutritional foods inside sweet treats. Carrots add moistness to these cupcakes, which have a rich cream cheese frosting. Now we can have our cake and eat our vegetables, too!

4 eggs
2 cups sugar
1 cup vegetable oil
2 cups all-purpose flour
2 teaspoons ground cinnamon
1 teaspoon baking soda
1 teaspoon baking powder
1 teaspoon ground allspice
1/2 teaspoon salt
3 cups grated carrots

Chunky Frosting:
1 package (8 ounces) cream cheese, softened
1/4 cup butter, softened
2 cups confectioners' sugar
1/2 cup flaked coconut
1/2 cup chopped pecans
1/2 cup chopped raisins

In a large mixing bowl, beat the eggs, sugar and oil. Combine the flour, cinnamon, baking soda, baking powder, allspice and salt; gradually add to egg mixture. Stir in carrots.

Fill greased or paper-lined muffin cups two-thirds full. Bake at 325° for 20-25 minutes or until a toothpick inserted near the center comes out clean. Cool for 5 minutes before removing from pans to wire racks.

For frosting, in a large mixing bowl, beat cream cheese and butter until combined. Gradually beat in confectioners' sugar. Stir in coconut, pecans and raisins. Frost cupcakes. Store in the refrigerator.

Chewy Brownie Cookies

—Joy Maynard
St. Ignatius, Montana

Prep/Total Time: 30 min.
Yield: about 4 dozen

These cookies are convenient and easy to make. So when you get the munchies, it doesn't take a lot of time before you have a tasty treat!

1 package fudge brownie mix (13-inch x 9-inch pan size)
1-1/2 cups old-fashioned oats
3/4 cup chopped nuts
3/4 teaspoon ground cinnamon
1/2 cup water
1 egg, lightly beaten

In a large mixing bowl, combine the brownie mix, oats, nuts and cinnamon. Add water and egg; mix well.

Drop by level tablespoonfuls 2 in. apart onto greased baking sheets. Bake at 350° for 12-14 minutes. Cool for 1-2 minutes before removing to wire racks.

My family can't possibly eat all of the sweets I whip up, so my co-workers are more than happy to sample them—particularly these rich chewy brownies that are full of gooey caramel, chocolate chips and crunchy walnuts.

Caramel Brownies

—*Clara Bakke*
Coon Rapids, Minnesota

2 cups sugar

3/4 cup baking cocoa

1 cup vegetable oil

4 eggs

1/4 cup milk

1-1/2 cups all-purpose flour

1 teaspoon salt

1 teaspoon baking powder

1 cup (6 ounces) semisweet chocolate chips

1 cup chopped walnuts, *divided*

1 package (14 ounces) caramels

1 can (14 ounces) sweetened condensed milk

In a large mixing bowl, combine the sugar, cocoa, oil, eggs and milk. Combine the flour, salt and baking powder; add to egg mixture and mix until combined. Fold in chocolate chips and 1/2 cup walnuts.

Spoon two-thirds of the batter into a greased 13-in. x 9-in. x 2-in. baking pan. Bake at 350° for 12 minutes.

Meanwhile, in a large saucepan, heat the caramels and condensed milk over low heat until caramels are melted. Pour over baked brownie layer. Sprinkle with remaining walnuts.

Drop remaining batter by teaspoonfuls over caramel layer; carefully swirl brownie batter with a knife. Bake 35-40 minutes longer or until a toothpick inserted near the center comes out with moist crumbs. Cool on a wire rack.

Prep: 20 min.
Bake: 35 min.
Yield: 2 dozen

Keeping Brownies Moist

If you can, make Caramel Brownies the day before your get-together. Keep them nice and moist by covering the pan tightly with foil—or put the pan in a large resealable plastic bag.

Frozen Ice Cream Delight

—*Susan J. Bracken*
Apex, North Carolina

Prep: **20 min.** + freezing
Cook: **10 min.** + cooling
Yield: **12-16 servings**

This recipe is a refreshing summer treat that dates back to before fast food ice cream. It's also handy—you can make it days ahead of time.

2-1/2 cups cream-filled chocolate cookie crumbs, *divided*

1/2 cup butter, melted

1/2 cup sugar

1/2 gallon chocolate, coffee *or* vanilla ice cream, softened

Chocolate Sauce:

2 cups confectioners' sugar

2/3 cup semisweet chocolate chips

1 can (12 ounces) evaporated milk

1/2 cup butter, cubed

1 teaspoon vanilla extract

1-1/2 cups salted peanuts

1 carton (8 ounces) frozen whipped topping, thawed

Combine 2 cups cookie crumbs, butter and sugar. Press into the bottom of a 13-in. x 9-in. x 2-in. baking pan. Freeze for 15 minutes.

Spread ice cream over crumbs; freeze until firm, about 3 hours.

Meanwhile, combine the sugar, chocolate chips, milk and butter in a saucepan; bring to a boil. Boil for 8 minutes. Remove from the heat and stir in vanilla; cool to room temperature. Spoon sauce over ice cream; sprinkle with nuts. Freeze until firm.

Spread whipped topping over nuts and sprinkle with remaining cookie crumbs. Freeze at least 3 hours before serving. Can be stored in the freezer for up to a week.

Oatmeal Raisin Cookies

—Wendy Coalwell
Abbeville, Georgia

I was given this recipe by a friend many years ago, and these cookies are as delicious as Mom used to make. The secret is to measure exactly (no guessing on the amounts) and to not overbake.

1 cup shortening

1 cup sugar

1 cup packed light brown sugar

3 eggs

1 teaspoon vanilla extract

2-1/2 cups all-purpose flour

2 teaspoons baking soda

1 teaspoon salt

1 teaspoon ground cinnamon

2 cups old-fashioned oats

1 cup raisins

1 cup coarsely chopped pecans, optional

In a large mixing bowl, cream the shortening and sugars. Beat in eggs, one at a time, beating well after each addition. Beat in vanilla. Combine the flour, baking soda, salt and cinnamon. Add to creamed mixture, beating until combined. Stir in the oats, raisins and pecans if desired.

Shape dough into 1-in. balls. Place 2 in. apart on ungreased baking sheets. Flatten with a greased glass bottom. Bake at 350° for 10-11 minutes or until golden brown. Do not overbake. Remove to a wire rack to cool.

Prep: **20 min.**
Bake: **10 min. per batch**
Yield: **about 3-1/2 dozen**

Lemon Sheet Cake

—Alyce Dubisar
Coos Bay, Oregon

Prep: **10 min.**
Bake: **20 min. + cooling**
Yield: **30-35 servings**

Lemon pie filling lends a splash of citrus flavor to convenient cake mix, and a rich cream cheese frosting gives it sweetness. My family likes this cake cold, so I cut it into squares and freeze it before serving.

1 package (18-1/4 ounces) lemon cake mix

4 eggs

1 can (15-3/4 ounces) lemon pie filling

1 package (3 ounces) cream cheese, softened

1/2 cup butter, softened

2 cups confectioners' sugar

1-1/2 teaspoons vanilla extract

In a large mixing bowl, beat the cake mix and eggs until well blended. Fold in the pie filling. Spread into a greased 15-in. x 10-in. x 1-in. baking pan. Bake at 350° for 18-20 minutes or until a toothpick inserted near the center comes out clean. Cool on a wire rack.

In a small mixing bowl, beat the cream cheese, butter and confectioners' sugar until smooth. Stir in vanilla. Spread over cake. Store in the refrigerator.

Crunchy Peanut Butter Cookies

—Lisa Brown, Iola, Kansas

Prep: **20 min.**
Bake: **10 min. per batch**
Yield: **about 5 dozen**

I developed this recipe when I was looking for a cookie with peanut butter taste but without the traditional peanut butter cookie texture. We call these cookies "I'll Have Another"—you'll find out why!

1 cup butter-flavored shortening
1 cup chunky peanut butter
1 cup sugar
1 cup packed brown sugar
2 eggs
3 tablespoons milk
1 teaspoon vanilla extract
2 cups all-purpose flour
2 cups quick-cooking oats
1-1/2 teaspoons baking soda
1 teaspoon baking powder
1/2 teaspoon salt
1 cup crushed cornflakes

In a large mixing bowl, cream the shortening, peanut butter and sugars. Add eggs, one at a time, beating well after each addition. Beat in milk and vanilla. Combine the flour, oats, baking soda, baking powder and salt; gradually add to creamed mixtures. Stir in the cornflakes.

Drop by tablespoonfuls 3 in. apart onto ungreased baking sheets. Flatten slightly. Bake at 375° for 8-10 minutes or until lightly browned. Remove to wire racks to cool.

Fresh Blueberry Pie

—Nellie VanSickle
Silver Bay, New York

Prep: **20 min. + chilling**
Yield: **6-8 servings**

As a fantastic finale to any special meal, surprise guests with this dessert—it'll remind them of the pies their mothers used to make. They don't have to know how simple it is!

4 cups fresh blueberries, *divided*
3/4 cup water
1 tablespoon butter
3/4 cup sugar
3 tablespoons cornstarch
1/8 teaspoon ground cinnamon
Dash salt
1 teaspoon lemon juice
1 pastry shell (9 inches), baked
Ice cream *or* whipped cream
Shredded lemon peel, optional

In a large saucepan, combine 1 cup blueberries, water and butter; bring to a boil. Reduce the heat; simmer, uncovered, for 4 minutes.

Combine the sugar, cornstarch, cinnamon and salt; add to the saucepan. Bring to a boil over medium heat, stirring constantly; cook and stir for 2 minutes or until thickened. Remove from the heat. Stir in lemon juice and remaining blueberries.

Pour into pie shell. Chill for 2-3 hours. Serve with ice cream or whipped cream. Garnish with lemon peel if desired. Refrigerate leftovers.

These mouth-watering cupcakes are guaranteed to satisfy the sweetest sweet tooth.

Chocolate Toffee Cupcakes

—Hershey Food Corporation Hershey, Pennsylvania

1-1/2 cups all-purpose flour

    1 cup sugar

1/4 cup baking cocoa

    1 teaspoon baking soda

    1 cup water

1/4 cup vegetable oil

    1 tablespoon white vinegar

    1 teaspoon vanilla extract

1/2 cup milk chocolate toffee bits

Frosting:

1-1/2 cups confectioners' sugar

1/3 cup baking cocoa

1/3 cup butter, softened

    2 tablespoons milk

3/4 teaspoon vanilla extract

3/4 cup English toffee bits *or* almond brickle chips, *divided*

In a large mixing bowl, combine flour, sugar, cocoa and baking soda. Stir in the water, oil, vinegar and vanilla until smooth. Add the toffee bits.

Fill paper-lined muffin cups two-thirds full. Bake at 350° for 20-25 minutes or until a toothpick inserted near the center comes out clean. Cool for 5 minutes before removing from pans to wire racks to cool completely.

For frosting, combine confectioners' sugar and cocoa; set aside. In a large mixing bowl, beat butter and 1/2 cup cocoa mixture until smooth. Add milk, vanilla and remaining cocoa mixture; beat until desired spreading consistency is reached. Stir in 1/2 cup toffee bits.

Frost cupcakes. Cover and refrigerate until serving. Top with remaining toffee bits before serving.

Prep: **20 min.**
Bake: **20 min. + cooling**
Yield: **about 1-1/2 dozen**

Cupcake Carrier

A disposable 13-in. x 9-in. foil pan *with a lid* makes an inexpensive carrier for transporting cupcakes. The lid is higher than the lid of a regular covered pan so it doesn't touch the frosted tops.

Bake-Sale Lemon Bars

—Mildred Keller
Rockford, Illinois

The recipe for these tangy bars comes from my cousin Bernice, a farmer's wife famous for cooking up feasts. This mouth-watering dessert is perfect year-round. It's also a best-seller at church mission sales.

1-1/2 cups all-purpose flour

2/3 cup confectioners' sugar

3/4 cup butter, softened

3 eggs, lightly beaten

1-1/2 cups sugar

3 tablespoons all-purpose flour

1/4 cup lemon juice

Additional confectioners' sugar

In a small bowl, combine the flour, sugar and butter until crumbly; pat into a greased 13-in. x 9-in. x 2-in. baking pan. Bake at 350° for 20 minutes.

Meanwhile, in a bowl, whisk the eggs, sugar, flour and lemon juice until frothy; pour over the hot crust. Bake 20-25 minutes longer or until light golden brown. Cool on a wire rack. Dust with confectioners' sugar. Cut into squares.

Prep: **10 min.**
Bake: **40 min. + cooling**
Yield: **3-4 dozen**

Banana Cream Pie

—Perlene Hoekema
Lynden, Washington

This fluffy, no-fuss pie is full of old-fashioned flavor. It uses instant vanilla pudding and is whipped up in minutes.

1 cup cold milk

1 package (3.4 ounces) instant vanilla pudding mix

1/2 teaspoon vanilla extract

1 carton (12 ounces) frozen whipped topping, thawed, *divided*

1 graham cracker crust (9 inches)

2 medium firm bananas, sliced

Additional banana slices, optional

In a large mixing bowl, whisk the milk and pudding mix for 2 minutes; whisk in vanilla. Fold in 3 cups whipped topping.

Pour 1-1/3 cups of the pudding mixture into pie crust. Layer with banana slices and remaining pudding mixture. Top with remaining whipped topping. Garnish with additional banana slices if desired. Refrigerate until serving.

Prep/Total Time: **10 min.**
Yield: **8 servings**

These brownies were enjoyed by everyone at our family's Fourth of July picnic. Mama always said that they didn't need frosting because they were the richest brownies around! I think she was right.

2/3 cup shortening

2 cups sugar

4 eggs

1 teaspoon vanilla extract

3/4 cup unsweetened cocoa

1-1/2 cups all-purpose flour

1 teaspoon baking powder

1/2 teaspoon salt

1 cup chopped nuts, *divided*

In a large mixing bowl, beat the shortening, sugar, eggs and vanilla until smooth. Combine dry ingredients; stir into batter. Fold in 1/2 cup nuts.

Spread into a greased 13-in. x 9-in. x 2-in. baking pan. Sprinkle remaining nuts on top. Bake at 350° for 20-25 minutes or until brownies pull away from the sides of the pan. Cool on wire rack. Cut into squares.

Chocolate Nut Brownies

—Sandra Anderson
New York, New York

Prep/Total Time: **30 min.**

Yield: **2 dozen**

I often make a big batch of these peanut butter-flavored cereal bars on days that I don't want to heat up the kitchen. Kids especially love them, so they're great for picnics, potlucks and school bake sales.

1 cup sugar

1 cup light corn syrup

1/2 cup peanut butter

5 cups crisp rice cereal

2 cups pretzel sticks

1 cup plain M&M's

In a large microwave-safe bowl, combine the sugar and corn syrup. Microwave on high for 3 minutes or until the sugar is dissolved.

Stir in peanut butter until blended. Add the cereal, pretzels and M&M's; stir until coated. Press into a greased 15-in. x 10-in. x 1-in. pan. Cut into bars.

Editor's Note: Recipe was tested in an 850-watt microwave.

Crispy Pretzel Bars

—Jane Thompson
Eureka, Illinois

Prep/Total Time: **20 min.**

Yield: **about 5 dozen**

Fresh Strawberry Pie

—Mary Egan, Carney, Michigan

Prep: **15 min.**
Cook: **10 min.** + chilling
Yield: **6-8 servings**

Each year we wait for strawberry time here in the Upper Peninsula of Michigan. After picking them, I can't wait to get home to make this pie.

Bottom Layer:
- 2 cups sliced fresh strawberries
- 1 pastry shell (9 inches), baked

Middle Layer:
- 2 cups halved fresh strawberries, mashed
- 1 cup sugar
- 3 tablespoons cornstarch

Top Layer:
- 2 cups halved fresh strawberries
- 1 cup heavy whipping cream
- 2 tablespoons sugar
- 1/4 teaspoon almond extract, optional

For bottom layer, place sliced strawberries in the pie shell. For the middle layer, combine the mashed strawberries, sugar and cornstarch in a saucepan. Bring to a boil; cook and stir for 2 minutes or until thickened. Cool for 15 minutes; pour over bottom layer. For top layer, arrange strawberry halves on top of pie. Cover and refrigerate for 2-3 hours.

Just before serving, in a small mixing bowl, beat cream until it begins to thicken. Add sugar and almond extract if desired; beat until stiff peaks form. Spread over pie or dollop on individual servings.

Crunchy Ice Cream Dessert

—Mildred Sherrer
Forth Worth, Texas

I like to start my meal prep with dessert. I sandwich vanilla ice cream with layers of cereal, peanuts and coconut. Then I put it in the freezer until it's ready to serve.

- 2 cups crushed Rice Chex
- 2/3 cup packed brown sugar
- 1/2 cup chopped peanuts
- 1/2 cup flaked coconut
- 1/2 cup butter, melted
- 1/2 gallon vanilla ice cream

In a large bowl, combine the cereal, brown sugar, peanuts and coconut. Drizzle with butter; stir until combined.

Press half of the mixture into an ungreased 13-in. x 9-in. x 2-in. dish. Cut ice cream into 3/4-in.-thick slices; arrange evenly over crust. Top with remaining crumb mixture; press down lightly. Cover and freeze until serving.

Prep: **25 min.** + freezing
Yield: **12-15 servings**

I like this cake because it's moist and rich. This from scratch treat is topped with a soft, silky chocolate frosting. You'll get a double dose of chocolate in every bite! It's great for large gatherings since it's made in a sheet pan.

Devil's Food Sheet Cake

—James Crabb, Greeley, Colorado

1-1/2 cups water
2 cups sugar
3/4 cup butter
2 eggs, lightly beaten
1 teaspoon vanilla extract
2 cups all-purpose flour
1/2 cup baking cocoa
2 teaspoons baking soda
1/2 teaspoon salt

Frosting:
1/4 cup butter, softened
2 cups confectioners' sugar
2 tablespoons baking cocoa
1/2 teaspoon vanilla extract
2 to 3 tablespoons milk

In a large saucepan, bring the water to a boil. Remove from the heat. Stir in sugar and butter until butter is melted. Add eggs and vanilla; mix well. Combine the flour, cocoa, baking soda and salt; add to butter mixture and mix thoroughly.

Pour into a greased and floured 15-in. x 10-in. x 1-in. baking pan.

Bake at 350° for 30-35 minutes or until a toothpick inserted near the center comes out clean. Cool completely on a wire rack.

For frosting, beat butter, confectioners' sugar, cocoa, vanilla and enough milk to reach a spreading consistency. Frost cake.

Prep: **20 min.**
Bake: **30 min. + cooling**
Yield: **16-20 servings**

Peanut Butter Ice Cream Topping

—Karen Buhr
Gasport, New York

Prep/Total Time: **10 min.**
Yield: **2-3/4 cups**

Whenever there's an ice cream social at church, this scrumptious topping is requested. It's easy to make.

1 cup packed brown sugar
1/2 cup light corn syrup
3 tablespoons butter
Pinch salt
1 cup creamy peanut butter
1/2 cup evaporated milk
Vanilla ice cream
Peanuts, optional

In a 1-1/2-qt. microwave-safe dish, combine the brown sugar, corn syrup, butter and salt. Cover and microwave on high for 4 minutes or until mixture boils, stirring twice. Add peanut butter; stir until smooth. Stir in evaporated milk.

Serve warm over ice cream. Sprinkle with peanuts if desired. Cover and store leftovers in the refrigerator. To reheat, microwave at 50% power for 1-2 minutes or until heated through.

Editor's Note: Recipe was tested in an 850-watt microwave.

Orange Chiffon Pie

—Tina Dierking, Canaan, Maine

Prep: **15 min. + chilling**
Yield: **8 servings**

You'll be greeted with smiles when you put this no-bake dessert on your menu. The pie is wonderfully refreshing in the summer. It's an old recipe that stands the test of time.

1 package (3 ounces) orange gelatin
1 tablespoon sugar
3/4 cup boiling water
1/2 cup orange juice
1 teaspoon grated orange peel
1 carton (8 ounces) frozen reduced-fat whipped topping, thawed
1 reduced-fat graham cracker crust (8 inches)

In a large mixing bowl, dissolve gelatin and sugar in boiling water. Add orange juice and peel. Refrigerate for 1 hour or until thickened but not set.

Beat on high speed for 3 minutes or until foamy and thickened. Fold in whipped topping until completely combined. Pour into crust. Cover and refrigerate for 4 hours or until set.

For a special, lovely treat, try this sherbet dessert. Our children have requested this treat many times over the years.

Triple Sherbet Dessert

—Mrs. Howard Hinseth
Minneapolis, Minnesota

1 package (14-1/2 ounces) coconut macaroon cookies, crumbled

1 carton (12 ounces) frozen whipped topping, thawed

1/2 cup chopped pecans, optional

1/2 cup flaked coconut

1 pint *each* orange, lemon and lime sherbet, softened

In a large bowl, combine the cookie crumbs, whipped topping, pecans if desired and coconut.

Spread half into a 13-in. x 9-in. x 2-in. dish. Spread with orange sherbet; freeze for 10-15 minutes. Repeat with lemon and lime layers. Top with the remaining cookie mixture. Cover and freeze until firm.

Prep: **15 min. + freezing**
Yield: **12-16 servings**

This peaches-and-cream pie once captured the blue ribbon at the Iowa State Fair. It always disappears fast!

Golden Coconut Peach Pie

—Gloria Kratz
Des Moines, Iowa

4 to 4-1/2 cups sliced fresh peaches

1/2 cup sugar

3 tablespoons all-purpose flour

1/4 teaspoon ground nutmeg

1/8 teaspoon salt

1/4 cup orange juice

1 unbaked pie shell (9 inches)

2 tablespoons butter

2 cups flaked coconut

1 can (5 ounces) evaporated milk

1 egg, beaten

1/4 to 1/2 cup sugar

1/4 teaspoon almond extract

In a large bowl, combine the peaches, sugar, flour, nutmeg, salt and juice. Pour into pie shell; dot with butter. Bake at 450° for 15 minutes.

Meanwhile, combine remaining ingredients. Pour over hot filling. Reduce heat to 350° and bake until coconut is toasted, about 40 minutes. Serve warm or chilled. Store in the refrigerator.

Prep: **20 min.**
Bake: **55 min.**
Yield: **8 servings**

Coffee Ice Cream Torte

—Janet Hutts
Gainesville, Georgia

Prep: 20 min. + freezing
Yield: 16 servings

Not only does this make-ahead dessert go over big with company, but it calls for only four ingredients. If you can't find coffee-flavored ice cream, dissolve instant coffee granules in warm water and stir into vanilla ice cream.

2 packages (3 ounces *each*) ladyfingers

1 cup chocolate-covered English toffee bits *or* 4 Heath candy bars (1.4 ounces *each*), crushed, *divided*

1/2 gallon coffee ice cream, softened

1 carton (8 ounces) frozen whipped topping, thawed

Place ladyfingers around the edge of a 9-in. springform pan. Line bottom of pan with remaining ladyfingers. Stir 1/2 cup toffee bits into the ice cream; spoon into prepared pan. Cover with plastic wrap; freeze overnight or until firm. May be frozen for up to 2 months.

Just before serving, remove sides of pan. Garnish with the whipped topping and remaining toffee bits.

Fluffy Cheesecake Dessert

—Rhonda Miller
Bethalto, Illinois

Prep: 20 min. + chilling
Yield: 12-16 servings

For this tasty treat, I prepare a light, creamy filling with mild citrus flavor, then spoon it over a simple vanilla wafer crust. It makes an appealing ending to a summer meal.

4 cups miniature marshmallows

1/3 cup orange juice

2 packages (8 ounces *each*) cream cheese, softened

1 carton (12 ounces) frozen whipped topping, thawed

2-1/2 cups crushed vanilla wafers (about 60 wafers)

1/2 cup butter, melted

In a large microwave-safe bowl, combine the marshmallows and orange juice. Microwave, uncovered, on high for 1-1/2 minutes. Stir until smooth.

In a large mixing bowl, beat cream cheese. Add marshmallow mixture; beat just until smooth. Fold in whipped topping.

Combine wafer crumbs and butter; set aside 3/4 cup for topping. Press remaining crumbs into an ungreased 13-in. x 9-in. x 2-in. pan.

Spoon cream cheese filling over crust. Sprinkle with reserved crumbs. Cover and refrigerate for 1 hour or until set. Store in the refrigerator.

Editor's Note: Recipe was tested in an 850-watt microwave.

I found this recipe in a rural newspaper years ago, and it's been a family favorite ever since. I like to serve it warm with vanilla ice cream but plain slices are just as tasty. If you don't want to make a homemade pie crust, you can use a frozen or refrigerated crust with equally good results.

Macaroon Apple Pie

—Frances Musser
Newmanstown, Pennsylvania

1-1/2 cups all-purpose flour

1/2 teaspoon salt

1/2 cup shortening

2 to 3 tablespoons cold water

Filling:

4 cups sliced peeled tart apples

1/2 cup sugar

1/4 teaspoon ground cinnamon

Topping:

1/2 cup all-purpose flour

1/2 cup sugar

1/2 teaspoon baking powder

1/4 teaspoon salt

1 egg, lightly beaten

2 tablespoons butter, melted

1/2 teaspoon vanilla extract

1/4 cup flaked coconut

In a large bowl, combine flour and salt; cut in shortening until crumbly. Gradually add cold water, tossing with a fork until a ball forms.

Roll out pastry to fit a 9-in. pie plate; flute edges. Toss apples with sugar and cinnamon; pour into crust. Bake at 375° for 20 minutes.

Meanwhile, in a bowl, combine the first four topping ingredients Stir in egg, butter and vanilla until smooth. Add coconut. Spoon over hot apples, carefully spreading to cover. Bake 30 minutes longer or until apples are tender. Store in the refrigerator.

Prep: **15 min.**

Bake: **50 min.**

Yield: **6-8 servings**

Subject Index

Alphabetical Index